MOUNTAIN FLOWER HOLIDAYS

IN EUROPE

by

LIONEL BACON

Hon. Editor: J. A. KELLY, F.L.S.

THE ALPINE GARDEN SOCIETY

This book is
DEDICATED
to the memory of
Dr. Hugh Roger-Smith
who encouraged and assisted so many Members
of our Society to see the flowers in the mountains

ISBN   0 900048 31 X

First Published 1979

Printed by
L. Baker (Printers) Ltd.
71 Lombard Street, Birmingham B12 0QU

CONTENTS

FOREWORD

For Members of our Society, the call to see and study in the wild the plants that grow in our gardens becomes ever stronger, and more and more Members travel to the mountains of Europe for this purpose. For many of us, an indispensable item in our travel kit has been Dr. Hugh Roger-Smith's *Plant Hunting in Europe*. It is nearly thirty years since the Society published this little volume, written by its former Director of Tours, and his own travels, upon which his book was based, date back in part to the years preceding the founding of our Society. It is inevitable that over so long a period there have been many changes in the countries and areas to which travellers have access, the facilities for travel, the range of plants known, and their nomenclature. The Society's Committee therefore, in considering the celebration of its fiftieth anniversary, felt it appropriate to publish another book on similar lines to *Plant Hunting in Europe*, updated and expanded. In the intervening years many Members of the Society have travelled in Europe, and not a few have written of their experiences in the *Bulletin*. As compiler of the present volume, I have drawn upon these sources of information as well as seeking contributions from other Members, but my primary source of material has been the 'logs' which my wife and I have kept of our plant-seeking holidays in Europe over the past thirty years.

A book of this type is bound to be selective. It can only be based on a sample of the many hundreds of hills and valleys where the mountain flowers of Europe bloom, and while it is hoped that the book will inspire Members to visit the mountains and assist those visiting an area for the first time, readers are most strongly urged to leave the well-worn paths and seek new fields and hills. The aim of the book is to inspire and assist, not to restrict.

There are other inevitable limitations. The book is not a flora, and though many plants (which are after all its main theme) are named, the coverage is not comprehensive. I have sought to give a full enough account of the plants to enable the reader to judge what each area has to offer, and to name the plants of special local interest. Long plant-lists can be tedious, and so far as possible they have been avoided, but some listing of names is inevitable if a reasonable overall picture is to be presented. Many plants have a wide distribution in Europe, and to name them afresh in every chapter would be irksome repetition. I have sought to make this unnecessary by giving in Chapter 1 an account of the typical flowers to be found widely in specified habitats throughout Europe—and these should be assumed to occur, unless the contrary is stated, wherever such habitats are found.

The order of presentation calls for explanation, and this is to be found in Chapter 1.

The method of presentation is not consistent. For some countries it has seemed better to select a few centres for description, and it should be remembered that these are but samples and usually there are many other possibilities. In other countries the reader is taken on a conducted tour—but here again by no means all possible routes have been travelled.

The area covered by the book (see map p. 8) is the whole of Europe except (i) the British Isles (ii) European Russia (iii) European Turkey and some Greek Islands off the Turkish coast (iv) the Azores. I admit to considerable regret at omitting the British Isles: Northern England, Scotland, Wales and Western Ireland have beautiful mountain flowers, including a number of the species characteristic of the mountains on the Continent; but two considerations have led to their omission—the overriding problem of keeping the book within reasonable size-limits and the primary purpose of assisting the traveller to the Continent. I regret also the omission of the Caucasus Mountains in Russia: again lack of space is a factor, but a no less important one is that the Caucasus is excluded from *Flora Europaea*, which is the authority on which I lean for plant nomenclature. There is in fact some doubt as to whether, or to what extent, these mountains are in Europe anyway. I was also influenced by their inaccessibility, but Mr. Gilbert Barrett, who has so valuably contributed the chapters on Eastern Europe, tells me that the Caucasus is now becoming much more accessible to the Western European tourist. Certain countries such as Belgium and the Netherlands receive no mention because they have little or no mountain flora. The omission of a chapter on Germany may at first sight occasion surprise, since it has considerable upland areas and in particular mountains along the Swiss and Austrian frontiers. These areas do not however carry, so far as I am aware, any alpine flora distinct from that of Northern Switzerland and Austria.

Though I have drawn upon past *Bulletin* articles in compiling this book, they contain far more information than is here included, and any traveller visiting a country for the first time is strongly urged to consult these earlier reports. To assist in this, a list of the major travel articles in past *Bulletins* is included at the end of each chapter. There are many other shorter ones, as well as paragraphs in the Alpine Anthologies with which all the *Bulletins* commence, and there is much interesting and valuable information in these. The three Indexes are an excellent investment, and back numbers of the *Bulletin* can frequently be purchased by Members of the Society from the Secretary, or they can be borrowed from the Hon. Librarian.

While I must take responsibility for the overall presentation and compilation of the material, the book is nevertheless the work of many hands. Indeed, some fifty Members of the Society have contributed in various ways to its production.

6

Chapters or sections written by other Members are attributed to them in the text, and in addition help or information has been received from Dr. J. G. Elliott, Mrs. C. Greenfield, Mr. W. Palmer, Mr. R. W. Richards, Mrs. P. Warburg and Mr. Z. Zvolanek, and many other Members have offered advice and help. Mr. Roy Metcalfe has provided the valuable Appendix and, thanks to his good offices, the regional maps in the text have been prepared by Mr. M. E. Barnes.

The photographic illustrations have been provided by a number of Members. Mr. Gilbert Barrett has contributed drawings to illustrate his chapters on Bulgaria and Romania. Except where otherwise attributed the illustrations have been provided by the author. In the drawings, the scale is indicated by a line representing one inch.

To all these Members, named and unnamed, I offer my sincere thanks, both personally and on behalf of the Society.

The production of this book has benefited from bequests from the late Mrs. Anna N. Griffith and the late Mrs. J. M. Gostling, and the Society is happy that the memory of these two past Members will be perpetuated in this way.

The mechanics of producing the book have likewise involved a team of people. I am grateful first to my wife Joyce for much practical advice, and for enormous toleration; to Mrs. Dora Parker for reading both the text and the proofs; to Mr. Michael Upward for reading the proofs; and lastly but by no means least to the Editor, John Kelly, who with our very helpful printers has turned the material into a book.

Lionel Bacon

Europe: the main mountain areas considered in this book.

1

FLOWERS IN THE MOUNTAINS

Much ink—perhaps a little blood—has been spilt over the definitions of 'alpines' and 'rock plants'. For the purposes of this book these terms are to be interpreted in the same broad way that the Society employs in its acceptance of plants as worthy of mention in the *Bulletin* or as suitable for display on the Show benches. Plants suitable for cultivation in a rock garden or alpine house grow at sea level by the Mediterranean and by the Arctic Ocean, as well as high in the mountains. Mountains have bottoms as well as tops: meadows, woodlands, stream-sides and bogs as well as rocks, cliffs, moraines and screes.

So the range of plants is enormous, but they are not scattered haphazardly. They are grouped by habitat, soil, and climate; confined by competition, grazing and man's cultivation of the soil, and by interesting and obscure factors which must somehow account for the occurrence of plants in particular situations and their absence from seemingly identical ones. The seasoned traveller in the mountains comes to recognise these groupings—to expect certain plants where he finds others—and to be eternally puzzled when he does not find them. For there are always surprises and always more to learn.

To seek successfully for alpine flowers, one must first learn the interplay of altitude and season. Many of the best-loved alpines—gentians, primulas, soldanellas, anemones and so on—appear early in the year in the lower valleys soon after the snow melts. Here they flower and pass, and it is only by finding their leaves buried under the coarser foliage and grass in the mown fields that the summer visitor can become aware of their presence. As the snows recede, these flowers appear higher up. In June and early July they fill the upper pastures—the 'alps' proper—and it is then that many of them are at their finest and most profuse. By mid-July, in most parts of Switzerland, the cattle have cleaned the upper pastures, and one must climb yet higher, to the rock-faces and screes inaccessible to cattle. By August these alpine flowers are to be found only in small numbers in the high places near to the permanent snow, and sometimes only on north-facing slopes where the soil has been slow to warm.

It would however be wrong to convey the impression that all, or even most, alpine flowers are to be found throughout the altitudinal range at appropriate seasons, though this is indeed true of many of them. There are in addition plants which are special to each season and altitude. In Switzerland in May you can find flowers in the lower valleys which will never appear very high up—particularly narcissi and other bulbous plants. Conversely there are flowers in the high screes in June and July which are not at any season to be found lower down.

Altitude and season are not the only variables: latitude is a factor. Some plants which are characteristic of the highest levels below the permanent snow in the Alps are to be found at or near sea-level by the Arctic Ocean, so that the season-altitude relationship is true only for each particular area. Of course, there are other climatic factors that exert their influence. Broadly speaking, European plants come into flower earlier on south-facing slopes or rocks than on north-facing ones; and there are areas, such as those around the Mediterranean, where temperatures are higher not only because of low altitude and southerly latitude, not only on southerly exposures, but also because of the moderating effect on temperature of the sea. So you may find, let us say, a frog orchid (*Coeloglossum viride*) flowering in May on a low hillside in Southern France, in June in an English meadow, in August near sea-level in Iceland or at 2500 m. on a glacier-moraine in Austria. The wide altitudinal range of some plants can be deceptive. Seeing *Anemone blanda* near sea-level in the warm sun of the Peloponnese, or *Chamaecytisus purpureus* among the oranges and lemons by Lake Garda, you might well suppose them to be frost-tender plants: but those same plants are to be found by the melting snow some thousands of feet higher in the same areas. It is of course the upper, not the lower range of a plant's distribution that indicates the potential hardiness of the species.

All this affects not only where, but also when, you may choose to go to the mountains. In the following chapters some indication is given as to the optimum time to visit each area; but as the foregoing remarks will have indicated, it is very often necessary to compromise, or to decide whether one is going to see the lower or the higher flowers. We cannot all choose the times of our holidays— but there are compensations. In fact, there is a great deal to be gained by and learned from 'out of season' visits. The Mont Cenis Pass, for instance, is a very different place in late April, in late June, and in September—and all are exciting.

An elementary knowledge, at least, of geology is of great value in seeking plants. The most obvious 'divide' is between calcareous and non-calcareous formations; for while there are plenty of plants which appear in our gardens to be equally at home on limy and non-limy soils, many of these seem in the wild to exhibit a clear preference for the one or the other type of rock formation. A few plants are decidedly happier, even in the garden, on limy soils, and there is a much greater number of plants which demand a lime-free soil. One result is of course that certain plants tend to be associated in the mountains, and others rarely occur together. Yet even here there are surprises. *Eritrichium nanum* is notoriously a calcifuge plant— nevertheless it is to be found, apparently quite healthy, on the dolomitic limestones. At least two factors seem to enter into this apparent anomaly. 'Limestone' may be pure calcium carbonate, and anathema to the calcifuge plant because the excess calcium interferes with the uptake by the plant of other essential nutrients such as magnesium; but dolomitic limestone contains a high enough proportion of magnesium to overcome this difficulty for many plants. The other consideration is that in many instances a plant which appears to be growing in limestone may in fact be growing in an acid, humus-rich wad of soil packed into a limestone crevice, so that the roots either do not reach the limestone or its effects are neutralised. Perhaps the most surprising thing is to find (as you may in the Picos de Europa) a reputedly calcifuge plant like *Lithodora diffusa* growing and flowering beautifully in a tight, apparently soil-free fissure in hard limestone cliff. Too hard to release its lime, perhaps—but not far away the lithodora grows in exceedingly soft limestone with calciphile orchids (see p. 132), so perhaps one must postulate that there are lime-tolerant forms of some generally lime-hating plants. This is not the place for a detailed discussion either of geology or of plant-physiology: the point to be made is that the plant-seeker, untrained alike in geology and botany, can by careful observation (aided by note-taking) add much to his and our Society's knowledge of how plants grow in the wild, and how therefore we should seek to grow them in the garden. While the distinction between calcareous and non-calcareous areas is perhaps the most obvious geological feature affecting plant-distribution, there is of course a wide range of rocks and soil-conditions to be observed and linked with the distribution, associations and health of the plants. The mountains are full of dead plants (a source of some comfort to the gardener!) and there is much to be learnt from observing the situations, condition, size and apparent age of the corpses.

The point has already been made that this book is not a flora, and it does not set out to assist the traveller in plant-identification. Nevertheless, in suceeding chapters the main plants endemic to, or particularly associated with, each area are named, and this should help the traveller towards identifying them from his 'pocket' flora. Happily there are now several good and well-illustrated books on European mountain flowers, which will go at least into the pocket of the car, if not one's own.

Nomenclature presents a problem. Plant-names are frequently changed, not simply to annoy the gardener (though it may sometimes seem like it!), but in a steady drive towards the praiseworthy objectives of securing an improved classification and a worldwide acceptance of one name for each plant and one plant for each name. When a new name is introduced he who uses it sounds pedantic, but soon he who doesn't sounds old-fashioned. So in this book, so far as possible, the currently correct botanical names are used, with *Flora Europaea* as the authority. In the Plant Index, however, well-known synonyms are included and cross-referenced to the correct names. In a few instances, where a well-known name has recently been changed, I have added the old name (in brackets) in the text. *Flora Europaea* (a book written for botanists, not gardeners) names species and subspecies of plants, and only rarely refers to varieties or forms: for the gardener on the other hand distinct forms can be of considerable interest. In this book, because the *Flora Europaea* nomenclature is followed, a third name, not in brackets, indicates a subspecies. In the Index this is stated, but in the text, to make for smoother reading, the indication 'subsp.' is omitted: e.g. *Pulsatilla alpina apiifolia* means *Pulsatilla alpina* subsp. *apiifolia*. Occasionally the third name is a form or variety, and this is stated. I have named the plants to the best of my ability, but it must be remembered that many of them were found on holidays taken years ago when reliable floras were less readily available, and also of course I must accept the names given by other contributors. I have however checked that whenever a plant-name is given for a location it does (according to *Flora Europaea*) grow there.

Unfortunately, at the time of going to print, the fifth volume of *Flora Europaea*, which contains the Monocotyledons, is not yet published. Thanks to the kindness of Professor Heywood and Professor Moore and their staff at the Botany Department of Reading University I have had access to much of the proof material for this volume but it is not finished and consequently the naming of the Monocotyledons in this book may prove to require correction.

A surprising number of the mountain flowers of Europe are to be found widespread over the length and breadth of the Continent. In a more restricted area, say from the Pyrenees eastward through the main alpine chain to Austria, the uniformity of the 'basic flora' becomes even more pronounced, comprising a large proportion of the plants of interest to rock gardeners. This is not so surprising when one considers that the latitudinal range is not very great and the types of habitat required by these plants are available throughout the Central European mountains. No attempts will be made in this book to list all the plants of interest to rock gardeners which fall within this 'basic flora', but in the ensuing paragraphs examples are given of the predominating plants, grouped according to their most characteristic habitats, that are likely to catch the traveller's eye. In the subsequent chapters, for each area or country the plants mentioned are in the main those which are of special and local interest— but these may make only a small contribution to the display that the visitor will meet there. Except where there is a specific statement to the contrary, it should be assumed that the 'basic flora' will be there, but this becomes less true as one departs from the main alpine chain. Differences of climate, altitude and soil no doubt account for the 'local interest' plants—but these, to emphasise the point again, are in many areas but a small part of the whole.

This 'basic flora' (not of course to be confused with the geological term 'basic' as opposed to 'acid') comprises the majority of the plants that will catch the eye of the traveller to European mountains. It is to a remarkable degree the flora of the Bernese Oberland in Switzerland. From the Oberland the flowers tend to change by the addition of new species in whatever direction one travels: the further that one is from

Central Switzerland the more does the 'basic flora' tend to be enriched by species which are not found in the Oberland. It is convenient to think in terms of four other broad types of flora as well as the 'basic flora' of the Alps—the Mediterranean, the Iberian, the Balkan and the Scandinavian. These are not clear-cut entities, sharply separated from one another geographically: on the contrary they merge into one another and overlap, and the map on p. 14 gives only a broad indication of the types of plants to be found in any particular country. The 'basic flora' is presented in this chapter: the Mediterranean flora is further considered on pp. 75, 105: the Iberian, Balkan and Scandinavian floras are indicated in the relevant chapters.

The order of presentation of the areas considered in this book is largely determined by what has just been said. Switzerland, starting in the Bernese Oberland, is presented first: the fact that many people travelling to the Continent to see the flowers go first to Switzerland is an added reason for this, but the primary one is that this is the centre of the 'basic flora'. From Switzerland we will first travel south and west through Italy and France (where we will first encounter the Mediterranean flora), across the Pyrenees, which are conveniently considered as an entity, and so into Spain and Portugal where the 'basic flora' gives way to the Iberian. Returning to the Central Alps we now travel eastward, through Austria and Jugoslavia to Greece where the Balkan flora predominates. In Eastern Europe (Bulgaria, Romania, Czechoslovakia and Poland) there are elements both of the Balkan and of the 'basic flora', and also some influence from a sixth type of flora, that of the Caucasus. Finally, we shall move away to the far north, to the vast area of Scandinavia, Iceland and Spitsbergen, where the plants of interest to us, though relatively few in number, include arctic as well as alpine elements.

THE 'BASIC FLORA' OF THE ALPS

The Alpine Pastures

The sheer quantity and variety of flowers in the mountain meadows takes one's breath away. The seasoned traveller may be seeking the rarities and the plants special to his chosen locality; but if he does not rejoice afresh at the common flowers of the alpine meadows each time he sees them, he would really do better to stay at home and play whist.

As the snow clears from the valleys in the spring, the flowers burst forth and rapidly mature in the rich lower pastures. The timing depends of course upon the locality and the season, and the flowers are not the same at all times and places, but there is a large common element. While the grass is still short after the snows come the soldanellas (in the Oberland it is likely to be *Soldanella alpina*), the crocuses (*C. vernus*), spring snowflakes (*Leucojum vernum*) and poet's narcissus. Primroses, oxlips and cowslips start the pageant, and among them the incomparable spring gentian (*Gentiana verna*), to be

The Major Components of the Rock and Mountain Flora of Southern Europe.

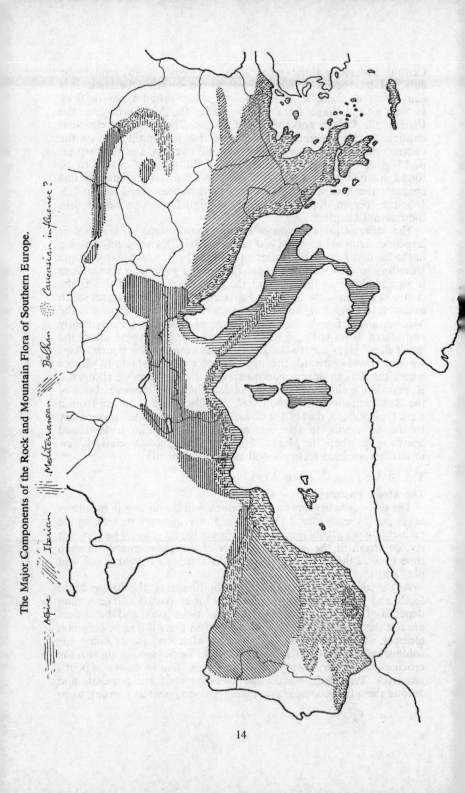

Alpine   Iberian   Mediterranean   Balkan   Caucasian influence ?

followed a little later by the bell-gentians (*G. acaulis* and *G. clusii*). In damper places are the bird's-eye primrose (*P. farinosa*), globe-flower (*Trollius europaeus*) and the lady's mantle (*Alchemilla "vulgaris"*—now much split up into many related species). Then, as the grasses grow lusher, St. Bernard's lily (*Anthericum liliago*) and St. Bruno's lily (*Paradisea liliastrum*) join the throng, with white *Pulsatilla alpina* or its sulphur-coloured subspecies *apiifolia* (the former tending to favour limy and the latter non-limy soils, though they may occur together). *Anemone narcissiflora*, martagon lilies (*L. martagon*), *Viola tricolor* in many colours, perhaps *Gagea fistulosa* (favouring the richly manured soil around cow-huts), tall many-flowered *Ranunculus aconitifolius*, the most handsome of the mountain rues (*Thalictrum aquilegifolium*), and the two odd little fern-relatives, adder's tongue (*Ophioglossum vulgatum*) and moon-wort (*Botrychium lunaria*)—inconspicuous in the grass. With all these there is a mass of orchids—early purple (*O. mascula*), burnt (or dwarf) (*O. ustulata*), vanilla (*Nigritella nigra* and the brighter-red subsp. *rubra*), green-winged (*O. morio*), spotted and marsh (*Dacty-lorhiza* spp.), butterfly (*Platanthera bifolia*), scented (*Gymnadenia conopsea* and *G. odoratissima*), and with them the somewhat orchid-like louseworts, *Pedicularis* spp. These latter sometimes make a great show in the meadows: they are held to be partially parasitic, and they are difficult in our gardens—perhaps we ought to try harder with them, for there are some lovely plants among the many kinds. In the same family (Scrophulariaceae), and also semiparasitic, are the yellow rattles (*Rhinanthus* spp.), sometimes one of the commonest plants in the lower alpine meadows, and the pretty little eyebrights (*Euphrasia* spp.).

As the season advances, many of these plants begin to appear in the higher alps—the upper pastures. At the same time new species come into flower at the lower levels. The summer visitor to the Bernese Oberland—in July or August—will miss the fine, lush display of the lower alps, for these will have been grazed or mown. But there will have been some regrowth of the meadows, as well as unshorn areas between the rocky outcrops. The bellflowers begin to take over; the little biennial *Campanula patula*, deep blue *C. scheuchzeri*, our own clustered bellflower (*C. glomerata*), and perhaps taller *C. persicifolia*. The common columbine (*Aquilegia vulgaris*) appears, and perhaps the rather less attractive *A. atrata*, with dark, brownish-red flowers. In high summer the rampions join the throng—purple and yellow, round headed and spiked (*Phyteuma* spp.)—and lilac meadow sage, *Salvia pratensis*. The pyramidal orchid (*Anacamptis pyramidalis*), the tall monkshoods (*Aconitum vulparia*, *A. anthora* and *A. napellus*), the pretty cypress spurge (*Euphorbia cyparissias*), its green flower-heads aging to red (and perhaps if you are lucky you may see on it the large and beautiful larvae of the spurge hawk moth), the orange-yellow flowers of arnica (*A. montana*) and the even deeper blood-orange of *Hieracium aurantiacum*, and the lovely blue flowers of the straggly mountain lettuce (*Lactuca perennis*). There are beautiful blue gentians too at the lower levels in high summer; the four-petalled *Gentiana cruciata*, and the fringed gentian (*Gentianella ciliata*), and in moister places the bladder gentian (*Gentiana utriculosa*). The last two tend to be annual or biennial, and so also are the little, mauve-flowered felworts (*Gentianella campestris*, *G. amarella* and *G. germanica*). In high summer too the 'alpenrose' flowers, the rusty-leaved *Rhododendron ferrugineum*, sometimes clothing the hillsides in red. It is a plant of acid soils, but its lime-tolerant counterpart, *R. hirsutum*, is commoner in the more easterly Alps. Finally, at these lower levels, in early September, the "autumn crocus" (*Colchicum autumnale*, not a crocus at all) sheets the meadows in soft lilac pink—one of the loveliest sights that the mountains have to offer.

Between, and just above the meadows at these lower levels there are rocky outcrops which, as summer advances, are liable to become hot and dry. They have their own special and attractive plants, many of which are good rock-garden plants at home. The little catsfoot (*Antennaria dioica*) with white woolly leaves and white or rosy flower-tufts, alpine harebell (*Campanula cochlearifolia*—so much better described by its old name, *C. pusilla*), pinks (*Dianthus carthusianorum*, *D. monspessulanus*, *D. superbus* and *D. sylvestris*), the neat blue *Globularia cordifolia*, *Gypsophila repens*, rockrose (*Helianthemum nummularium*), the variable but always beautiful silver saxifrage, *S. paniculata* (*aizoon*), stonecrops (*Sedum album* and *S. reflexum*), houseleeks (*Sempervivum tectorum*, *S. montanum* and *S. arachnoideum*), the delicate yellow *Biscutella laevigata*, and the alpine cinquefoil, *Potentilla crantzii* are all to be found here.

The Upper Pastures

We have followed the seasons through at the lower levels. Let us now instead climb upwards into the higher alps—from the spring pastures to the summer—and here are many of the same plants again flowering later, sometimes perhaps a little more dwarf, but with their flowers no smaller and indeed by contrast seeming bigger. The turf is shorter here, and the spring and bell gentians show to better advantage. Other plants join them—*Androsace chamaejasme*, the alpine aster (*A. alpinus*), the much exploited 'edelweiss' (*Leontopodium alpinum*), *Polygonum viviparum*, *Pulsatilla vernalis*, and among the rocks between the alps the thornless alpine rose (*Rosa pendulina*). The alpine clover (*Trifolium alpinum*) gives a fruity smell to the high meadows. *Viola calcarata* in many colours tends to take over from *Viola tricolor*. The orchids of the lower meadows are still with us, and in many areas they are joined by the misnamed elder-scented orchid (*Dactylorhiza sambucina*), with flowers of yellow, red or a wonderful intermediate rosy-salmon. The lady's mantle (*Alchemilla 'vulgaris'*) is here joined by the silvery *A. alpina*. Blue bugle (*Ajuga genevensis*) is in stony places and in the damper

16

spots in the meadows is another of the little semiparasites, *Bartsia alpina*, attractive in a slightly sombre way. As summer advances the bearded bellflower, *Campanula barbata*, opens its soft blue (or white) stiffly down-turned flowers, and with it there may be the most un-bellflower-like *Campanula thyrsoides*, its greeny-yellow flowers in stiff fat spikes and the tiny, brilliant blue flowers of the annual *Gentiana nivalis* open (if the sun shines) in the short grass. Two conspicuous plants of the higher pastures are the great yellow gentian (*G. lutea*) and the poisonous *Veratrum album*, rather similar in leaf and both a yard or more high.

The Mountain Woodlands

Happily for the summer visitor, the alpine meadows and hillsides are in many areas well wooded, and the paths tend to run through these woods, providing shade for the upward trudge. At the lower levels the trees are mainly deciduous; at the higher levels mainly coniferous. Among the many plants to be found in these woodlands are the beautiful alpine clematis (*C. alpina*), *Corydalis bulbosa*, *Cardamine pentaphyllos* (with white, pink or purplish flowers), *Erica herbacea* (*carnea*) (the 'winter heather' of our gardens, but spring-flowering in the mountains), *Hepatica nobilis* in many colours (but unless you go early in the year you will find it in flower only in the highest woodlands), the related *Isopyrum thalictroides*, charming early in the year at the lower levels, the spring vetchling (*Lathyrus vernus*), beautiful deep blue gromwell (*Buglossoides purpurocaerulea*), *Polygala chamaebuxus* in its two very distinct colour forms, the May lily (*Maianthemum bifolium*), lily of the valley (*Convallaria majalis*), Solomon's seal (*Polygonatum odoratum* and *P. verticillatum*), the poisonous bane-berry (*Actaea spicata*), amelanchier (*A. ovalis*), *Aruncus dioicus*, masterwort (*Astrantia major*), the wintergreens (*Pyrola minor*, *P. media*, *P. rotundifolia*, *Orthilia secunda* and *Moneses uniflora*) and two large and handsome Composites, *Adenostyles alliariae* and *Prenanthes purpurea*. There are several orchids of light woodland which are widespread in the Alps, and three of the loveliest are the butterfly orchid (*Platanthera bifolia*), the rose helleborine (*Cephalanthera rubra*) and the lady's slipper orchid (*Cypripedium calceolus*).

Viola biflora

Damp Rock Faces

Within the woodlands there are damp, shady rock faces, and it is here that one may find such plants as the yellow mountain saxifrage (*S. aizoides*) (sometimes orange or blood-red rather than the typical

17

yellow), another yellow saxifrage, the rather scarcer *S. mutata* with beautiful rosettes but rather squinny flowers, the grass of Parnassus (*Parnassia palustris*), the common and alpine butterworts (*Pinguicula vulgaris* and *P. alpina*) with their star-fish rosettes of insectivorous leaves, and the pretty and distinct little yellow *Viola biflora*.

Marshes and Stream-sides

On the hillsides, both in the open and in the woods, there are damp, marshy areas. Some of the loveliest flowers here are British natives—the kingcup (*Caltha palustris*), globe-flower (*Trollius europaeus*), marsh orchids (*Dactylorhiza incarnata* and *D. majalis*), and the bird's-eye primrose (*Primula farinosa*); and in moist or shady places by stream-sides and in light woodland is the lovely willow gentian (*Gentiana asclepiadea*).

Turfy Screes

The higher alps reach up towards the rocks, and at their junction with the cliffs and screes there is a particularly interesting area, where the mineral-rich soil is stony and fast-draining. Many of the higher meadow plants are still with us, though very few are those which we encountered at the lowest alpine levels. But in the sparse stony turf *Gentiana verna* is still brilliant, now joined by *G. brachyphylla* and *G. bavarica*. *Myosotis alpestris* assumes its dwarfer and more compact form, *M. a. rupicola*. *Ranunculus alpestris* is here, *Draba aizoides*, the moss campion (*Silene acaulis*), alpine campion (*Lychnis alpina*), mountain avens (*Dryas octopetala*), *Androsace villosa*, and (a little surprisingly perhaps) the mezereon (*Daphne mezereum*). Another eye-catching plant with a surprising altitudinal range is the martagon lily, which is to be found in these high turfy screes (and even sometimes in the rocks above them) as well as in the lower alps and woodlands. The alpine avens (*Geum montanum*), though it occurs at lower altitudes as well, shows to best advantage here. Yellow *Vitaliana primuliflora*, and the pretty little alpine 'chrysanthemum' (*Leucanthemopsis alpina*), white or pink-tinged and a devil to grow in an English garden, spread down from the screes above.

Snow Valleys

Among these areas of high rocky turf are pockets in which the snow lies longer, and as it melts the soil stays moist while the turf around begins to dry off in the summer sun. Here, at the edge of the snow, the visitor in July may find spring in summer. The white and purple flowers of *Crocus vernus*, purple, orange-lipped alpine toadflax (*Linaria alpina*), *Pulsatilla vernalis* at its loveliest as it almost explodes through the snow, *Soldanella alpina* (which we met weeks ago in the lower meadows), *Homogyne alpina* (rather a dowdy little plant whose leaves make you think you are finding soldanella—or even cyclamen!), oxlip (*Primula elatior*) and forms of the cowslip (*Primula veris columnae*), seeming to an Englishman ridiculously out of place here, *Ranunculus alpestris*, *Silene acaulis*, and many more

18

that we have met in the turf, or are about to meet—for now we come to the screes.

Scree and Moraine

Screes—areas of broken stone—grade from the stony turf that we have just left to the open soil-less unstable rock piles at the feet of the cliffs. Here there is little or no grass, and the plants tend to be isolated from one another, with long anchorage roots to stabilise them in the moving stones. Despite the fast drainage, there is moisture on the under-surfaces of the stones in the screes, and sometimes (particularly as the snow just above is melting, and in the specialised type of scree which forms the moraines at the edges of glaciers) water is abundant. Such wet screes are the specially favoured home of the alpine toadflax (*Linaria alpina*)—though you may find it sometimes, looking very hearty, in a pile of roadman's grit by the roadside! Another delightful little plant which favours glacier moraines is the alpine rosebay (*Epilobium fleischeri*), a good garden plant in spite of its restricted habitat in the mountains. The purple saxifrage (*S. oppositifolia*) prefers moister or more shady screes, and on acid soils the somewhat similar *S. retusa* may be found. Moss campion (*Silene acaulis*) favours more stable, soil-rich screes; while the beautiful sweet-scented *Thlaspi rotundifolium* is especially to be found in coarse open soil-less limestone scree. Some of the highest and barest places, on non-calcareous screes, are the home of the glacier buttercup (*Ranunculus glacialis*), white or rose-pink (and some say that it changes colour after the flowers are fertilised), and with it in these same high acid screes is the magnificent *Geum reptans*, with huge golden flowers, crimson running stems, and tousled seed-heads rather like those of the mountain avens (*Dryas octopetala*), which also can occur in high screes, usually on limestone.

Rock-fissures

Some of the most specialised plants grow in crevices or fissures* in the cliff-faces at high altitudes, often on aspects which are at least partially shaded. Many of these are rare or local plants, to be mentioned as we reach them in their respective localities. A few are widespread in the Alps, and are appropriately included in this general survey. Yellow *Draba aizoides* in its various forms, white *Hutchinsia alpina*, and pink, scented *Petrocallis pyrenaica*—three beautiful little plants in the much-maligned race of crucifers—are mainly crevice dwellers in the wild, but take well to the garden scree. The edelweiss (*Leontopodium alpinum*), by no means rare in the high turf, sometimes conforms to its popular image as a high cliff dweller, tending then to be (or to seem) neater, whiter and woollier. Some of the scree plants, such as *Saxifraga oppositifolia* and *S. retusa*, grow also in rock-crevices.

* In this book the term 'crevice' is used to mean a V-shaped cleft usually packed with soil (often a rich acid humus), and 'fissure' refers to a virtually soil-less hair-crack in the rock.

Acid Heaths

One other habitat remains to be mentioned. There are upland heaths, more or less stony, on acid soils, which are remarkably reminiscent of our own British mountains and carry a generally similar flora. The common heather (*Calluna vulgaris*) is here, bearberry (*Arctostaphylos uva-ursi* and *A. alpinus*), whortleberry (*Vaccinium vitis-idaea*), crowberry (*Empetrum nigrum*), alpine campion (*Lychnis alpina*), and the charming little creeping azalea (*Loiseleuria procumbens*).

Other reading:

Huxley, A. *Mountain Flowers* Blandford

Polunin, O. & Huxley, A. *Flowers of the Mediterranean* Chatto & Windus

Polunin, O. *Flowers of Europe* O.U.P.

Polunin, O. & Smythies, B. E. *Flowers of South-West Europe* O.U.P.

Roger-Smith, H. *Plant Hunting in Europe* A.G.S. (out of print)

2

TRAVELLING TO THE MOUNTAINS

This book is written with the car-traveller primarily in mind, because the great majority of Members of our Society who travel independently to the mountains either take their own cars or hire them on arrival. The convenience of having a car is beyond question; you are free to go anywhere where there is a negotiable road, and can cover a wider area and reach places beyond the range of public transport. If the car is your own, you have the advantage of being able to increase the quantity and range of your clothing and equipment. Otherwise there are decided advantages in a hired car; car-hire is usually associated with flying to one's destination, thus effectively extending the holiday, and most of us are likely to be rather happier wearing out a hired car on rough mountain roads than our own! Costs of course vary tremendously, but by the time you have allowed for the considerable expense of getting your car across the Channel, and paying for petrol to your destination, and have allowed also for the fare-reduction which is now generally available with a 'Fly-drive' holiday, and for the additional genuine holiday-time that you obtain, there is usually not a great deal to it as regards the relative costs of driving your own car and hiring one. If your own vehicle is one in which you can eat and sleep, then of course the balance-sheet is quite different, and after the initial outlay it is doubtless the most economical way to travel.

Though writing with the car-driver primarily in mind, one must emphasise that looking for plants from a car is not an efficient method. It is true that a knowledgeable and alert passenger (not the driver!) can become remarkably adept at spotting plants from the car, as well as recognising a 'likely place' to stop and search—but there is no doubt that really to find plants one should be on foot, and the car should be used to get to a place to start walking, not as a substitute for it.

By whatever method you travel, there is much to be gained by consulting the National Tourist Office (in Britain) for the country you propose to visit. There is a list of these in Appendix I. While as much information as possible is given in this book about local travel facilities, it cannot be complete and it cannot long remain up-to-date. Travel agents are likely to have a certain amount of literature, and are usually helpful, but there is far more to be gained by going to the National Tourist Office.

Mountain roads vary from magnificently engineered highways to barely negotiable tracks—'routes jeepables' as they are sometimes nicely described on the maps—and some of them have a disconcerting way of fluctuating unpredictably from one state to the other. If there is a doubt one of course attempts inquiry, but it has been our experience that local advice, even if one has enough of the language to follow it, can prove quite misleading, usually (we have found) in the direction of over-caution. We have tackled pretty well everything, never got irretrievably stuck, and only once did our rather under-powered car refuse to face the gradient. The gradients are in fact usually very good, even though the surface be bad. In some countries and areas the maps fall short of British standards, and if there is any doubt it is as well to inquire whether the road really does go through —in particular does this apply to roads across passes subject to closure by snow. Foreign touring guides, such as are available from the A.A. and R.A.C., give valuable information about the usual times of opening and closure of the main passes, but seasons vary, and sometimes one can be frustrated. It is in any case wise to allow a little latitude, or provision for alternatives, in planning one's route. Our own practice has always been to plan beforehand the broad pattern of our holidays. To drive 'wheel-loose and fancy-free' into the hills sound delightful as you sit planning at home, but when you are among them, having little idea where you want to go can lead to much argument and wasted time. Conversely being too rigidly tied to a precise schedule can also lead to frustration; not only may roads be blocked (or even non-existent), but the time taken to traverse a planned route in the mountains may prove very much longer than you had supposed—the state of the road, of the traffic, of the weather, and above all the delays arising from plant-seeking, can often mean that a journey takes twice as long as you allowed for. We have generally found it better not to be booked into an hotel when travelling to a new destination, but there are exceptions.

Map names and spellings can be very confusing, particularly if one knows little of the local language. We have on two occasions (in Majorca and Jugoslavia) been utterly confused to find all roads leading to 'Ronda' and 'Izlaz' respectively—till at last it dawned on us that they meant 'Ring Road' and 'Exit'! It is particularly desirable to have good maps (or exercise considerable caution) when near national frontiers: a road leading towards the frontier (so often a mountain ridge—just where you would like to be) is liable to end at some sort of military installation and the army personnel—though we have found them courteous and helpful—do not seem readily to understand plant-seeking as an adequate explanation for being up in the wilder hills. (The two words 'English' and 'botanist' can be useful as conveying alternative explanations of the visitors' apparent madness!)

This is not the place to attempt any detailed advice as to how to prepare the car, mechanically speaking, for the journey, but it is as well, if it is your first drive into the mountains, to seek advice from a motoring organisation, and follow it. Even an ordinary puncture on a mountain road can make you feel terribly lonely if your wheelnut spanner does not fit. In most countries good repair garages are not too far to seek, but this is not always so; the comment made in a guide book on a certain country that 'trained mechanics are rare but would-be mechanics abound' has a wider application than the particular country to which it referred.

It is difficult in a book of this sort to advise on hotels and other types of accommodation, because people's tastes and standards differ so, and also the hotels themselves tend to change, so that information becomes out of date. In this book therefore the practice adopted is simply to indicate the presence or absence of hotels in the areas discussed, and not to specify or assess them. Similarly no indication is given of charges or costs (for hotels or anything else) except in the most general terms: these again are matters on which the traveller should seek information from Tourist Offices or travel agencies before he sets off. Most Tourist Offices (see Appendix I) have hotel lists, with indications of the standards, if not of actual prices. In several countries both the standards and the prices are government-controlled, and lists are available. Mountain huts and refuges, usually maintained by the national alpine club, can be most useful for a night's stay for those who are active enough to walk or climb into the hills. Again the National Tourist Office will probably be helpful and give the address of the headquarters of the alpine club, whence information about the use of the huts can be obtained. Even if you do not intend to stay overnight when you visit a mountain hut, it is wise to be prepared to do so, in case you should find yourself weather-bound.

Advance booking of hotel accommodation will bring peace of mind to those who wish to be certain of their next night's rest and (since language difficulties are magnified over the telephone) hotel staff are usually very obliging in 'phoning to one's next port of call and making a booking. Advance booking is advisable in most countries at the height of the holiday season (generally July and August) but at other times this is seldom necessary, and there is much to be said for leaving one's choice of destination (both place and hotel) open when moving on from one place to another. As in England, hotels are more crowded at week-ends—and so are the roads—so it is better to avoid both main road travel and changing hotels at the week-end if possible. Popular beauty spots and picnic areas also of course are more crowded at week-ends, but it is remark-able how in the mountains one has only to go a couple of hundred yards from the road to be more or less alone with the flowers. It is advisable to inquire as to local feast days, holidays, saints' days, etc., for at such times the roads and beauty spots are liable to be congested—and the banks closed. If you are going to spend more than a day or two in one spot (and this can be much more restful and rewarding than pressing on from day to day, and may also enable you to obtain more favourable *pension* or *demi-pension* terms) it is worth making an early visit to the local Tourist Information Bureau and finding out about local transport, ski-lifts, holidays, opening hours of banks, shops, museums, show-places, etc., and the weather in the mountains. Check too that your watch is adjusted to the local time.

Language problems must of course arise if one has nothing but English, though such problems tend to be less than the inexperienced traveller might anticipate. It is still usual, at least as far east as Greece and Jugoslavia, to be able to find someone in the vicinity who speaks English (or American), and the local inhabitants confronted by a dumb tourist are ready enough to rush off and find an interpreter if possible. If you have German or French, then it is still more likely, even in countries where these are not the native tongue, that someone can be found who speaks one or other of them. Nevertheless, it is a very sensible precaution to try and learn at least the alphabet of the country you are visiting (which helps you to read the road-signs among other things) and to carry a phrase-book: such books often seem to provoke mirth when they are produced, but the reaction is always friendly and helpful.

In a few parts of Europe you can drive to the high passes and even in late July be among the flowers not far from the snow's edge, but in most places and at most times to see the highest flowers it is necessary to leave the car and either climb on foot or take a mountain railway, cable car, or ski-lift. Railways and cable-cars have for the most part been provided primarily for summer visitors, and are likely to be running when the plant-seeker wants them; even so it is as well to inquire at the National Tourist Office before leaving, and to confirm in the local Tourist Information Bureau on arrival. Ski-lifts are a different matter. They are provided, of course, for winter sports, and unless there is summer ski-ing they will probably not be running in the summer. Before taking any of these forms of transport high into the mountains it is advisable to inquire as to the snow conditions up there, or you may find yourself landed on a slab of rock with snow all round you and no plants. Some ski-lifts do run in the summer. If you are not accustomed to these and want to be helped on or off (the lifts do not stop) ask for this help as you get on; do not ask for the lift to be stopped for you. Inquire as to the time of the last lift down, and when you arrive at the top immediately check the location of the path down, in case the lift is not running when you return.

A rapid ascent to high altitudes, by whatever method, can impose a strain on the heart and lungs if you are not acclimatised and it is well to take it quietly until you get your 'second wind'.

If you are going off the beaten track (and especially if alone) let the hotel staff know where you are making for.

Winter sports have made their mark in most of the mountain ranges in Europe. The hotels, ski-shops, ski-lifts, etc. continue to proliferate. They are often ugly and tawdry, and the peaceful alpine villages of Roger-Smith's day are now ugly beyond recognition. Nevertheless it must be conceded that in terms of accommodation, transport and communications the summer visitor can benefit from them.

The weather in the mountains is notoriously unpredictable, and it can be very wet, cold and cloudy. In some areas, such as the Pyrenees, violent thunderstorms are commonplace. A bitter wind may howl across a saddle or col, yet drop to a balmy breeze a hundred feet above it. A dry ravine can rapidly become a raging torrent as a result of rain or snow-melt above. So plant-seeking requires a good deal of determination, tolerance of discomfort, and the right equipment.

To some extent equipment is a matter of personal choice, and the requirements certainly depend upon how active one is and in the conditions one is likely to find. However, anyone who intends to walk, even a little, in the hills should carry appropriate clothing and protection and this means having some sort of rucksac. These come in a wide range of sizes, weights and cost. The 'casual' walker will probably want only a small and light rucksac, but even so there is much to be said for having one with a frame that holds the sac away from one's back. This makes for much better weight-distribution and comfort; the weight is distributed between the hips and the shoulders. Clothing is a problem, especially if you are flying to your destination (with a weight-limit on your luggage) or carrying your pack on your back. The weather may be as just described, or it may be very hot, changing at the same place within a few hours. In addition to the normal range of clothing which you would need for any holiday in England, take a pair of good stout climbing boots, a pair of strong walking shoes, thick long socks, a good light-weight wind- and rain-proof anorak or wind-jacket (preferably with a hood), a light-weight close-woven nylon cape or raincoat, a sou'wester type hat, and a pair of gloves. Ladies should remember that while trousers are excellent for the mountains they are unacceptable in church—whether for worshipping or for sight-seeing.

Other equipment should include sunglasses (to avoid snow-glare), a reliable compass, and a stout walking-stick or, better, an ice-axe. The latter has many uses, from driving off obstreperous cattle to clearing rocks or snow off a mountain road to get your car through. If you travel by plane you should pad the point and blade, or you may have to hand it over to the steward as an offensive weapon. Take too a good insect-repellant; horse-flies can be a nuisance in hot weather. If you use mains-powered electrical equipment (e.g. a shaver or an immersion heater for making tea) you will need a set of continental plugs or adaptors—and see that they are up-to-date, for continental electrical fittings, e.g. in France, appear to be undergoing change.

A first-aid box in the car is as valuable on holiday as at home. When walking, carry a few adhesive dressings, some sterilised gauze, a 1-inch and a $2\frac{1}{2}$-inch cotton bandage, a triangular bandage, a $2\frac{1}{2}$-inch calico or elastic bandage (for sprains) and some safety-pins. On a long trek, always carry chocolate or glucose, and a drink, as 'reserve energy'. Mr. H. Taylor (who contributes a note on camping to this chapter) recommends muesli mixed with dried milk as being light in weight and requiring only the addition of snow to make a delicious meal. Mountain travellers are not immune from the 'D. & V.' that threatens holiday-makers abroad; see what your family doctor advises, and do not drink unboiled unsterilised milk. It is wise to carry a suitable cream for the prevention and treatment of sunburn.

For those who are prepared really to study the growing conditions of plants, a small hand-fork or fern-trowel (with a brightly painted handle or marker on it) is useful for investigating the soil.

Most of the flowers we grow in our rock gardens and alpine houses are the wild flowers of the mountains, including those of Europe. In Roger-Smith's day plant-collecting was an accepted practice—though his whole emphasis was on restraint, responsibility, courtesy and selectiveness in so doing. Gardeners owe a debt of gratitude to those who in past decades have travelled, often in conditions of hardship such as we rarely encounter now in Europe, and introduced these plants to our gardens. Without them our Society would not have come into being.

But times are changing. The alps are still massed with flowers, to a degree hard to imagine for anyone who has not seen them. Yet these flowers are threatened, for man is steadily encroaching upon their living-space and destroying their habitats in order to meet his own needs for housing, crops, roads, amusements and factories. Many species are still abundant, but others have become scarce and more limited in their distribution.

Except in a few instances, the collection of plants for botanical or horticultural purposes has probably not hitherto been a significant factor in reducing the populations of mountain flowers, but as the destruction of habitats progresses the effects of any additional assault upon the plants become greater, and rare or local species (whose rarity indicates that they are already failing to compete successfully with other species) may be extinguished.

More and more the governments or local authorities in Europe are seeking to conserve their rarer species. In some areas the collection or picking of any kind of flower is forbidden, while in others there are lists of plants, publicly displayed and depicted, which it is forbidden to collect.

It is no part of the Society's policy to encourage the collection of plants by its Members, and in this book no precise plant locations are given. The decision whether to collect is of course a personal one but the Society hopes that its Members travelling abroad will at least accept the following restraints.

First, if plants are to be imported it is necessary to obtain a permit from the Ministry of Agriculture, Fisheries and Food, Eagle House, 90–96 Cannon Street, London EC4N 6HT: the requirements specified in the permit should be observed in every detail. There are certain 'vulnerable species' (of which cyclamen and all species of orchids are most likely to be of interest in the context of alpines)

26

whose importation requires in addition a licence from the Wildlife Conservation Licensing Section, Department of the Environment, 17–19 Rochester Row, London SW1P 1LN. Attempts to import plants otherwise than under licence run the risk of bringing the Society as well as the Member into disrepute; and to collect species, or in areas, where this is locally prohibited is in addition a discourtesy and a breach of the trust which is implicit when any country admits a foreign visitor. The importation of 'vulnerable species' requires permission from the exporting country, so application should be made in good time.

Apart from legal restraints, the picking of plants, even of species and in areas where it is permitted, under the eyes of local people can cause resentment and is a discourtesy. The picking of flowers or collecting of plants by paths or roads or in popular beauty-spots—anywhere where people gather and the flowers are a part of the scene—is also discourteous and inconsiderate.

There remain in the mountains vast areas where these considerations do not apply, but even in such areas the visitor if he collects at all should do so responsibly and with restraint. This means taking no more than very small numbers of specimens of plants which, even though abundant in the area where they are found, have a limited distribution, and refraining from collecting plants which are locally scarce even though they have a wide distribution elsewhere.

Of special importance is the need to refrain from collecting plants which one has no hope of growing at home and this means making a careful study of the plants and their cultural requirements, and ensuring that suitable growing conditions can be, and are, provided for them.

The foregoing relates to the uprooting of plants (and local regulations may apply also to the picking of flowers). But two forms of collection are in the writer's view permissible, provided that local restrictions are not infringed—moderate seed-collecting and cuttings. For cuttings, if you have a car, take a propagating tray with a plastic cover, containing a mixture of two parts of sand and one of vermiculite (the small-granule type 'suitable for horticulture', not the coarser builder's stuff, which may be poisonously alkaline) suitably moistened, some labels and a gardener's pencil, a razor-blade to trim the cuttings, and a note-book. If you are flying and hiring a car take a small quantity of vermiculite in a plastic bag (it is very light); the rest of the equipment can be improvised and discarded for the return journey, when the cuttings are packed in polythene bags. It is of course necessary to ensure that the cuttings receive adequate light in the car, and are not subjected to drying out or overheating. In the plane, they should be carried as hand-luggage in the pressurised cabin. This method can be highly successful, and the range of plants that can be propagated by cuttings in this way is very wide. A permit to import cuttings should be obtained in the same way as for rooted plants.

The serious student of plants may also wish to carry an altimeter, but if one has a good map, showing contours, it should be possible to calculate altitudes (in relation to plant-distribution) adequately from this. Altitudes are of course shown in metres on continental maps, and for this reason are similarly given in this book. A simple but adequate method of converting metres to feet is to divide by three and add a nought—e.g. 3069 metres = 10230 feet.

This chapter has so far been directed mainly to the traveller visiting a country for the first time independently with a car. Much of it of course applies equally to him who travels by public transport, and walks, but he will need to seek information beyond the scope of this book, as to availability and times of public transport. Tourist Information Bureaux are frequently very helpful.

Finally, let it be said that an excellent introduction to mountain holidays is to travel the first time with an organised party—and what better than an A.G.S. party for this purpose? Information on the proposed Tours is given every year in the *Bulletin* and *Newsletter*. Most of the difficulties of foreign travel in Europe occur in anticipation rather than in reality, but they can be discouraging to the complete beginner, and to go the first time with an A.G.S. party will show how very unreal are most of the difficulties—and how very friendly and helpful are most foreigners.

A mountain holiday is a wonderful cure for despondency. The first fresh breeze stirring the flowers at 1500 m. makes the whole world seem a richer and better place—and you will wonder why you ever had misgivings about coming.

Camping in the Mountains*

Camping has the great advantage of easy mobility to the next pass if the first chosen is lacking in flowers. Pitch a small dark green tent at dusk, arise with the dawn, and you can camp anywhere. When camping at low altitude, detailed maps are a help. Look for a small side road, keep clear of villages, and camp in the entrance to a little-used field. Shun cows; they swallow equipment, and in the mountains they jangle those cracked bells at night.

Try to camp at the highest possible altitude, as this helps acclimatisation. In the high mountains you will be alone at dusk (8 p.m. approximately) as the locals all live down in the valley.

Do not leave litter or light fires. For cooking, a Primus is useful, or a small butane gas burner. In France paraffin comes from the Droguerie where it is known as 'pétrole'. Butane gas in small containers is now widely available, but becomes less so as you go further east. A camping shop is then the best bet, but the small containers do not appear to be obtainable in Jugoslavia.

Ample warm bedding is required as even in July you may wake to find the tent dusted with snow, but for compensation you are off

* Contributed by Mr. H. Taylor

long before the valley folk and in these early hours you may spy timid animals such as the ibex.

For the gregarious, campsites in the valleys are plentiful and always have room for one more, if you avoid France on 14th July and the following week. The sites signposted with a 'Slavia' beer sign are cheap and good in my experience. Before venturing into remote high places, exercise your languages by stocking up with food from the village shops.

Avoid camping in the dried-up bed of a stream or you may find yourself pelted by hail when awash in a midnight thunderstorm.

Finally, camping in the wilds is inexpensive. Think of being able to afford extra croissants, or maybe even a ride on one of those exorbitantly-priced chairlifts.

3
SWITZERLAND

Before the war Switzerland was the country most often visited by those who wanted to see alpine flowers in the wild and this probably still remains true, though it became very expensive. In recent years costs have so risen in other countries that Switzerland is no longer as disadvantageous on this account. Cost apart, it is an excellent country for one's first visit to Europe's mountain flowers. Tourism has been one of its major industries for decades, with the result that problems of accommodation and of language are minimal and both its scenery and its flowers are magnificent.

The country consists of a relatively low-lying plateau, running from W.S.W. to E.N.E., bounded to the north by the Jura, which form part of the frontier with France, and to the south by the main mountain block of the Central Alps. The Alps are again divided along this same axis by the valleys of the Rhône and the Rhine, two valleys whose heads are separated by high land at the St. Gotthard Pass. The mountains to the north of the Rhône valley constitute the Bernese Oberland and those to the south are the Pennine Alps which in part form the frontier with Italy, and their northern (Swiss) slopes are in the Canton Valais. In this book three main areas are considered, the Oberland and the Valais and a third area at the eastern end of the country, the Engadine. These three areas, while they have a large flora in common, also have some very distinct features for the plant-seeker, so that all are separately worth visiting. It would however be quite misleading to suggest that only these three areas are of interest; apart from some industrial zones in the north, the whole country is at least hilly, with flowers to please the rock-gardener and two more areas, the Jura and the lake district of Ticino, will be briefly considered under France and Italy (into which they overlap) respectively.

Communications are good. Most towns and villages are accessible by road, and the roads are generally well engineered and reasonably well surfaced. However, many of the roads traverse high passes, and these are subject to blockage by snow and by rock-falls. The lower passes are usually open, but the higher ones are closed by snow for as long as nine months (October to June) and even longer in abnormal weather conditions. The motoring agencies (A.A. and R.A.C.) list the expected closure times but it is as well, in planning a day's journey which may take one across such a pass, to make local inquiry in advance. Visitors coming from England by car are most likely to enter Switzerland from the north-west, between Geneva and Basel, across the Jura mountains, and main road passes here are normally open.

The visitor travelling by train will most likely enter at Basel, and from here a network of railways reaches most of the major towns and tourist centres, and in addition there is a good public coach service along many of the mountain roads. Funicular and cable-railways and ski-lifts abound, and full particulars of these, with other local transport services, and usually useful local maps are available in the Tourist Information Bureaux. 'Package holidays' can be arranged which include rail travel concessions.

Switzerland is famous for its footpaths, which are abundant, well-maintained and clearly marked.

Language presents few problems to the English visitor because English is so widely understood. Western Switzerland is French-speaking and most of the rest Swiss-German-speaking, but many Swiss are at least bilingual. Parts of South-East Switzerland (particularly the Ticino) are Italian-speaking, and in the Engadine the commonest native language is Romansch.

Accommodation is, as would be expected in a country so fully developed for the tourist, abundant and generally good, with good service and good food. The Swiss Alpine Club (S.A.C.) provides and maintains many Club Huts high in the mountains; members of the Club (which can be joined in England) have priority and lower charges than non-member tourists, but the latter are not excluded from using the huts. Local Tourist Offices can advise as to whether the huts in their areas are open.

The best time to visit ranges from May to September, according to what you want and how high you are prepared to go. The lower valleys can be delightful in May, and we have found plenty of interesting flowers in the Valais in early September. Late June and early July is an excellent time in a typical season, for the lower alps are still in fine form and the higher passes and valleys sufficiently clear of snow to make flower-seeking rewarding—but the seasons do vary a very great deal, and if it is the higher levels that call you, you will be safer in mid-July but you will have to pay more.

THE BERNESE OBERLAND

This title is used here to include the great block of mountains forming the north side of the Rhône valley and the extreme upper reaches of the Rhine valley. The mountains include the famous trio—the Jungfrau, the Mönch and the Eiger—and the highest is the Finsteraarhorn (4274 m.). There are vast glaciers. It is an area that displays in typical form all the main zones and habitats of mountain flowers—the more lush, lower alpine meadows and the more sparse (though flower-rich) higher alps, which are respectively the winter and summer cow-pastures; deciduous woods (not many of these) and above them coniferous forests; hot, low-level rocky outcrops; high rock-faces, creviced and fissured, both wet and dry; turf at the upper levels of the alps grading into 'fixed scree' with a high soil-content; above this, and below the rock-faces, almost soil-less open unstable screes; wet slopes at the snow's edge, and gullies where the snow lies late; streams and waterfalls; marshy stream-side meadows, and high acid bogs. It is a country of great beauty, long and fully developed for the tourist.

The geology of the Oberland is, I believe, mixed and complicated, but undoubtedly there is a predominance of limestone areas, which is one of the factors that produce differences in its flora from that of the Valais.

The flora of the Oberland has been discussed at some length in Chapter 1.

There are dozens of centres where one can stay in the Oberland. To the north of the mountains lie the great lakes—the Thunersee and the Brienzersee with Interlaken between them, the Sarnersee, and the Vierwaldstättersee (the Lake of Lucerne)—and the many towns and villages round these are especially popular centres; but if it is the higher mountain flowers that you seek—and particularly if you have no car—you will waste a lot of time getting into the hills each day. So for Members of our Society, higher centres are likely to be more attractive. Only a small sample can be given here, and I have chosen Kandersteg and Wengen, which lie in fairly well-separated parts of the Oberland.

Kandersteg was acclaimed by Roger-Smith. My own memories of it go back more than fifty years—but my records, alas, do not. Its altitude is 1176 m., and it is reached from the north by road or rail running south from Spiez on the Thunersee. It is at the head of a narrow valley, and though the road does not penetrate southward into the high mountains, the railway continues through the Lötschberg tunnel under the mountains to Goppenstein in the Rhône Valley; and cars are transported by this railway so that there is in effect a car approach from the south as well—the ferry-service is speedy and frequent.

There are plenty of hotels and there is ready access to a considerable number of mountains and high valleys. Around the little town itself (and in the valley below it) are lush alpine meadows

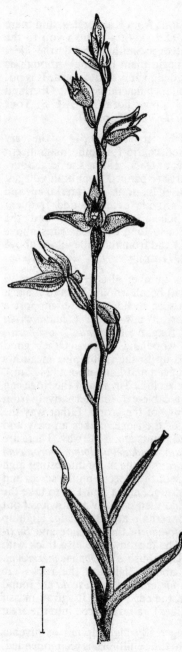

Cephalanthera rubra

carrying the typical rich flora of the lower alps. A fine path and a chair-lift lead up to the Oeschinensee, a beautiful lake set in the mountains, where many orchids grow including the rose helleborine, *Cephalanthera rubra*. The path goes on and up to the Blümlisalp Hut, where there is a pass over into the next valley (the Kiental).

Above the village a toll road runs along the Gasterntal to Selden. This wild valley, interesting for its flowers, is a long one and runs up to the summer snow level; it furthermore appears to be mixed geologically, the plants there including on the one hand *Primula hirsuta* and *Androsace alpina* and on the other *Cypripedium calceolus*. Consequently the range of plants is tremendous, comprising the vast majority of the 'basic' alpine plants of all habitats mentioned in Chapter 1.

Another branch valley, running southwestwards from Kandersteg, is the Ueschinental, which can be reached by road (toll) as well as footpath.

There are four main routes for walkers into the high mountains. Those to the Blümlisalp Hut and to the Lötschen Pass (2690 m.) have already been mentioned. Another good path leads over the Bonderkrinde (2384 m.) to Adelboden, and perhaps the most popular one is the old through-route from the Oberland to the Rhône Valley—a long high track leading past the Daubensee and over the Gemmi Pass and so down (by cable-car if you wish) to Leukerbad. There is a fine selection of high-level plants here.

33

These are only some of the excursions from Kandersteg, and there are now several mountain railways and ski-lifts to take you to the higher slopes. All in all, it is as Roger-Smith claimed 'the ideal centre from which the novice may begin plant-hunting'—though as he said, it is inclined to be a bit crowded in July and August. It is not a place for special local plants, but offers a fine range of the Oberland flowers which comprise the 'basic' alpine flora. An A.G.S. Tour visited Kandersteg in 1977 (see *Bulletin* Vol. 46, p. 64).

Wengen* (1163 m.), also chosen by Roger-Smith, is in the very heart of the Oberland and is a good centre for some magnificent walks. There is no need for a car here, or when visiting the neighbouring resort of Mürren, and indeed cars are banned from both villages. Both are readily reached from Basel by train to Interlaken and Lauterbrunnen. Local trains also provide excellent and frequent service to Grindelwald, Kleine Scheidegg (2061 m.) and the Jungfraujoch (3454 m.). There are also long cable-car runs above Wengen to the Männlichen (2230 m.) and from the valley-floor above Lauterbrunnen to the Schilthorn (2971 m.).

Around Wengen itself there are a number of easy and attractive walks through pine and (lower down) beech woods. Even in August (when the plants here named were seen in flower) these support a rich and varied flora with masses of cow-wheat (*Melampyrum pratense*), *Lilium martagon*, yellow foxglove (*Digitalis grandiflora*), *Gentiana asclepiadea* and smaller woodland species. Other good walks start in these woods and lead up to the rich alpine meadows running under the cliffs of the Tschuggen and Lauberhorn (2472 m.). Chamois are a common sight on these cliffs. The top of the ridge can easily be reached by the Männlichen cable-car, or alternatively from Kleine Scheidegg at the southern edge of the group. Either way the path, which skirts the eastern side of the ridge, makes an easy and spectacular walk with plenty of good plants along the way. There are masses of gentian, and *Viola calcarata*, *Soldanella alpina*, *Doronicum grandiflorum* and *Hypochoeris uniflora*, but the more interesting high alpines are not so easily found. Some of these occur on the screes and moraines below the Eigergletscher station, and a 'must' is to take the train right up to the Jungfraujoch and then on the way down get out and walk back to Wengen over Wengernalp and Biglenalp. High up there are masses of *Thlaspi rotundifolium* in the moraine and *Saxifraga caesia* in some of the screes. The meadows are also thick with *Nigritella nigra*, and there are some large bushes of *Daphne mezereum*. Coming into the thin woodland above Biglenalp the rocks are studded with primulas, and both *P. hirsuta* and *P. auricula* are found in the area. These high pastures on the edge of the Jungfrau massif are a favourite place for steinbock (ibex), re-introduced into the area.

For some of the more interesting really high alpines or niveous plants of the rocks and screes a trip to the Schilthorn is recommended.

This is worth it for the view alone, but there are interesting plants around the summit restaurant, and if the path down looks too much of a scramble for some (and it is often covered by snow through much of the year) it is possible to descend to Birg and walk from there down to Mürren in about two hours. Above the Schilthorn Hut there is a rather flat valley where there is a carpet of interesting plants.

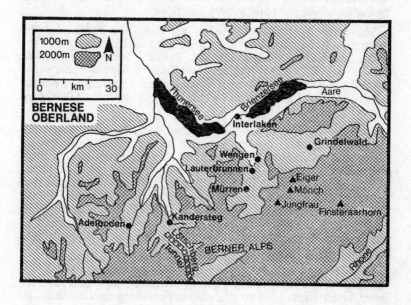

Ranunculus glacialis and *Androsace alpina* are in abundance, and there are occasional good patches of *Geum reptans*. Below the hut there are cushions of *Androsace helvetica* wedged in the crevices, and there are many other interesting plants, as well as superb views, on the descent to Mürren, whence return to Wengen is quick and easy by the railway via Lauterbrunnen.

Wengen is a good centre for a holiday, there are plenty of good trips around the spectacular Lauterbrunnen valley to keep the visitor occupied for a full fortnight and, if the weather is bad, which is not so unusual in mid-summer, it is still possible to visit the Lakes of Thun and Brienz and the town of Interlaken in between.

The Canton Valais is in effect the valley of the Rhone from the Simplon and Furka Passes to the Lake of Geneva, and the mountain slopes on either side of the valley—the limestone southern faces of the mountains that we have already met as the Bernese Oberland and the mainly siliceous northern faces of the great mountains of the Pennine Alps which here form the frontier between Switzerland and Italy. The area to be considered here is the Pennine Alps from the Val d'Hérens to the Saastal, but there are other parts of the Valais that are exciting for both scenery and flowers.

The main approach by road is via Lausanne and round the eastern end of Lake Geneva. A good road and a railway run the whole length of the Rhône valley, and branch roads run southwards into the side valleys that lead up to the Pennine Alps and northward toward the Bernese Oberland. The other main approach is from the north (Basel and Bern) by rail or car ferry through the Lötschberg Tunnel from Kandersteg (q.v.).

Broadly, the flora of the Valais includes all that of the Oberland, but limestone areas are less frequent on the Pennine side, where gneiss and schists are widespread, and consequently strictly lime-demanding plants are more rarely met with and calcifuge plants predominate. This, with perhaps climatic factors as well, means that a number of plants scarce in the Oberland are abundant in the Valais. Furthermore the Valais has a number of southern species absent from the Oberland, making its alpine flora the richest in Switzerland. Two centres, both on the Pennine side, are here singled out from many others.

Saas-Fee is approached from Visp on the main road and railway. A beautiful ride takes one to Stalden, where the valley forks and the more westerly arm goes up to Zermatt. Following the other arm, by car or post-coach, one arrives at Saas-Grund, and from here a fine road runs steeply up to Saas-Fee (1790 m.) set on a hill in a magnificent hanging valley, surrounded by some of the finest scenery in the Alps. Saas-Fee has plenty of hotels, and is developed as a winter-sports as well as a tourist and mountaineering centre. The streets of the old village are very narrow, and cars are not allowed: there is a large car park at the entrance to the village, and transport within the village is by small electrically-powered vehicles.

There are good easy walks in the meadows and woodlands immediately round the village, and plenty of exciting mountain paths up to the lower peaks and to the mountain huts to the west and south, as well as the cable-cars to the Langefluh and Plattjen, and further walks and climbs from Saas-Almagell in the Saastal below.

Two charming little veronicas, *V. aphylla* and the crimson-eyed, deep blue *V. fruticans*, grow close to the village. On the wooded

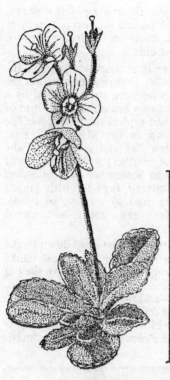

Veronica aphylla

slopes to the north-west *Linnaea borealis* and *Polygala chamaebuxus* are to be found with many other woodlanders. *Primula hirsuta* is magnificent by the stream that runs through the valley, as well as on the rocks around.

A popular excursion is to the Langefluh, by foot or using the cable-railway. This is an enormous ridge of black rock, reaching 2870 m., between the arms of the Fée Glacier, which comes down almost to the valley. Many of the higher turf and snow-valley plants grow here, and it is a site for *Lloydia serotina*—fairly widespread on the acid rocks—and for one of the specialities of the district, *Campanula excisa*, which at its best (though not always) is an exceedingly beautiful plant distinguished by the little punched-out notches between the bases of the petals. Another high point which can also be reached by cable-car (but the path is easy, pleasant and interesting) is Plattjen, where there is a restaurant set upon a promontory over-looking the Saastal and from here there is a fine walk, more or less level at first, leading to the Britannia Hütte (3029 m.). Hereabouts grows *Eritrichium nanum*, that loveliest of high alpines—a plant usually of siliceous rocks, though we shall meet it again on the dolomitic limestone. Also in the rocks by the path is *Androsace alpina*, here growing as a cushion plant, a perfect twin in white or rose to the eritrichium's blue, but continuing to flower even into September, when the eritrichium has set its seed. It is a plant remarkable not only for its long flowering season but also for its diversity of habit; for further along, where a stream crosses the path and trickles through wet scree, the androsace spreads diffusely through stones and runnels, where also (and doing the same thing) is the soft grey-blue *Campanula cenisia*, crimson-eyed with fresh pollen, and likewise still flowering in September. I remember an attractive hare's-ear here too (*Bupleurum stellatum*), and in the screes near the Britannia Hütte the magnificent *Geum reptans*, a widespread but by no means common plant of the acid soils.

Returning to the slopes below Plattjen, *Dryas octopetala* is found, for the schists of this area are rich in lime and support a display of lime-loving plants among which are many astragalus, oxytropis, *Hedysarum hedysaroides* and martagon lilies.

On the west side of the valley there is pleasant walking on the lower slopes of Melig, and into the valley that runs down from the Hohbaln glacier. *Androsace vandellii* is here, on rocks reached by a path through stony turf where there is a very beautiful dwarf form of *Dianthus carthusianorum* (var. *vaginatus*) typical of the Valais. The more strenuous will take the path up to the Mischabel Hütte (3329 m.)—a climb which will fill your day and give you all the flowers and (if you are lucky with the weather) some of the finest views that the Valais can offer. Even in September *Senecio halleri* (*uniflorus*), a lovely dwarf golden-flowered ragwort with jagged white-felted leaves, was in fine flower, and so was the edelweiss, *Leontopodium alpinum*, here dwarfed and cotton-wool-leaved against the turf, browned by recent snow.

On the eastern side of Saas-Fee there is a steep drop down to the Saastal—the way you came up. You can drive down past banks filled with superb *Campanula barbata*, or you can walk down the old track (Roger-Smith's Kapellenweg) among the *Ononis rotundifolia*, and along the valley to Saas-Almagell—and from here there is a long, relatively level, walk to Mattmark. The track goes on from here right up to the Italian frontier at the Monte Moro Pass (see p. 50). Roger-Smith reported *Campanula cenisia* and *Primula halleri* at Mattmark

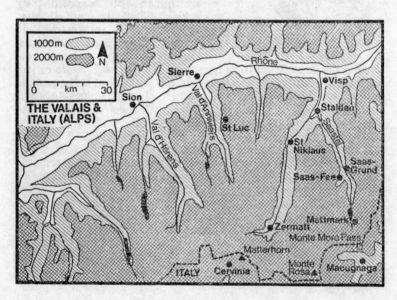

and we found a fine display of *Primula farinosa* and *Pinguicula alpina* growing together. The walk up the Almagellertal from Saas-Almagell is described in the *Bulletin* (Vol. 25, p. 314) where *Eritrichium nanum* is mentioned as growing in the rubble among stream-silt.

Zermatt, lying at the head of the next valley to the west, is famed alike as a tourist and a mountaineering centre. It is reached by train from Visp, but cars are not allowed further up the valley than St. Niklaus. It is dominated by the Matterhorn, and is more shut-in than Saas-Fee, and at a rather lower level. Its flora is similar, but additional plants of interest which have been reported there (they may well be around Saas-Fee too, for the searching) are *Viola pinnata, Pulsatilla halleri, Callianthemum coriandrifolium, Anemone baldensis, Viola cenisia, Saxifraga biflora* and *S.* x *kochii* (*S. oppositifolia* x *biflora*).

St. Luc* (1652 m.) is perched on the east flank of the Val d'Anniviers, which runs into the Rhône Valley near Sierre. From Sierre a good road with splendid views of the Bernese Alps and the terraced vineyards of the Central Valais climbs by hairpin curves to Niouc, and thence to Vissoie where it trifurcates; straight on along the bottom of the valley to its head at Zinal (1678 m.); left, zigzagging up to St. Luc and Chandolin (2000 m.); and right, across the torrent to Grimentz (1572 m.) and up the Val de Moiry to the foot of the glaciers just beyond the artificial Lac de Moiry (2249 m.). All three branches are served by postal coaches.

Two other good 'corniche' roads run, one almost level from St. Luc to Ayer, the other from just past Ayer to Grimentz, Vercorin and down to Sierre. So from Sierre a circular drive of the Val d'Anniviers, mostly around 1500 m., is possible. It gives easy access to all types of montane vegetation, particularly spruce forests and meadows, in part on limestone. Many other forestry roads, mainly above St. Luc and Grimentz to Vercorin, enable the tree-line to be reached by sturdy car.

Three chairlifts, at St. Luc, Grimentz and Chandolin, and two cable-cars from Zinal to Sorebois and from Vercorin to the Crêt du Midi, also give access to the alpine zone.

St. Luc is ideally located, not only for the interesting botanical areas immediately above it, but also as a base for approaching by car or postal coach all other parts of the Val d'Anniviers. The varied geology—gneiss, calceschists and limestone—makes the valley one of the richest in montane and alpine plants in Switzerland, though its much drier climate makes for a less spectacular display of colour in the meadows than in the Bernese Alps. The limestone north-west flank of the valley up to 2700 m. is the habitat for some rare and strictly protected orchids; in the widespread belt of calceschists from above St. Luc to above Zinal and back on both flanks of the Val de Moiry one finds almost all the alpines of neutral to basic soils of the

Central Alps, and the siliceous rocks of the higher slopes, the quartzites here and there, the acid turf, bogs and springs are the homes for lime-intolerant plants.

The ascent to the Alpine Club huts, three of which are in majestic settings (Tracuit, 3256 m., Mountet, 2886 m., Moiry, 2825 m.), demands no more than endurance and ordinary mountain hiking training. Singled out here are less strenuous walks on well-marked tracks within most people's ability.

1. Prilet, Gilloux, Alpe Nava. 25 minutes' level walk or 5 minutes' drive to the camping ground of the Prilet, then footpath to Gilloux. The usual flora of meadows, and a good area of *Linnaea borealis* and other spruce woodlanders. By gullies with springs, orchids, pinguiculas, adenostyles, etc. The view is superb.

2. Pointes de Nava, Col de la Forclettaz. A long whole day, with outstanding views and a great variety of plant habitats. From St. Luc on foot, or by chairlift via Tignousa, or by car on a rough road, to Alpe Tounot; continue to Hotel Weisshorn and then round the west side of Pointes de Nava (where there is an eagle-eyrie) up to the Col de la Forclettaz (2900 m.) and back via the Alpe Fachet. The Forclettaz is the westernmost station of *Eritrichium nanum* in the Valais. This tour includes steep acid turfy screes, with *Primula hirsuta* and *Gentiana purpurea*, a spring, and less acid rocks with a good display of the high alpine form of *Dactylorhiza majalis*, high neutral turf, and alpine scree with *Gentiana terglouensis schleicheri, G. brachyphylla, Androsace alpina, Geum reptans, Myosotis alpestris, Ranunculus glacialis* and *Linaria alpina*. This wild area is patronised by a large herd of chamois, and ptarmigan are not uncommon. The descent from Alpe Tounot to St. Luc via the waterfalls is well worthy of the extra effort.

3. Tignousa to Alpe Roua. A half-day. From the top of the chairlift, wander through the pastures just above the tree-line (Arolla pine and larch) towards the Châlet Blanc at the Alpe Roua. The plants of the acid alpine turf are all here.

4. The Bella Tola (3025 m.) and the Pas du Boeuf. From the top of the chairlift, or from the Châlet Blanc, the Bella Tola can be reached in three hours on a well-beaten track. On the way up, a bog at about 2500 m. has a striking display of the cotton-grass *Eriophorum scheuchzeri*. The real treat comes on the way down via the Pas du Boeuf (2897 m.), with a full display of the neutral to basic soil high alpines where schists and quartzites meet near the pass.

5. The calceschists of the Tounot (3018 m.). From the Alpe Tounot, reached by sturdy car from St. Luc or on foot from the chairlift, walk up the pastures among the big boulders to the Lac de Combavert (2441 m.) and further up on the north-east side of the Tounot. This is an area where a floor of ancient acid moraines is strewn with huge blocks of calceschist fallen from the Tounot. So one finds the craziest mosaic of vegetation: *Dryas octopetala* on a calceschist boulder and *Loiseleuria procumbens* on the acid turf a few feet away; *Aster alpinus* and *Leontopodium alpinum* next to *Salix herbacea* and *Alchemilla pentaphyllea*. In one day in this area from 2200 m. to 2800 m. one can find all but the few strictly lime-demanding alpines of the Valais.

Among other areas in the Val d'Anniviers of scenic or botanical interest, which can be visited from St. Luc by car or postal coach, are the slopes near Zinal with an exceptionally rich vegetation of montane tall herbs, including *Aquilegia alpina* (strictly protected); the Val de Moiry, where there are both limy and acid glacier moraines and *Anemone baldensis*, *Campanula cenisia*, *Ranunculus glacialis*, and *Achillea nana* are among the plants to be found, and a little lower down *Campanula thyrsoides* and *Lychnis alpina*; near the Basset de Lona, *Androsace alpina* and *A. obtusifolia* and their hybrid *A.* x *aretioides*; the area of the Lac des Autannes and the approaches to the Col de Torrent high up in the Val de Moiry where in the slaty screes and schists the plants rival those of the Alpe Tounot and the scenery also is magnificent.

THE ENGADINE

The Engadine is the south-east corner of Switzerland, in the Canton Grisons, and is in effect the upper valley of the River Inn before it flows into Austria. Like the Valais, it has an intricate mountain frontier with Italy; this is traversed by two main roads which enter Italy respectively at Tirano (having traversed the Bernina Pass) and by the Umbrail Pass. The main road and rail approach from the north-west is via Zürich and either Chur or Davos.

Scenically the Engadine is beautiful. For the most part it is rather more gentle and less abrupt than Western Switzerland, though the Bernina Group of mountains are as awe-inspiring as anyone should need. As elsewhere in the Alps, the 'basic flora' flourishes but in the Engadine, and particularly in that part of it which lies to the south-east of the Inn, plants more characteristic of the Eastern Alps begin to appear—many of which become more abundant as one crosses into Northern Italy or Western Austria.

Pontresina (1850 m.) lies near the mouth of the Val Bernina, a southern side-branch of the Inn Valley near St. Moritz. It is reached from Chur by either the Julier or the Albula Pass, or from Davos by the Flüela Pass—or by rail from either of these two towns. A road runs through Pontresina south-eastward up the Bernina Valley to the Bernina Pass. So, lying at a junction of valleys, it offers a very wide range of excursions on foot or by car, rail or ski-lift. It has been a popular centre for A.G.S. Tours.

Pontresina is a solid little town and with modern traffic somewhat congested but there are plenty of hotels, and for those who shun

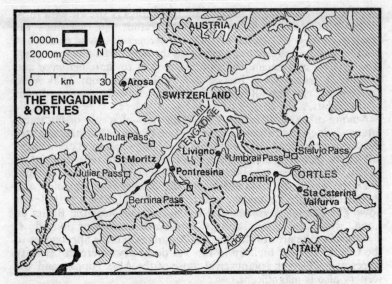

towns when on holiday there are a few isolated hotels up the Bernina Valley, for example at Morteratsch, some three miles from Pontresina.

At the head of the valley are very high mountains, reaching 4049 m. in Piz Bernina, and including the notorious Piz Palü. These summits are under permanent snow, and there are large glaciers with tongues extending down the side-valleys towards the Val Bernina; scenically the area is magnificent. The rock is predominantly acid, though varying in form, including granite, shales and schists, but there are also calcareous areas, notably the Piz Alv. The lowest parts of the valley are wooded. This combination of varieties in altitude, aspect and soil means that most of the plants of the Central Alps are to be found.

Probably in an average year the best time to visit is about the end of June, but the seasons vary tremendously. At this time in 1975 the Heutal and Val Minor were inaccessible because of snow, but others have found them beautifully flowered in late June.

In the woods to the east and north of the town, and around Morteratsch, there are to be found *Linnaea borealis* (not very common in Switzerland), *Maianthemum bifolium*, *Trientalis europaea*, *Moneses uniflora* and *Senecio incanus carniolicus*.

From just below the town (at Punt Muragl, where there is a railway station) one may take the footpath or the rack-railway to Muottas Muragl (2453 m.)—a magnificent viewpoint—whence there are fine walks up the Val Muragl and to the Val Languard. The characteristic 'upper alp' and snow-edge plants are here, and of special note is the pretty little *Soldanella pusilla*, near the western limit of its distribution. A fairly level path from Muottas Muragl follows the hillside southward to the Alp Languard, whence one may drop by footpath or ski-lift to Pontresina. *Hedysarum hedysaroides*, a leguminous plant with dark purplish flowers (and quite a good garden plant) grows here. From the Alp Languard one can walk (snow-conditions permitting) up to the Piz Languard (3261 m.) where *Campanula cenisia* and *Papaver rhaeticum* grow, or take the steep path to the Chamanna Segantini (2731 m.), where there are thirst-quenching facilities, and by the path from here back to Pontresina. *Androsace helvetica*, *Eritrichium nanum* and *Saxifraga oppositifolia* all grow within a few feet of one another.

From Pontresina the road and railway up the Val Bernina bring one shortly to the Val de Morteratsch, a side-valley to the south. This is a fine and spectacular valley, of which the upper part is filled by a great long tongue of glacier, and a footpath following the lateral moraines of the glacier takes one without too much effort to the Boval Hut (2495 m.). Two beautiful plants on the moraine are *Geum reptans* and *Primula latifolia*, and by the footpath in its final climb to the hut there are masses of excellent forms of *Primula hirsuta*.

Higher up the Val Bernina is another railway station at Bernina Suot, the starting point for a number of outstanding excursions. A very distinctive pyramidal mountain on the north-east side of the main valley is the limestone Piz Alv, among whose many plants are *Saxifraga squarrosa* and *Draba aizoides*. In dark contrast are the acidic Piz Albris and Piz Lagalb on either side of the Piz Alv, and the two valleys between these three mountains are especially famous for their abundance of flowers. The Heutal (Val dal Fain) is the more northerly; its special plants include *Allium victorialis*, *Sempervivum wulfenii*, *Pedicularis rostratospicata* (*incarnata*), *Gentiana terglouensis*, *Senecio abrotanifolius* and the hybrid *Primula* x *berninae* (*hirsuta* x *latifolia*). The other is the Val Minor which, having limestone rocks on one side and acid on the other, offers a particular profusion and variety of flowers. Both valleys are protected areas for plants. There is an aerial railway and a ski-lift to the restaurant at the top of Piz Lagalb.

On the other side of the valley, near Bernina Suot, a magnificent cable railway goes up to the hotel and ski-centre at Diavolezza (2973 m.). It is a stupendous ride, and at the top, where the acidic rocks break through the snow, are *Ranunculus glacialis*, *Androsace alpina* in both colours, and fine specimens of *Eritrichium nanum*. We were surprised to find *Primula latifolia* also growing at this altitude.

Pursuing the main valley, by foot, road or rail, one comes at last to the Bernina Pass, with its hospice. It is a fine wild area, somewhat marred as so often by the works of man, with two spectacular lakes—both of which we found iced over at the end of June. The upper valley and the pass are beautifully flowered, especially with spring and bell gentians, but the speciality is the primulas. Three species grow here; *P. integrifolia* tends to favour grassy slopes, *P. latifolia* more shaded

43

areas, and *P. hirsuta* rock crevices, but there is no rigid adherence to these habitats and the three plants are to be found in close proximity, with the result that the area is famous for its primula hybrids. We spent much time examining them. There was certainly a great deal of variation among plants, but we could not really satisfy ourselves that we had found any of the named hybrids. All were (more or less) beautiful, all approximated to one or other of the three species, and we saw nothing which we regarded as an improvement upon a good form of one of the species. There is a full account of these primulas on the Bernina Pass by Richard Nutt in the *Bulletin* (Vol. 33, p. 286).

Beyond the pass the road drops steeply, and on the south-facing rocks and turf the plants are appreciably more advanced. A notable area here is the Alp Grüm, reached by footpath or railway. The three primulas and their variations are abundant here, as is *Androsace obtusifolia*.

A short way down the south side of the pass there is a fine drive up the Val Agone, over the Forcola di Livigno into the Livigno valley. This valley is in Italy, but is easily reached by car from Pontresina. We found no formalities at the frontier post. There is a fine deep blue form of *Pulmonaria angustifolia* here and on the Italian side of the frontier there is an interesting area of grey-white limestone scree, with *Dryas octopetala* and *Saxifraga squarrosa*. The Val di Livigno was interesting in that the valley was full of snow and the east-facing hillside above the road became progressively clearer as one climbed higher. It is unusual to find the plants more advanced in flower as one climbs. Watched by ibex and shrieking marmots we found *Pinguicula leptoceras*, *Veronica fruticulosa*, arnica, martagon and edelweiss among many other plants.

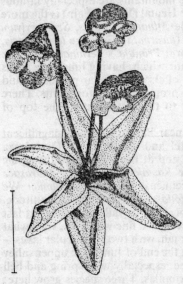

Pinguicula leptoceras

These are a few of the many excursions from Pontresina (a leaflet lists 79!). For the car-driver, the Inn valley is at his disposal, with the famous resorts of St. Moritz and Silvaplana beautifully set beside their lakes, but somehow tame after the Bernina valley. Two passes running westward from the Inn valley are however well worth a visit—the Julier (Giulia) and the Albula, both about 2300 m. On the Julier Pass the typical snow-valley plants are to be seen, and on the rocks of the Valetta, high above the pass, *Eritrichium nanum* is in fine form. Just below those rocks is *Myosotis alpestris*, becoming ever more dwarf and compact as one climbs up— so that at last it is the true *M. rupicola* of gardens (not a distinct species botanically), and here the myosotis and the eritrichium grow within a few feet of one another and one has to look very closely at the foliage to see which is which. There is an interestingly analogous situation on the Albula Pass, for here as you scramble steeply and uncomfortably up the steep shales, *Androsace villosa* all about you becomes progressively more compact and cushion-like, and seems almost to grade into *Androsace helvetica* in the rock-faces above.

Arosa* (1825 m.) lies at the top of the Plessur Valley in the Grisons. It can be reached by road or rail from Chur (Coire) up a picturesque valley. It has been a centre for three A.G.S. Tours and offers much for the plantsman. The town is situated on a steep slope, which means some hard walking, but there are buses and taxis available to take you to the cable-car stations. There are two cable-cars, one to the top of the Weisshorn and the other to the Hörnlihütte, both to the west of the town.

The best time to visit this valley for flowers is probably early July, though on a later visit the snow still blocked the Carmenna Pass, making higher walking impossible.

There are many possible walks. The Weisshorn is of distinct interest, with a varied flora due to the geological make-up. The cable-car can be picked up at the half-way stage. On the summit of the Weisshorn *Androsace helvetica* is plentiful. Just down from the summit is an area of black schist in which *A. alpina* thrives, and their hybrid *A.* x *heeri* grows in the rocks to the north. The east-facing slopes down to the town offer pulsatillas in variety—*PP. alpina, apiifolia* and a double form of *vernalis*, which was a disappointing curiosity. *Gentiana clusii* was to be found on the limestone and *G. acaulis* on the serpentine, and *Dianthus glacialis*, probably near its westernmost limit here.

Another walk back to the town from the Weisshorn is via the Carmenna Pass, subject to snow conditions. The walk down is steep, but full of delights, particularly the good forms of *Viola calcarata*. At the pass itself can be found *Globularia nudicaulis* and an excellent form of *Primula auricula*. Back across the damp meadows to the Mittler Hütte there are masses of soldanellas, including *S. pusilla*.

The Welschtobel is well worth exploration, but requires a long day. It is reached by walking down to the Isel woods, and where they thin out *Clematis alpina* may be found, and further on *Primula auricula balbisii* and *Saxifraga caesia*. Pyrolas, fragrant orchids, frog orchids and moonwort were some of the other items of interest along the path.

Aquilegia alpina is in the area, but rare. However, you can view it with ease in the slightly disappointing 'Botanic Garden'. This can be reached by taking the bus to Maran and walking across the golf course—an excellent afternoon outing, leaving just enough energy for the consumption of strawberry tarts and tea at the hotel before returning on the bus.

Switzerland in the Bulletin:†

There are over 20 articles on Switzerland in the *Bulletin*. The following articles relate to the centres chosen in this chapter—

*Sections marked with asterisks were contributed as follows:—
        Wengen: Mr. E. M. Upward
        St. Luc: Professor G. Pontecorvo
        Arosa: Mr. E. M. Upward

†Throughout this book, the 'Bulletin' referred to is the *Quarterly Bulletin of the Alpine Garden Society*.

4

ITALY

Italy is, except for the great Plain of Lombardy, a mountainous country, and its flowers range from the highest alpines in the north to a Mediterranean flora in the south.

The mountains are conveniently thought of as two large groups; the Alps bounding the north and west of the Lombardy Plain and the Apennines running along the 'leg' of Italy, though the two groups are linked by the Ligurian Apennines around the Gulf of Genoa.

In a country so diverse, few generalisations are permissible, but it can be said that the Italian roads and other services are as a rule good, and in the mountainous areas the tourist is well provided for. It is usually possible, at least in the towns, to find someone who speaks English, and along the northern frontiers there are many who speak French or German. Winter sports facilities, often of assistance to the summer tourist, are developing apace in the higher mountains.

THE ITALIAN ALPS

The Italian Alps form Italy's frontiers with France, Switzerland, Austria and Jugoslavia. They are more or less a continuous chain, the chief break being in the lake district which Italy shares with Switzerland, but they are conveniently considered as a number of separate ranges. The most westerly, from the Maritimes to the Graians, are shared with France and will be treated in Chapter 5, except however that the Italian Graians form a distinct group round the Gran Paradiso, about which Professor Pontecorvo writes in this chapter. Along the Swiss frontier lie the Pennine Alps, the lake area, the Alpi Orobie and the Ortles Group. The Oetztaler Alps are considered with Austria in Chapter 9 and the remaining mountainous area of North-East Italy centres upon the Dolomites and Lake Garda, and is included here.

The flora of the Italian Alps embraces that of the Western, Central and Eastern Alps, so that it is very varied indeed, but it is nevertheless built upon the 'basic flora' described in Chapter 1.

THE GRAN PARADISO*

This is a superb massif of glaciers and green, mainly unspoilt, valleys entirely in Italy a little way from the main watershed of the Graian Alps. The three main valleys—Cogne, Savaranche and Locana—converge towards the highest peak (the Gran Paradiso, 4061 m., the highest mountain wholly in Italy). The first two are easily reached by car from Aosta and have plenty of tourist accommodation in the two main centres—Cogne (1534 m.) and Valsavaranche (1540 m.) respectively. In the third (on the south side of the massif) the road continues up to 2612 m. at the Colle del Nivolet, but is still (1978) under construction.

A National Park has replaced what was a Royal Hunting Reserve. It includes a substantial part of the massif, and adjoins the French National Park of the Vanoise. It has an interesting alpine garden at Valnontey near Cogne. Before the recent successful reintroduction of ibex into various French and Swiss reserves the Gran Paradiso was the last remaining area where they had persisted in large numbers.

The geology is very varied, a core of gneiss making up the highest peaks, surrounded by calcareous schists, and even some dolomitic outcrops, and serpentines here and there. The flora is accordingly rich, with all the alpines of the Graian Alps added to the 'basic flora.' Especially interesting local plants include *Aethionema thomasianum* (a distinct form, if not a subspecies, of *A. saxatile*) on calcareous

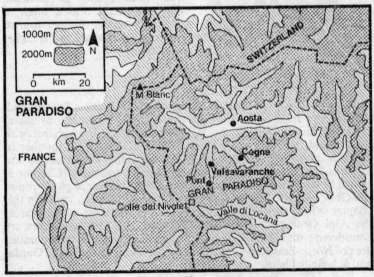

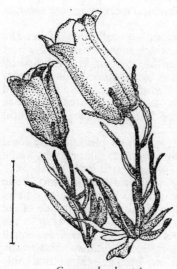

Campanula alpestris

sunny screes, *Astragalus centralpinus* (whose other location is Bulgaria), and *Campanula excisa* of the Pennine Alps, which also has an outlying area here. *Saxifraga retusa* and *Campanula alpestris* (*C. allionii*) are common and beautiful in slaty screes at high altitude. Most of the alpine astragalus and oxytropis, and *Pulsatilla halleri*, are found as one climbs to the Col Lauson (3296 m.), botanically one of the most rewarding walks, with magnificent views of the amphitheatre of glaciers. Another rich area is that of the Alpe Grauson (2271 m.) and the corries of the north slope of Mt. Greya. *Saponaria lutea* grows in the interesting dry and sunny screes of the south slopes of this mountain.

The vast network of well-built mule-tracks of the time of the Royal Reserve must be used with caution; that is, only where confirmed by present tourist maps. Some have fallen into disrepair and may lead the walker astray.

In addition to the plants mentioned above by Professor Pontecorvo, Mr. R. W. Richards mentions *Primula pedemontana*, *Androsace chaixii*, *Pulsatilla montana* and *Viola pinnata*, and Dr. H. S. Wacher (*Bulletin*, Vol. 30, p. 236), mentions *Silene vallesia* and the yellow-flowered *Sempervivum grandiflorum*.

Our own attempts to explore the Gran Paradiso have been foiled by bad weather but we did reach the little village of **Pont** (1892 m.) at the head of the Valsavaranche, where there are pleasant small hotels, and it appeared to us that this would be an excellent centre.

THE PENNINE ALPS

These great mountains form the frontier between Italy and the Valais in Switzerland. The flora is very similar on the two sides of the range, and has already been considered in Chapter 3 (see pp. 36–41). Monte Cervino (the Matterhorn) (4478 m.) and Monte Rosa (4633 m.) both lie on the frontier, and on the Italian side of each there is a valley running up into the mountains with a village at its head. These are, respectively, Cervinia and Macugnaga, both of which have been selected for A.G.S. Tours. Both have adequate hotels and a range of excursions into the mountains. Cervinia gives better access to the Aosta valley, but the village itself is highly developed as a ski-centre, to its detriment as a centre for the summer visitor.

Macugnaga (c. 1300 m.) is a very diffuse collection of hamlets near the head of the Valle Anzasca, which branches off to the west at Piedimulera from the Brig-Simplon-Milan road. It is reached by the motorist either through Switzerland by the Rhône valley or from the Turin-Milan motorway in Italy. Piedimulera can also be reached by train from Brig, Turin or Milan, and there is a coach service along the Valle Anzasca. The latter is an exceedingly beautiful valley.

There are several hotels in Macugnaga, and pleasant easy local walks along the valley between the three communities (Borca, Staffa and Pecetto) of Macugnaga. From Borca a path leads up through woods past a pleasant little lake (and restaurant) into Valle Quarazza, giving access to the slopes of Pizzo Bianco, which dominates the village on its south side. A footpath on the north side of the valley, between Staffa and Pecetto (the start of the walk up to the Alpe Bil) takes one under rock-faces shaded by shrubs and small trees, and here grow *Prenanthes purpurea*, *Lilium bulbiferum*, *Phyteuma hemisphaericum*, *Saxifraga cotyledon* and (at a remarkably low level) *Androsace vandellii* is abundant. Reports of a yellow sempervivum here probably relate to the scarce *S. grandiflorum*, though *Jovibarba allionii* is also reported in this area.

A footpath from Pecetto follows the valley upwards to the Albergo Belvedere on the terminal moraine of the Belvedere Glacier, and continues upwards along the lateral moraine to the Rifugio Zamboni. There is also a ski-lift to the albergo, though neither this lift nor the Rifugio Zamboni is always manned in the early summer (see *Bulletin*, Vol. 28, p. 82). These areas are reported as presenting good examples of acid glacier moraine flora.

The special excursion from Macugnaga is to the Monte Moro Pass (2868 m.). An aerial railway runs from Staffa to the Alpe Bil, and another proceeds from there up to a point just below the pass. It is a magnificent journey, with stupendous views of Monte Rosa and the neighbouring mountains. From the upper station (rather a messy place, where there is also a rifugio) it is a short and easy walk to the pass itself. Here one stands beneath a beautiful statue in dark metal of the Madonna, and looks down into the Saas Valley in the Swiss Valais, where the fine artificial lake above Mattmark enhances the view. There are lovely flowers, including *Gentiana brachyphylla*, *Ranunculus glacialis* and *Senecio halleri* (*uniflorus*). To see them at their best one should either clamber up the ridge between the pass

Senecio halleri

50

and Monte Moro, or follow the footpath down to Macugnaga instead of taking the 'funivia'. It is easy and pleasant going (given kind weather—see Richard Nutt's account of the upward journey in *Bulletin* Vol. 30, p. 164). *Campanula excisa* is abundant here, and some of the forms are magnificent.

For the motorist a fine drive, but one to be avoided at a week-end, is down the valley to Piedimulera and then northward, leaving the main Simplon road north of Domodossola to follow the Toce valley up to its head at the Passo San Giacomo on the Swiss frontier. In the snow-valleys at this pass, close by the roadside, *Androsace alpina* is abundant, with *Arenaria biflora* and *Senecio incanus* as well as the typical snow-valley flora.

Cervinia (2006 m.) presents a flora similar to that at Macugnaga, though there are indications, such as fields of *Colchicum autumnale*, including white ones, of lime lower down the valley around Valtournanche. Plants recorded when the A.G.S. visited Cervinia included *Androsace lactea*, *Aquilegia alpina*, *Campanula cenisia*, *Dryas octopetala*, *Epilobium fleischeri*, *Lychnis flos-jovis*, *Petrocallis pyrenaica* and *Primula pedemontana*. Two other interesting little plants, neither in the first rank of beauty, to be found above Cervinia are *Saponaria lutea*, which is plentiful in the rocks to the north-east of the village, and *Saxifraga biflora*.

For the motorist there is ready access to the Aosta valley. The old road is relatively quiet now that the motorway to Aosta has been completed. Just above Aosta a small road runs northward to the Valpelline, which in September we found to be a peaceful, though foodless, little valley with some interesting plants in the rocks by the roadside; *Androsace vandellii*, *Juniperus sabina*, an erysimum which was probably *E. helveticum*, and *Silene vallesia*, which was attractive in the dusk, but closed its flowers during the day.

The Lake District and the Alpi Orobie

To the east of the Pennine Alps are the lakes—Maggiore, Lugano, Como and others. Set among hills, they are very beautiful, but are in a popular area much developed for the tourist. The mountains round these lakes, and particularly to the south and east of Lake Como, are of limestone, and they contain a few very special rarities, such as *Campanula raineri*, *Saxifraga vandellii*, *Androsace brevis* (*A. charpentieri*) and *Silene elisabetha*. *Physoplexis* (*Phyteuma*) *comosa* is here too, and there seems to be a tendency towards continuity in the flora from this area through the hills to the north of Bergamo to Monte Tombea by Lake Garda. We drove through these hills in late June one year. It was a journey that took us across the Passo Croce Domini, and we encountered within a short space *Cyclamen purpurascens*, *Primula halleri*, *P. spectabilis* (or was it *P. glaucescens*?), *Ranunculus seguieri* and *Fritillaria tubiformis* (*delphinensis*).

51

Running eastward from Lake Como is the Valtellina, a populous valley with the Alpi Orobie (or Orobiche) forming a wall on its south side and on the north side the Bernina Alps which we have met at Pontresina. Of the Alpi Orobie one reads remarkably little, though the Pizza di Coca reaches a respectable 3052 m. Small roads run into them from the south, and we drove as far as we could northward from Clusone. It was a disappointing journey. The only interesting find was the normally calcicole *Rhododendron hirsutum* growing with the normally calciphobe *Primula hirsuta*. The whole area on this very dull day was somewhat uninspiring, and I cannot recommend a centre there. Nevertheless I hope that somebody will explore and report upon the Alpi Orobie more fully than has yet been done in the *Bulletin*.

THE ORTLES GROUP

To the north-west of the Alpi Orobie lie the Ortles group, reaching 3899 m. It is an area well worth visiting, where the flora of the Eastern Alps begins to assert itself. The main centre is **Bormio**, developed now as a major ski-centre, with all the advantages (including plenty of hotels) and disadvantages that this entails. Eastward from Bormio the Valfurva valley runs up into the mountains, and some 11 km. from Bormio is the much smaller and attractive village of Santa Caterina Valfurva, which for those with a car is a very pleasant and convenient centre.

Santa Caterina has at least one excellent hotel, whose name (Sobretta) does not, as at first we feared, indicate that it is a temperance establishment; it is the name of the mountain opposite. The most direct route by car from Switzerland is via Davos, the Flüela Pass, Zernez, and the Umbrail and Stelvio Passes. The last two are high passes, not usually open till late June, and liable to be closed by snow even later. An alternative approach is over the Bernina Pass, normally open in mid-May, to Tirano. There is a coach-service from Bormio to Santa Caterina.

Running southward from the village is the Gavia Pass (2621 m.), cutting across the south-western end of the Ortles group to join the Bolzano-Tirano road. It is reached by a small, rather rough, road, and is liable to closure, but it is worth going up as high as you can. The area immediately around Santa Caterina is non-calcareous, and a special feature on this pass is the abundance of *Primula hirsuta* and *P. glutinosa*. Their habitats are somewhat different, *P. hirsuta* in the rock-crevices and *P. glutinosa* in the high turf as the snow clears, but they are in sufficient proximity to produce interesting hybrids. *Ranunculus glacialis* is here, and a fine display of *Soldanella pusilla*.

Running eastward from the village is a small road, remarkable for its steepness and its scenery, leading to the Albergo Forni. Never have we seen better *Clematis alpina* than along this road; it is widespread in the European mountains, but it has always seemed to me

52

a considerably better plant in the Eastern Alps. High in this valley the common red primula seems to be *P. daonensis*, a very local species, though truth to tell it is not easy to distinguish from the somewhat variable *P. hirsuta* which is also about. Above the albergo a 'jeepable' route (a walk for most of us) leads up to the Rifugio Pizzini. This is a fine valley, beautifully flowered, where in the turf below the snow *Primula glutinosa* joins *P. hirsuta* and *P. daonensis* and above the hut, in the screes between the snow-fields, there is a remarkable range of forms of *Saxifraga oppositifolia*.

From Bormio the main road runs up to and over the Stelvio Pass. This magnificent pass is entirely in Italy, but near the top the Umbrail Pass branches off straight into Switzerland. The Umbrail is not a very good road down a not very impressive valley, but the Stelvio (2757 m.) is wonderful. The road itself is a fine one but snow, ice and cloud can make it quite an adventure even in July. We calculated that in a drive from Bormio to Solda and back, with a diversion down the Umbrail, we negotiated over 200 hairpin bends, but the views and the flowers were worth every one of them. The western (Bormio) side of the pass is mainly open country, and a mass of flowers. Nowhere else, except perhaps on the Mont Cenis Pass, have we seen *Viola calcarata* so profuse and many-coloured, nor *Geum reptans* so fine on the high crags. A great hillside glistened heliotrope with *Soldanella pusilla*, wet from recent rain, and in the snow-water runnels through the screes loose mats of *Androsace alpina* mingled with *Ranunculus glacialis*. Only a little lower down, by melting snow, were *Primula veris columnae*, *P. hirsuta* with white forms, and *P. daonensis*. On the eastern side of the pass the aspect changes. The road drops steeply through pine-woods, and the north face of Ortles, with vast steep cliffs and tongues of glacier, seemed on a dull day almost to overhang the pass. Here among the crocuses, above the trees, grows again that magnificent deep blue *Pulmonaria angustifolia*, and on the edges of the woods the widespread but by no means common Jacob's ladder of our gardens, *Polemonium coeruleum*, accompanied by *Ononis rotundifolia*, suggests that we are now entering limestone country.

The valley warms and widens as we drop. At Gomagoi a side-road runs southward up to the little village of Solda, where the A.G.S. has based a Tour. Although it is attractive, it is a dead-end for the motorist.

A road to the north-west from Bormio forks to offer two attractive possibilities. The more spectacular is a steep, wild road running northward to the Val di Fraele, with two great reservoirs high in the hills. This is limestone country, with *Dryas octopetala*, *Daphne striata*, and *Polygala chamaebuxus*, and butterfly and scented orchids. The other branch continues westward along the Val Viola, at first through wonderful alpine meadows, then up to the Foscagno and Eira Passes leading over to the Livigno valley. This is acid soil again, with *Primula hirsuta*, and pedicularis that looked like early purple orchids. Here, if you wish, you are on your way to the Bernina Pass and Pontresina (see p. 44).

The Dolomites

'The Dolomites' is a mountainous region of North-East Italy, running up to the Austrian and Jugoslavian frontiers. It is a scenically distinctive and beautiful area, whose name derives from the predominant local rock-formation, *dolomite*, which is a crystalline magnesian limestone. These mountains are wonderful and exciting to see; great pinnacles and castellations of rock with vertical and horizontal cleavages. The crystals have curved surfaces which catch the light giving constant changes of colour. The Dolomite mountains are not so high as the Central Alps, reaching only some 3,300 m., and there are only small areas of glacier and permanent snow.

Road communications are good, and the Dolomite Road (Strada dei Dolomiti, Dolomitenstrasse) runs through the Dolomites from south-west to north-east, and good branch roads lead across the mountain passes on either side. Probably the quickest road-route from England is via the German autobahn to Innsbruck, entering Italy at the Brenner Pass. Bolzano (Bozen), lying to the west of the main Dolomite mountains, and the biggest town in the area, is also accessible by rail, as are the mountain towns of Predazzo, Selva and Cortina. There are public coaches on the Dolomite Road and a number of other main roads.

The flowers are abundant and varied, the alpine pastures at both lower and higher levels vying with anything that the Swiss Alps can offer, but presenting in the main the same plants as are found in the Eastern Alps. Above the valleys the mountains are wooded, coniferous forests predominating, and here again one meets the flora of the Eastern Alps. Over the forests the great limestone mountains tower into the sky, glaring white in the midday sun, grey in the cloud, glowing red at dawn and sunset. It is here, in the limestone crevices of the cliffs, and in the jumbled screes at their feet, that the special dolomitic plants are to be found. A few are endemic to the area, others spreading into the neighbouring limestone mountains, for the magnesian limestone is not confined to the Dolomites, but forms a component, in varying quantity, of the other limestones in neighbouring districts. This no doubt is one of the factors that determine whether plants which one associates with the Dolomites are totally confined to that area. An example is *Physoplexis comosa* (better known to alpine gardeners as *Phyteuma comosum*) centred in the Dolomites but extending westwards to the lake district as well as into Austria and Jugoslavia.

Plants which grow in dolomite are obviously tolerant of magnesium carbonate (which is very alkaline) and it is likely that those which are confined to the dolomite actually need it. It seems that an excess of lime (calcium carbonate) impairs the ability of some plants to take up their magnesium requirement (as well as iron), so that the Dolomite endemic plants are by no means always tolerant of lime or chalk in the garden, and indeed some appear to do better in an acid or peaty soil. Calcifuge plants are to be found in the Dolomites for quite another reason. The dolomite, probably of marine origin, was deposited over non-calcareous primary rocks, and there are areas in the Dolomites where these rocks break through the limestone crust so that the two types of rock, each with its characteristic flora, are to be found within a small area. The Pordoi and Rolle Passes provide well-known examples of this.

The largest town is Bolzano, and here are the fleshpots. But it is on the edge of the area and Merano, further to the north-west, is even more remote from the flowers. Cortina d'Ampezzo is on the Dolomite Road, and for those who like to stay in a town and yet be among the mountains this is perhaps the best centre. It provides good access to the north-east part of the area, and the Pordoi and neighbouring passes are accessible by car: a magnificent drive. It lies in a wide hollow in the mountains, but there are several funicular railways leading up into the hills. There are many smaller centres giving still closer access to the mountains, and well provided with hotels. They tend to be in the valleys, but there are also hotels of varying standards placed away from the villages on the high passes, as at Pordoi and the Rolle. The three centres here chosen for description are well known to the writer to be among magnificent scenery and with fine flowers.

An area of less renown is the wide mass of mountains between Misurina and the Jugoslavian frontier beyond Tolmezzo, bounded on the north side by the Carnic Alps. A correspondent writes that the area south and east of San Martino, centering on Belluno, is very beautiful and florally interesting. These areas may well merit exploration.

As to the time to visit, I would suggest late June and early July. In early June the meadows will be magnificent, but the more specialised flora of the dolomite cliffs and screes may still be inaccessible. As always in the European mountains, a later visit—late July or even August—will offer its rewards, but the main show will have passed and to find the specialised flowers the visitor must use a lift or his legs into the mountains high above the passes.

Misurina (1755 m.) lies to the east of Cortina and is reached by the Dolomite Road from the south-west or from the Brenner Pass via Dobbiaco, or by railway following the latter route as far as Carbonin, which is about 5 miles north of Misurina. It is set along a lovely lake in the mountains. Farrer's description of the Lago di Misurina in *The Dolomites*, glowing though it was, seems to have been no exaggeration, but subsequent accounts in the *Bulletin* have told a sad tale of uncontrolled building on the west side of the lake. We have seen this unhappy 'progress' from a series of four visits between 1958 and 1971, but despite this I would still recommend it as a fine centre from which to see this beautiful corner of the Dolomites. Go if you can no later than early July, and avoid the week-end. We stayed at a small hotel at the northern end, with a lovely view down the lake towards magnificent Sorapis. Indeed, the lake is surrounded by beautiful mountains, of which the most spectacular is (or are) the Tre Cime di Lavaredo (Drei Zinnen) to the north. They are famous for their startling magnificence, as a challenge to climbers, and for the flowers at their feet. The road towards the Tre Cime passes the lovely little Lago Antorno, backed by the inviting white cliffs and pinnacles of the Cadini. All this is now a 'scenic area', entered by a great new toll-road, a *strada panoramica*. On a Sunday in August in 1971 (begrudging the toll-fee, which would have taken all my lire) I left the crowds and clambered up the lower cliffs of the Cadini, alone among the flowers, and these, even in August, were well worth the effort. At the foot of the cliffs were the dark purple *Horminum pyrenaicum* and the orange *Senecio abrotanifolius* in pleasing contrast, brilliant blue *Gentiana utriculosa*, and in the crevices above the charming silver-leaved, rose-flowered *Potentilla nitida* and the ever odd and eye-catching *Physoplexis comosa* tightly gripped in its fissures. These last two plants are among the Dolomite 'specials', though neither is in fact endemic to the area. The potentilla flowers far more freely in the wild than in most gardens at home, but you must go in high summer to see the best display. The physoplexis flowers over a long season, varying somewhat with altitude as one would expect. The fine flowers to be found on the Forcella Longeres at the foot of the Tre Cime represent as good a sample of the higher dolomite flora as you could hope to meet in one place, including

Primula halleri

Androsace hausmannii, *Primula minima* (the rare white form has been reported here), *P. halleri*, *P. auricula balbisii*, a fine full-petalled form of *Ranunculus parnassifolius*, and the lovely *R. seguieri*. The occurrence here of the calcifuge *Primula minima* (the 'smallest primula'—with the largest flowers!) is interesting; perhaps it is an example of a plant which is tolerant of magnesian limestone but not of ordinary lime. As it is not widely distributed through the Dolomites it is perhaps more likely that it is growing here in acid humus overlying the limestone.

There is a good path from the northern end of the lake running at first through magnificent sheets of *Primula farinosa* and numerous

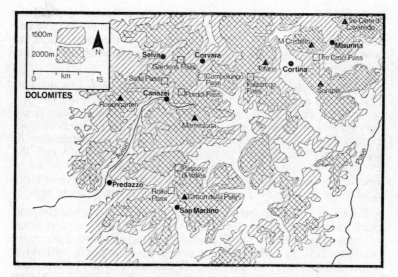

Lilium martagon and then rising steeply to the Passo dei Tocci. This is not to be compared with the Forcella Longeres for plants, but leads one into a high wilderness of jumbled stark desolation, dolomite rock at its most fantastic and cruel. It is quite an experience to be up there on a stormy day, and the views across the lake to the whole panorama of the Dolomites are incomparable.

In peaceful contrast, one may follow a footpath round the unspoiled eastern side of the Lago di Misurina and ramble about in the woodland, finding *Erica herbacea* (*carnea*) mixed with *Daphne cneorum* and the beautiful *Rhodothamnus chamaecistus*, *Polygala chamaebuxus* in both its yellow and its purple forms, some magnificent *Clematis alpina*, pretty cream *Pinguicula alpina*, and the tiny, delicate *Soldanella minima*. Clambering up through the woods one comes to lightly shaded scree where the sweetly scented *Thlaspi rotundifolium* is especially fine, though indeed it achieves exceptional beauty throughout the dolomitic screes. *Anemone trifolia* is the common wood anemone here; it is very close to our *A. nemorosa*, but with three undissected leaflets, and soft blue forms may be found.

South of the lake a short fine drive (or a long fine walk) leads to the Tre Croci Pass (1809 m.) between Monte Cristallo and Sorapis. The spring gentian on the pass is lovely, and here, as often in the Dolomites, you may find soft mauve and violet flowers among the blue. There is a cable railway up to the heights of Monte Cristallo, and fine mountain walks to the hut and lake below the glacier on Sorapis. This is one of the stations for the endemic *Primula tyrolensis* —rather like a short-stalked *P. hirsuta*, but characterised by the persistence of the withered leaves.

57

Cortina lies a few miles beyond the Tre Croci Pass, and from here there are funiculars and chair-lifts to the lower levels of the three fine mountains that make up Tofana, to the west of the town. There are also marked paths leading into these mountains, one of them leading to the summit of Tofana di Fuori at 3237 m.

Beyond Cortina, the Dolomite Road runs westward to the Falzarego Pass, and thence on to Pordoi and our next 'centre'. This is a magnificent drive, for flowers and scenery alike. The distance is not very great, but it is not a road for fast travel: steep gradients, hairpin bends and flowers by the roadside should combine to detain you. In fact it is perfectly feasible to visit the group of passes of which the Pordoi is the first from Misurina and return the same day, or of course you can do the reverse. But only by staying for three or more days in each of these areas can you see what it really has to offer.

Pordoi and the Four Passes. Halfway between Cortina and Bolzano (and also accessible from Brunico in the north) there is a great block of dolomite mountains, the Gruppo di Sella; a solid spectacular mass reaching 3151 m., which Farrer described as a plinth without a statue. It is encircled by a road which can conveniently be described as a 'square,' though indeed it is neither circle nor square, but 48 km. of twisting and exciting road climbing over four passes and dropping steeply between them: a wonderful drive. Along its southern side is a stretch of the Dolomite Road, crossing the Pordoi Pass (2239 m.), the highest point on this fine road. On the west side of the 'square' the road traverses the Sella Pass (2214 m.), the saddle between the Sella Group and the great spike of the Sasso Lungo, Farrer's statue without a plinth. So to the north-west corner of the square where, leaving on your left the road which runs away down the Val Gardena, you turn eastward to cross the Gardena Pass (2121 m.), and on the fourth (eastern) side of the 'square' you cross the lowest of the passes, the Campolungo (1875 m.) and drop down to the Dolomite Road at Arabba, ready to climb again to the Pordoi. The 'square', as well as having a pass on each of its sides and a road going off from each of its corners, also takes you through or near some villages and hotels. It is a wonderful area, with much to see and fine flowers but no obvious central point to stay. There are several hotels on the Pordoi Pass itself, which is in fact rather an untidy aggregation of buildings now, and this is perhaps the nearest place to the finest flowers in the Dolomites. But it is exposed and very high, so perhaps it is better to stay a little lower, at least until you are acclimatised to the hills. **Selva,** in the upper reaches of the Val Gardena, and **Corvara,** at the north-east corner of the 'square', are both centres with hotels which Members have visited and found comfortable. For ready access to the hills and flowers, particularly if you have no car, Selva can probably best compete with the Pordoi Pass, for it is a centre from which you can climb to the foot of the Sasso Lungo or walk along the Val Lungo (said to be remarkable for the variety of flowers you can see with a minimum of effort). Or you may climb up to another high dolomite group, Le Odle, to the north, but wherever you go you will be starting 800 m. lower than if you stay on the Pordoi Pass.

So Pordoi let it be, even though on a summer Sunday afternoon you may have to walk all of a quarter-mile to get away from the crowds.

From Pordoi you can, of course, drive to any of the passes and valleys on and around the 'square', and spend as long as you can spare doing it.

Or you can take the track (or the funicular) up to the Rifugio Forcella Pordoi, and thence to the Rifugio Boé and its glacier, but unless you go late in the season you will probably be amid snow rather than flowers.

Running southward from the pass is the Vial del Pan—the famous 'Bindelweg' extolled by Farrer and many others since: and it is this relatively level track which has lured so many of the Society's Members to the Pordoi Pass. It has everything; scenery, dolomite flowers, calciphobes. First it skirts the Sasso Becce, an isolated block where much of the dolomitic flora is gathered together. *Anemone baldensis* is at your feet as you leave your hotel. *Leontopodium alpinum* is here to be found as a true crevice plant on the cliffs, in company with *Paederota bonarota*, *Saxifraga crustata*, *Potentilla nitida*, *Rhodothamnus chamaecistus* and *Thlaspi rotundifolium*. In the rough grassy scree below the cliffs are *Primula halleri* and *Soldanella minima*, but the most remarkable thing here (provided only that the sun be shining) is the variety of colour of *Gentiana verna*. Among the deep glowing blues are purples no less intense, soft greys and violets, and we have even seen a plant on which every flower had each petal divided along its length—half blue, half purple.

Then the path begins to curve away to the east, crossing a neck of black schistous scree, and this is the eastern end of the Sasso di Capello, the outcropping of igneous rock whose vast sheer cliffs drop down towards the main road as it runs from Pordoi to Arabba. On and among these rocks and screes are to be found many of the finest calcifuge flowers of the high places of the Eastern Alps. There are yellow mats of *Vitaliana primuliflora* (*Douglasia vitaliana*) and with them purple mats of *Saxifraga oppositifolia*, the great golden salvers and red trailing stolons of *Geum reptans*, *Ranunculus glacialis* in white and pink, *Primula minima*, *Leucanthemopsis* (*Chrysanthemum*, *Leucanthemum*) *alpina*, *Androsace alpina* (generally white-flowered and tight-clumped here) and further to the east the *pièce de résistance*, *Eritrichium nanum* in as fine a form as you will find anywhere, growing among the wire netting of old gun-emplacements in loose schist from which we have seen whole plants kicked out by the sheep.

All this lies above you and to your left as you follow the Bindelweg, for it skirts the southern slope of the Sasso di Capello, where the curious blue-and-white striped form of *Gentiana acaulis* which is one of the oddities of the area may be found. The path at long last drops to the Lago di Fedaia, and from here you may climb, or take the chair-lift, into the great glacier-crowned mass of the Marmolada (3342 m.), the highest mountain in the Dolomites, and one of the sites for *Primula tyrolensis*. You can of course scramble up from the Bindelweg to the crest of Sasso di Capello to see the eritrichium, but on a fine day (they are not so very common in June and July in this area) it is the views across to the Marmolada, and far away to the east, that are the special attraction of this part of the Bindelweg. Nearly all the flowers may be found near the neck where the Bindelweg runs between the Sasso Becce and the Sasso di Capello, and from here too you can look away westward steeply down the valley that runs behind the Sasso Becce to Canazei in the Val di Fassa, a thousand metres below. A chair-lift follows this valley, so that if you are staying at Canazei you can come up to the Pordoi with little effort, but it is a valley to walk in, full of flowers. *Pulsatilla alpina* and *P. apiifolia* grow here together, with *P. vernalis*, *Soldanella alpina*, *Pulmonaria angustifolia*, *Ranunculus pyrenaeus*, *Crocus vernus* and *Primula elatior*. This is an association of plants to be met with frequently in the Alps, where they spring to life together as the snow recedes from the high passes around the end of June. The one that has always intrigued me is the last. By what freak of nature has the oxlip of our East Anglian woodlands become a snow-breaker at 2100 m. in the European mountains?

While this does not complete the list of interesting and lovely plants to be found on and around the south side of the Pordoi Pass (for instance the androsaces *AA. chamaejasme, lactea, hausmannii* and *helvetica* have all been mentioned by visitors to the area) it should be sufficient to justify a choice of the Pordoi Pass, or somewhere in its vicinity, as a place to stay.

If you do so, and have a car, do please drive round the 'square'. Even in the worst of weather it is a day well spent, and there are some plants of special interest, though not many, to be found on or around the other passes which so far as I know are not on the Pordoi. *Ranunculus seguieri* on the Sella Pass is as beautiful as *R. glacialis*, and a good deal easier to grow. In rock crevices on the north side of the pass is *Campanula morettiana*, one of the few true endemics of the Dolomites, to be seen in flower only by those who go late in the season. Great stout orange-red *Lilium bulbiferum croceum* is by the roadside in many parts of the 'square', and from the Gardena Pass *Campanula caespitosa* has been reported, here surely nearing the western limit of its distribution, a pucker-mouthed version of *C. cochlearifolia*. And if, as has happened to many, you tire of driving in the rain, you can turn down the Gardena Valley to Ortise, where there are reports of tea and good shops.

The Rolle Pass. Here is the *crème de la crème*—at least for us. Yet, in spite of Farrer's eulogies, the Rolle does not seem to have been as popular a centre as those in the more northerly mass of the Dolomites, for there are few *Bulletin* references. Perhaps it seems a little more remote and difficult of access, though indeed for the motorist at least it is reached by easy and lovely drives, and there are regular coaches between Predazzo and San Martino di Castrozza. In fact it is only some 70 km. from Bolzano, and whether you come from there or from the Pordoi area you will travel down the Dolomite Road and down the Val di Fassa to Predazzo, and here turn eastward into the Val Travignolo. The latter valley is delightful. I have never seen roadside meadows more rich with flowers. The orchids in particular—dwarf, marsh and scented and *Dactylorhiza sambucina*—are magnificent in late June, and the military orchids a little earlier. Fine *Pedicularis* species pretend to be orchids, the St. Bruno's lilies are superb, and here and there the huge flowers of *Lilium bulbiferum croceum* stand out brilliantly on the roadside slopes. Higher, you drive through fine forest alongside the Lago di Forte Buso before the road finally zigzags up to the Rolle Pass over the rolling alps. Farrer, seeing them only from the coach, was rude about these 'dull green' alps, but if he had got out and walked he would have found them studded with gentians (the *G. acaulis* is especially fine here), pulsatillas, *Loiseleuria* and *Pinguicula leptoceras* with white-blotched, purple flowers.

Alternatively, you may come to the Rolle from the north-east, from Cortina, leaving the Dolomite Road at Andraz and travelling via Falcade to reach the Passo di Valles and so join the Rolle road above Paneveggio. This too is a lovely drive, especially after Falcade, with spike after spike of the great Pala range on your left. It is as you turn up towards the pass from Paneveggio that you may catch your first glimpse of the Cimon della Pala. Misurina and the Pordoi are beautiful places, and their mountains magnificent, but the soul of the Rolle lies in the Cimon and lifts it high above the others. I have never seen another mountain so beautiful. I shall not attempt to describe it, for Farrer has done so as only Farrer can. But perhaps I should venture a warning or two. Hold on to your steering wheel as you drive up from Paneveggio lest your first glimpse of the Cimon throw you off the road. Leave your camera in the hotel, or you will find that, as it were in a trance, you will point its lens at the Cimon and go on exposing film after costly film. At dinner, drink your coffee *before* you go out to watch the lurid sunset glow on the Cimon, otherwise it will be stone-cold when you get back. Take plenty of wine to make you sleep through the night, or you will be up at 4 a.m. to see the Cimon dark against the dawn sky. And one other warning—you may not see the Cimon at all, for it can rain in torrents on the Rolle!

You can stay on the pass itself. At 1970 m. it is lower than the Pordoi. There are several hotels; we have stayed in two and found them both comfortable. Although there are a good many buildings on the pass, yet it is somehow less of a mess than the Pordoi. It is narrower, the mountains overhang it more immediately, and the road makes a right-angled twist on the pass. But if you feel that you will sleep more snugly at a lower level, there is a hotel at Paneveggio and plenty of them at San Martino. We have visited San Martino, but not stayed there. It is beautifully placed for looking at the mountains, and there are chairlifts and a funivia to take you high among them, and a fine drive through the woods to the pass above. But it is around the pass itself that the greatest variety of flowers is to be found. On the Rolle Pass, as on the Pordoi, the igneous rocks break through the dolomite—the easternmost end of a long chain on the south side of the Travignolo valley. Around the pass itself the igneous rocks predominate, but it is only a short way to the outliers of the dolomitic Pala group. A list of the flowers to be found within a short range of the pass would be very much a repetition of what has been said of the Pordoi, and few if any names would be missing from the list.

A profitable day can be spent on Cavalazza (2324 m.) to the south of the pass—a great outpost above the San Martino valley with all the Pala range spread out before you. Here, among *Soldanella pusilla*, *Primula glutinosa* and *P. minima* and the occasional hybrid, is *Saponaria pumilio*—though you must go late in the season to see it in flower. And here too, among the tunnels and galleries of the 1914–18 war, is *Eritrichium nanum*.

The drive down to San Martino is delightful—first over rolling alps covered with blue and violet spring gentians, past screes where *Anemone baldensis* and *Ranunculus seguieri* grow, and then steeply down through beautiful coniferous woods where among *Daphne striata*, *Anemone trifolia* (sometimes blue) and many other fine flowers is the lady's slipper orchid, *Cypripedium calceolus*, which used to keep the restaurant flower-vases filled in San Martino. One may hope that this is no longer so, for the Italians are becoming more conscious of the need to protect such plants as this.

From near the top of the pass a small road winds past the Baita Segantini over a ridge of igneous rock and then down steeply to the Val Venegia at the foot of the Pala range. Here in fine abundance is the whole flora of the Eastern Alps and the dolomite specials as well. I know no finer place. Of special interest here is *Eritrichium nanum* growing in the dolomitic cliffs; it is perhaps a little paler and smaller than the best forms, but still a lovely plant. Presumably it is exposed to limestone at its roots, but it is magnesian limestone, and it appears to grow in fat chunks of humus-rich soil in V-shaped crevices rather than penetrating the true fissures of the rock. The little road is rough, but (once the snow has cleared—it lingers late here) it is perfectly negotiable; and after running down the Val Venegia it joins the upper reaches of the Val Travignolo and the Passo di Valles. A great red ridge (the Cima Valles and the Cima di Venegiotta—2403 m.) runs on the south side of the Passo di Valles. It is well worth the effort of climbing, for it commands magnificent views of the Pala range and of the south face of Marmolada.

While the main mass of the Dolomites, including the centres so far described, lies to the east of the Adige Valley, there are also limestone mountains in the Trentino to the west of that valley. One group of these is the Brenta Alps, where the village of Madonna di Campiglio has been visited by an A.G.S. Tour.

Madonna di Campiglio* (1550 m.), well known for winter sports, has more recently developed also as a summer resort, so that more hotels and other facilities are now open in the summer months. As a centre it is well supplied with cable-cars and chair-lifts, allowing one to climb rapidly to over 2000 m., while the paths and tracks are plentiful and usually well-marked. A considerable part of the area, with much of the interesting flora, is thus of easy access. To the east, once up on M. Spinale by cable-car, there are gently undulating rich alpine meadows for the less energetic to explore, and they can be quickly crossed to reach the screes and cliffs beyond. A similar situation exists at the terminus of the Predalgo cable-railway on the north-western side of the town. There are also easy but interesting low-level walks up to the Lago di Nambino or down to the water-falls of the Vallesinella, both of which can lead to higher levels, while the possibilities for other more energetic scrambles are endless. So much is on the doorstep that one could find plenty of interest for a week or a fortnight without having to use a car to travel further afield, although the Val di Genova, which climbs westward from the road about 5 miles south of the town, is well worth a visit, and if one fancies a more distant day excursion, the famous rock-carvings of Capo di Ponti near Edolo are within easy reach by car. Late June and early July would usually be the best times to go, but not all the hotels will be open nor all the cable-cars running at the beginning of this period.

From the plant point of view the Campiglio area may not be quite so rich as some other parts of the Dolomites—it is surprisingly poor in *Primula* species—but it does gain something in variety from being situated right on the western margin of the Brenta Dolomites and at their junction with the granite and other acid igneous rocks to the west. There is, for instance, an abundance of *Soldanella pusilla* in suitable areas on the slopes to the west of the town, together with small quantities of *Eritrichium nanum*, *Primula hirsuta*, *Lloydia*, *Loiseleuria*, *Geum montanum* and *Phyteuma hemisphaericum*, while on the eastern side of the valley most of the soldanellas are *S. alpina*, and one finds a few *Physoplexis* (*Phyteuma*) *comosa* and *Androsace helvetica* as well as many of the usual plants of dolomitic areas. *Pulsatilla alpina* and *P. apiifolia* are both common in the area but their relative abundance is markedly different on the two sides of the valley. The meadows in and around Madonna itself, and especially at Campo Carlo Magno, are rich in flowers, and the open coniferous woodlands to the south of the town and into the lower reaches of the Vallesinella are also full of interesting plants including at least a dozen species of orchids. The centre is therefore ideal in demonstrating a range of habitats and flowers, but nevertheless many of the 'specialities' are uncommon around Campiglio and one hopes that they will not suffer from depredation by tourists.

LAKE GARDA

The Lago di Garda is a large lake, a little above sea-level, running from south-west to north-east from the Lombardy Plain into the heart of the limestone mountains which extend southwards from the Dolomites. The hills around its southern end are low, but the northern part of the lake is flanked by the Monte Baldo range to the south-east and the Monte Tombea range to the north-west. The altitudinal, and to a less extent the latitudinal, range are such that the flora round the southern end of the lake has a Mediterranean quality, while there are true alpines on the mountain tops.

There are two main approaches, from the south and the north. The autostrada across Northern Italy, accompanied by a railway, lies close to Desenzano and Peschiera on the southern end of the lake. A road, in many places scenically beautiful, but somewhat built-up now, particularly on the eastern side, runs right round the lake. There is no railway except along the southern end, but there are coaches running along both sides of the lake up to Riva and Torbole at its northern end. Passenger steamers serve many of the towns on the shore, and there is a car-ferry (Maderno to Torri) across the lake. From the north there are a main road and railway from Bolzano via Trento to Rovereto, whence Riva is easily reached

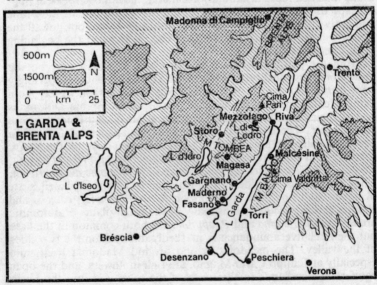

by road. A smaller, more beautiful, route from the north to Riva runs past the Brenta Alps via Molveno.

Two main valleys run parallel to the lake—the valley of the Adige on the south-east side of Monte Baldo, and the higher-level valley of Ledro and Idro to the north and west of Monte Tombea. Both these are reached by good roads from Riva, and also by a series of small roads threading their way along and across the mountains. There is a funicular running from Malcesine on the east side of the lake up to the ridge of Monte Baldo, and also a chair-lift from behind Torri. The small mountain roads vary a good deal in quality, but in the main they are perfectly negotiable and scenically beautiful.

There are plenty of hotels all round the lake, and some in the side valleys. The problem is to achieve optimum access to both mountain ranges. Riva is most conveniently placed for this, but it is a hot, enclosed, close-packed little town. **Malcesine** also has good accommodation, and for the pedestrian it is well-placed with its funicular railway for reaching the highest peaks of Monte Baldo. Using the steamer gives access to the Tombea side too. There are mountain huts (rifugios) in both ranges. An interesting account in the *Bulletin* (Vol. 41, p. 165) is based on a stay at **Fasano** in mid-June. This centre provided ready access by car both to Monte Tombea and also, by taking the ferry across to Torri, to Monte Baldo. Another useful and pleasant centre for the visitor with a car is **Mezzolago** on the Lago di Ledro at the northern end of the Tombea range. This is readily reached from Riva, and gives easy access to Monte Tombea from its north-west side and rather less easy access to Monte Baldo via Riva and Mori. An A.G.S. Tour was based partly on Riva in 1961.

Because of the wide range of altitude and climate round the lake, the best time to visit is difficult to specify. Mid-April for the lower levels and more southerly parts and late June for the higher levels are certain to be rewarding times.

The flowers round the lake, while not in a narrow sense 'alpine', include many good rock garden plants. Among the oranges and lemons, oleanders, lizards, cicadas and swallow-tail butterflies are to be found *Dianthus sylvestris*, *Petrorhagia saxifraga*, *Teucrium chamaedrys*, *T. montanum* and *Chamaecytisus* (*Cytisus*) *purpureus*. These plants spread up the hillsides (so that they are not tender as might be supposed from seeing them only by the lakeside) accompanied by orchids; *OO. militaris, simia* and *coriophora* and various species of *Ophrys*, and bright purple *Legousia speculum-veneris*. The two lovely flaxes *Linum tenuifolium* and *L. viscosum* are on these hillsides, small gladioli (*G. illyricus* and the more rare and local *G. imbricatus*), *Ajuga genevensis* and *Ononis natrix*.

MONTE BALDO

Monte Baldo is an undulating ridge with no one distinct summit; rather a series of knobs, of which the Cima Valdritta (2218 m.) is the highest. There are tracks along and across the ridge and an erstwhile military road well below the crest on its southeast side. This is entered from various points in the Adige valley, the most northerly being Mori, or from Garda or Torri on the lake. To reach the crest itself one must walk from the road or take the 'funivia' from Malcesine, certainly the quickest route to the highest flowers. But by the road there are plenty of flowers to be seen, for it climbs out of the valley through fine alpine meadows full of *Arnica montana*, *Campanula glomerata* and *C. barbata*, *Phyteuma ovatum*, *Lilium bulbiferum* and its variety *L. croceum*, *Paeonia officinalis*, *Aster alpinus* in varied colours, *Gentiana lutea* and *G. utriculosa*, and *Lilium martagon*. In these same meadows the leaves of snowdrops tell of earlier flowerings and in the woods between the meadows are the rose helleborine, *Cephalanthera rubra*, *Melittis melissophyllum*, *Lathyrus vernus*, *Hepatica nobilis*, *Daphne mezereum* and the orchid *Traunsteinera globosa*.

Higher still, among the rocks and tunnels and the scars of two world wars are the pretty little *Silene saxifraga*, the handsome-leaved (but rather squinny-flowered) *Saxifraga mutata*, edelweiss, and (to our surprise when we first saw it) *Corydalis lutea*. This common 'cottage garden' plant acquired a new status in our eyes as it hung from the high limestone crevices which it shares on Monte Baldo with *Physoplexis comosa*. All these (and Roger-Smith mentions also *Daphne alpina* and *Dictamnus albus*) are to be reached by the old military road, but for the real high specialities of Monte Baldo you must take one of the paths up towards the ridge. *Anemone baldensis* and *Carex baldensis* acclaim the mountain, though they are not confined to it, *Geranium argenteum* called forth one of Farrer's clearest paeans, *Callianthemum kerneranum* is rare and beautiful, and there are reminders of the Dolomites in *Rhodothamnus chamaecistus*, *Potentilla nitida* and *Daphne cneorum*.

MONTE TOMBEA

Monte Tombea, like Monte Baldo, consists of many peaks with no clear summit but it is a less well-defined ridge; rather a great elongated jumble of beautiful limestone hills, the highest being M. Caplone (1977 m.). Like Monte Baldo, it has seen service, and military roads wind among the peaks. A fine new road runs up from Gargnano on the lake to Magasa, a remarkable mountain village from which the Cima Tombea is reached easily (in two hours or less) on foot. It is a wonderful drive to Magasa, worth making alike for the flowers and the scenery; nevertheless the approaches to the Monte Tombea group from the north-west have even more to commend them. The drive from Riva up to the Lago di Ledro (655 m.) and then down via Storo to the Lago d'Idro is beautiful and in places spectacular. A road climbs steeply up from the little Lago d'Ampola to the Passo di Tremalzo, and from here there are tracks by which various of the peaks, including the Cima Tombea, may be reached by foot, and three mountain huts. The road continues over the Passo di Tremalzo, down to Lake Garda. It is however a military road, and we found ourselves barred from using it but others seem to have got through. From Idro a little road runs steeply up to Capovalle, and ultimately, by two alternative routes, to Magasa, so that it is possible to complete the circle to Gargnano. The roads up from Idro are small and rough but negotiable.

The flowers on the Tombea range are to a very large extent the same as those on Monte Baldo, though there are some interesting differences, particularly among the plants near the summits. Our first approach to Magasa was from Gargnano at the end of June, and *Cyclamen purpurascens*, very sweetly scented, grew in the roadside grit. *Physoplexis comosa* was in the cliffs overhanging the road, with masses of its seedlings, doomed to an early death, germinating in the three-inch-deep moss in the ditch below. In the same cliffs was the very pretty little *Aquilegia thalictrifolia*, with neat leaves and clear deep blue, wide, flat-faced flowers. These flowers are still there in places, but with the cutting of the new road at a higher level the cliffs and banks are inevitably for a time unclothed. At Magasa you must take to your feet and follow the path leading up from the village among *Geranium phaeum* and the leaves of *Helleborus niger*, until you come to the limestone faces. Here, flowering together with *Physoplexis comosa*, are *Ranunculus bilobus* and *Primula spectabilis*, both beautiful and the latter varied in form and colour and giving a lovely show on the white rocks. In the grass and among the shrubs between the rocks are *Fritillaria tubiformis* (*delphinensis*) and *Cephalanthera longifolia*, one of our scarcer British helleborines. A special plant of the highest rock faces here is *Silene elisabetha*, but the *pièce de résistance* is of course *Daphne petraea*, confined to a small area centred on the Lago d'Idro and reputedly abundant in a few places within this area. White and double forms are reported, as well as the large form *D.p. grandiflora* which is common in cultivation.

Further to the north, down by the Lago d'Idro, *Physoplexis comosa* is abundant in the cliffs by the roadside, and is accompanied by very good forms of *Paederota bonarota*, which is somewhat similar in foliage, and by that charming and distinct form of *Primula auricula* f. *albocincta*, white-ringed both at the throat of the flower and at the edges of the leaves. Here in April *Primula*

Silene elisabetha

spectabilis is to be found growing by the roadside among scrub, and higher up *Leucojum vernum*, magnificent *Helleborus niger* and *Cardamine heptaphylla*. In June, *P. spectabilis* flowers up on the pass with that most beguiling and cheeky little pansy *Viola dubyana*. Hereabouts too are the attractive white-flowered sedge *Carex baldensis*, and the neat domes and large white flowers of *Saxifraga tombeanensis*.

Before leaving this area, let us briefly visit the Roccia Campei, an outlier of the Cima Pari to the north of the Lago di Ledro. It is reached by footpath from Mezzolago, and many of the Tombea flowers are here. The ascent is wooded, and in June these woods are lovely with the flowers of *Laburnum alpinum* and *Amelanchier ovalis*, and under the trees are *Polygala chamaebuxus*, *Erica herbacea* (*carnea*), *Convallaria majalis* (Lily of the Valley), *Cyclamen purpurascens*, and the little coralroot, *Corallorhiza trifida*, a saprophytic orchid. In the meadows above are many of the flowers already seen on Baldo and Tombea, with the attractive *Scabiosa graminifolia*, *Muscari botryoides* and *Chamaecytisus purpureus*; and so up to the ridge where *Saxifraga tombeanensis* adorns the soldiers' trenches.

THE APENNINES

The Apennine chain runs down the length of the 'leg' of Italy, reaching 2914 m. in the Gran Sasso, the highest peak in the Abruzzi mountains, in the middle of the chain. Its flora is largely Mediterranean in type, progressively more so as one proceeds south-eastward, but there are considerable elements of the 'basic' alpine flora in the more northerly Apennines. In general these mountains have a pleasant but not a distinct flora, though there are a few special plants in the Abruzzi.

The Apennines are divided into many named groups. The only ones which will be briefly considered here are the Tuscan Apennines in the north, the Apuan Alps, and the Abruzzi.

THE TUSCAN APENNINES

Lying to the north-west of Florence, these form the most northerly part of the main 'backbone' of the Apennines, reaching 2165 m. in Monte Cimone. We were there at the end of April, when the summit of Monte Cimone was still under snow. It was a beautiful countryside in the spring; a land of lightly wooded hills and valleys, with rocky outcrops; a land no doubt soon to become hot and arid. We stayed at **Séstola**, in a comfortable little hotel, and visited Monte Cimone and the surrounding area.

In the valley woodlands were the hellebores *H. viridis* and *H. foetidus*, hepaticas, *Corydalis bulbosa* in an interesting range of colours, *Asarum europaeum*, yellow *Anemone ranunculoides*, and (our most exciting find), *Cyclamen repandum*, as well as the leaves of *C. hederifolium*. In the higher woodlands, not far below the snow, were *Scilla bifolia* with white-flowered forms, *Gagea lutea*, *Cardamine*

Anemone hortensis

kitaibelli, and the leaves of martagon lilies. In places there was a scrub of the large heaths, *Erica arborea* and *E. multiflora*. There was *Arabis caucasica* (*albida*) on the rocks, and in the soft turf lilac *Anemone hortensis* and many orchids—*Orchis morio*, yellow *O. provincialis*, *Dactylorhiza sambucina* in both yellow and purple and possibly *D. sulphurea* too, and we were delighted to see for the first time the magnificent lady orchid, *Orchis purpurea*, as well as some fine *O. militaris*. Up near the snow *Pulsatilla alpina* was starting into flower among gentians (*G. verna* and *G. utriculosa*) and beautiful crocuses. These were presumably of one of the forms of *C. vernus*—very large-flowered, with petals approaching 8 cm. in length, white, purple or subtly feathered.

No doubt the higher levels of Monte Cimone had more to offer as the snow receded but we felt that the season was likely to be short and the flora limited.

THE APUAN ALPS*

This compact range of low elevation (highest peak 1945 m.) lies between the Tuscan Apennines and the Tyrrenian Sea just a few miles away, which ensures abundant precipitation and a mountain climate. During the summer thunderstorms are a regular feature in the afternoon. The central core of the range is the famous Carrara marble, surrounded by schists, more or less slaty and in places calcareous, with acid volcanic rocks here and there.

The sea, the rugged profiles, the snow-white marble screes, the villages precariously perched high up, and the intensely green chestnut forests merging downwards with olive trees and vineyards, combine to make the Apuan scenery most attractive. The best time to visit is the end of May.

There is easy access by road to the subalpine zones. An interesting drive is from Massa to the Pian della Fioba where there is an alpine garden with exclusively local plants. Professor E. Ferrarini, now at the Instituto Botanico, Universita, Siena, can advise about visits. The road, rough in parts, tunnels through the mountains to reach the inland side of the range in the Serchio valley and from Arni one may

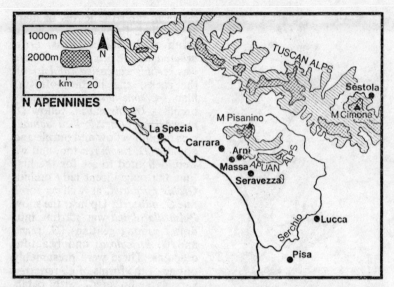

return, through another tunnel, to the coastal plain at Seravezza. At several points along this road one can walk up to the main ridge.

All the mountain plants of the Northern and Central Apennines occur in the Apuan Alps. The Orchidaceae are particularly abundant, and there are superb alpine meadows with martagon lilies on the steep northern slopes of Monte Pisanino, approachable by the road which climbs up from Piazza al Serchio. Special plants of the area are *Globularia incanescens* and *Moltkia suffruticosa* in cracks on the marble rocks. *Saxifraga aizoides* is here predominantly orange-flowered.

The Abruzzi*

In early June go due east from Rome on the A24 Autostrada, and after some eighty miles the road passes under the Gran Sasso d'Italia. If you are not in a hurry, however, you will go to L'Aquila (600 m.), the capital of Abruzzi province, and from here it is half an hour's drive up to **Fonte Coretto** (1200 m.), where there is an hotel at the lower station of the funicular.

We drove up the road to the Gran Sasso, but stopped first at the Valle Freddo, which cuts through the limestone. The pink flowers of *Lamium garganicum* and *Ononis rotundifolia* were out at the sides of the stream, *Saxifraga callosa callosa* was in masses on the rocks, and less spectacular, but delightful to see in the wild, was the small *S. porophylla*. The sides of the newly repaired road provided an endless array of plants; *Euphorbia myrsinites*, *Cerastium tomentosum* var. *columnae*, the exciting *Viola eugeniae* in yellow or deep purple,

Erodium alpinum in pink providing a contrast with *Muscari botryoides* and *Edraianthus graminifolius* in blue, but *Polygala major* in pink, blue or white was the most colourful of them all. *Calamintha grandiflora* was in masses, as was *Alyssum alpestre*.

As we passed above the Campo Imperatore to the east, *Globularia cordifolia* and *Androsace villosa* abounded. *Gentiana acaulis* was the prevalent gentian here. High up there was plenty of *Dryas octopetala, Gentiana verna* and *Erysimum helveticum. Iberis saxatilis* was difficult to spot in the scree—unlike *Dactylorhiza sambucina* which was conspicuous in both yellow and red. We found *Scilla bifolia* in flower in muddy areas and *Doronicum columnae* in the screes. *Ranunculus hybridus* (like a small *R. thora*), *Orchis pallens* and *Gentiana brachyphylla favratii* were to us rare and exciting. *Saxifraga oppositifolia* comes as far south as this.

Sheep had come up to the high plains of Campo Imperatore very early; they and their shepherds were the only people we saw in this wild, desolate but beautiful part of Central Italy. *Armeria maritima* was in sheets by the roadside. *Ononis cristata* (*cenisia*) with red and white flowers was new to us. The scent of *Matthiola fruticulosa*, a perennial stock, I shall not forget; it was growing on pure gravel in the old river bed. The little *Dianthus deltoides* contrasted with the metre tall *Salvia argentea*, which is not easy to identify immediately.

The north side of the range is approached by going up to Pietra-camela and so to Prati de Tive, a newly developed ski resort where there were several hotels open in June. The area was wetter, green, and the flora different. *Primula auricula* was there, sometimes farinose and sometimes efarinose and so were *P. vulgaris* and *Daphne mezereum*. We had not met *Arabis alpina* before, but *Anemone ranunculoides* was an old friend, and here a good yellow. At a lower level *Paeonia officinalis* was in full flower.

SICILY*

Sicily is the largest island in the Mediterranean. It lies across latitudes 37 and 38° N., and thus has a typical Mediterranean climate, though cooler than, say, Greece. The island has a pronounced spine of limestone mountains along its north side, reaching 1979 m. south of Cefalu but the highest point is the peak of Mount Etna (3323 m.), which of course is still an active volcano, towards the north-east corner.

There are regular scheduled charter-flights to Palermo and Catania but it is cheaper by train to Taormina. It is a long way by car, but crossing from the mainland by car-ferry is easy; there are frequent services. Cars can be hired on the island, which is cheaper but riskier, or by a 'Fly-drive' arrangement or, if you go by rail, through Italian Railways. There is a motorway from Enna to

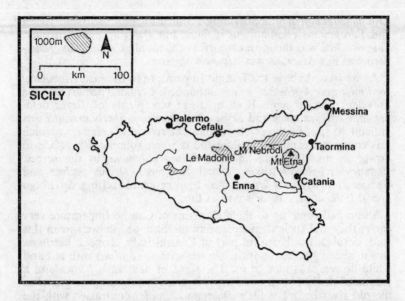

SICILY

1000m

N

0   km   100

Messina

Palermo
Cefalu

Taormina

Le Madonie   M Nebrodi
Mt Etna

Enna

Catania

Palermo and from Messina to Catania, with others under construction or planned, otherwise the roads vary from poor to terrible, and distances covered in a day will be short. Garage facilities are not frequent in the mountains; one wary eye on the petrol gauge and the other on the road is essential.

Sicily has a fascinating history and many wonderful archaeological sites, but nearly all these are on or close to the coast, so the touring facilities are not ideally suited for alpine plant hunters. It would be possible, though difficult and rather uncomfortable, to explore the mountains by bus, or by train and bus, but a car is best.

Probably the best centres for plant hunting in the mountains are **Taormina** (for Etna and the Peloritani), **Cefalu** (for the Nebrodi and Madonie) and **Palermo** (for what is left). Hotels or motels of fair quality can be found in these towns, as well as in Acireale, Randazzo, Messina, Milazzo and Enna. The Madonie are being developed for skiing, and new hotels are being built there.

The best time to visit depends on your taste in flowers and holidays. The winter and early spring are wet and mild. In May the rainfall decreases sharply, but not necessarily in the mountains, and temperature rises.

As to the flowers, they are not conspicuously different from those of other Mediterranean countries. Nobody should make Sicily his first choice for plant-hunting in that area; equally it should not be overlooked. In one short day in May, in a small area of woodland in the Nebrodi, I found *Cyclamen hederifolium, C. repandum* (in flower but no white ones), ornithogalums, *Narcissus tazetta*, a white-flowered primrose, and *Paeonia mascula russii* in all shades from pure white to a delicate pink. Elsewhere were found *Orchis tridentata* and *OO. provincialis, italica, morio* and several others. *Crocus vernus, Romulea bulbocodium, Muscari* and *Bellevalia* species were not surprising. On some poor overgrazed hillsides were great masses of *Spartium junceum*; large bushes ten or twelve feet high.

Sicily is now generally recognised as a site for autumn-flowering snowdrops, which occur quite low down on the north-facing slopes of the northern mountains (see *Bulletin* Vol. 45, p. 273). The most interesting find for me was a form of *Galanthus* which looks exactly like *G. nivalis corcyrensis*, but flowers in January and February. These slopes could reveal many interesting plants, as much of the weather comes from the north or north-west resulting in wetter conditions and richer vegetation.

Lithodora rosmarinifolia

Etna of course is a special case. Above a certain height one feels one is walking on the largest slag-heap of all time. It is not surprising that this unusual habitat gives rise to several endemics. There are species or forms of *Betula, Erysimum, Berberis* and *Viola*, as well as *Genista aetnensis*. Oxford ragwort, *Senecio squalidus*, also grows there! One can get to the top from Catania by car and ski-lift or walk and climb from Linguaglossa—but take advice first.

Apart from orchids and shrubs, there is a plant of special interest in the central plateau, *Lithodora rosmarinifolia. Convolvulus cneorum* is said to grow on the little island of Marettimo off the western end of Sicily.

SARDINIA*

Sardinia is interestingly placed in the West Mediterranean between Sicily, Corsica and Majorca. It is largely mountainous, the highest peak reaching 1834 m. It would be expected to have, and indeed has, a large number of the Corsican and Sicilian plants, and some Balearic ones as well. Yet, to judge from the absence of references in the *Bulletin*, it has been little visited by A.G.S. Members.

It can be reached by car ferry from Genoa to Porto Torres on the north-west of the island. There is a network of railways and roads.

The lower levels carry a typical Mediterranean flora, and a special plant on the sand-dunes is an attractive ophrys, peculiar to Sardinia and Sicily, *O. lunulata*, with a dark red lip, yellow-tipped and with a small sickle-shaped blue patch. The beautiful *Rosmarinus officinalis*, cascading down the white limestone cliffs, and *Arenaria balearica*, growing surprisingly in full sun, are reminiscent of Majorca. A special plant of the Central Mediterranean islands is *Pancratium illyricum*, sweetly scented and at higher levels reduced in size; truly an alpine plant. At the beginning of May it was flowering in bog and even in

Morisia monanthos

running water: no doubt it would dry out later. In the same place was a yellow bunch-flowered narcissus, *N. cupularis*, a Sardinian version of *N. tazetta aureus*. Among boulders in 'a weird landscape like a moonscape with vegetation' was *Brimeura* (*Hyacinthus*) *fastigiata*; another plant shared with Corsica. On shady roadside banks, and in cork oakwoods too, was *Cyclamen repandum*, with flowers of a good rosy pink. *Ornithogalum exscapum* grew in boggy conditions, and with it, surprisingly, *Morisia monanthos*. Yet another plant associated with Corsica was the beautiful *Crocus minimus*, and *Paeonia mascula russii* is shared with Sicily.

Italy in the *Bulletin*:

3, 99 Seligman, R. Abruzzi
3, 307 Seligman, R. Abruzzi
10, 54 Mountfort, C. C.
 Dolomites
17, 121 Seligman, R. Tombea
18, 165 Cumming, P.T.
 Macugnaga
21, 50 Bartlett, N. M.
 Dolomites
21, 273 Spencer, E. Dolomites

28, 312 Elliott, R. C.
 Dolomites
30, 164 Nutt, R. D.
 Macugnaga
30, 236 Wacher, H. S.
 Cervinia, Cogne
30, 319 Barrett, G. E. Baldo
31, 110 Nutt, R. D. Dolomites
36, 54 Gorer, R. Macugnaga
36, 289 Harding, W. F. W.
 Abruzzi

*Sections marked with asterisks were contributed as follows:—
The Gran Paradiso: Prof. G. Pontecorvo
Madonna di Campiglio: Mr. T. S. Crosby
Apuan Alps: Prof. G. Pontecorvo
Sicily: Mr. F. F. H. Charlton
Sardinia: Mrs. S. Maule
The Abruzzi: Mr. R. D. Nutt

5

FRANCE

The mountains of France lie in the south and east, and this mountainous part of the country is cleft by the north-south valley of the great rivers Saône and Rhône. To the west of the Rhône lies the vast upland area of the Massif Central, within which are to be distinguished a central block, the Auvergne, and the Cévennes which form the western rim of the lower Rhône valley. The Pyrenees, on the frontier with Spain, are separately considered in Chapter 6. To the east of the Rhone lie the French Alps, an area of high mountains comparable in size to the whole of Switzerland, increasing in altitude as one goes eastward, and at their highest levels forming the frontier with Italy. Beyond this frontier they drop fairly steeply to the Plain of Lombardy. North of the Alps, and forming part of the frontier with Switzerland, is a line of rather lower hills, the Jura.

For the purposes of this book the main area (other than the Pyrenees) to be considered in France is the vast mass of the French Alps. The Auvergne however also merits and receives separate consideration. The Cévennes and the Jura, though not separately treated here, are both beautiful areas, well-flowered though not distinctively so.

France presents few problems for the British traveller abroad. Communications are good, the roads generally well-surfaced. and there is a good railway network. English is taught as a second language in the schools, so that generally someone can be found who speaks it. Hotels vary in standard but are generally comparable with those in England; there are usually one or two even in smaller towns and often in villages too, but this cannot be relied upon. A very useful book is the *Guide des Logis de France*, which is obtainable in England.

The flowers of the Alps and the Auvergne are considered below but before reaching these areas a driver from the Channel ports will find the roadsides (unless he be on the motorway) becoming progressively more beautiful, with an abundance of orchids in the calcareous areas. Short incursions into the woods in such places are likely to reveal the lizard orchid, *Himantoglossum hircinum*, which is widespread. There are many beautiful Leguminosae, of which *Coronilla varia* is outstanding, and here and there the colourful crested cow-wheat, *Melampyrum cristatum*. More local are the tassel hyacinth, *Muscari comosum*, the lovely yellow *Halimium alyssoides*, and the related *Tuberaria guttata* with blotched flowers.

In Southern France—the Corbières, the Cévennes and the lower and more southerly hills of Provence and the Alpes Maritimes—the flora is predominantly Mediterranean in type. This flora contains two main elements—summer-resting plants, mainly tuberous or bulbous, which flower in the autumn or spring (*Orchis* and *Ophrys* species are an important group of these) and summer-flowering plants tolerant of hot dry conditions, such as *Linum narbonense* and *LL. suffruti-cosum* and *tenuifolium*, cistuses, *Convolvulus cantabrica*, *Helichrysum stoechas*, *Iris lutescens*, *Colutea arborescens*, *Leuzea conifera*, *Digitalis lutea*, *Lavandula stoechas*, *Teucrium polium*—and many more (see p. 105). While many of these are good garden plants in England, others are happy only in warmer gardens or the alpine house.

The traveller to Switzerland is likely to cross the more northerly parts of France. He too will find fine roadside flowers and a foretaste of the alpine flora as he crosses the Jura, but he will find little there that is not also present, and more abundantly, on the lower levels of the Swiss and French Alps.

THE AUVERGNE

In the Auvergne the Massif Central reaches 1886 m. at the Puy de Sançy. It is an area of acid rock, distinctive and beautiful. It is also a tourist area, with plenty of hotels, and accommodation problems are unlikely except in August.

Latour d'Auvergne, lying among fields of poet's narcissus, and sweetly scented with *Spartium junceum*, is a convenient centre for the motorist. It lies to the south-west of Clermont-Ferrand, and can be reached by rail from there to Mont-Dore, and thence by bus. For the visitor without a car **Mont-Dore** is perhaps a better centre.

The outstanding local visit is to the Puy de Sançy, reached from Mont-Dore by a road to the foot of the mountain and then by foot-path or cable-car to a station near the summit. A plant of special beauty here, glowing from the rocks as you sweep past them in the *téléférique*, is *Androsace carnea rosea*. White *Pulsatilla alpina* and its sulphur-yellow subspecies *P.a. apiifolia* grow intermingled and on the lower slopes this yellow and white theme is taken up by sheets of daffodils and poet's narcissi.

There are fine drives from Latour west and southward along the Gorge de la Dordogne, the Vallée de Falgoux, and the area of Pas de

Peyrol and Puy Mary. In the woods we found *Scilla lilio-hyacinthus*, and by the roadsides the little, spiked *Anarrhinum belli-difolium*, but on the whole this was not a well-flowered area. Far better is the drive eastward from Mont-Dore over the Col de la Croix St. Robert towards Besse-en-Chandesse. In late June in this beautiful rolling upland country we found a large white 'anemone',

Scilla lilio-hyacinthus

like a small *Pulsatilla alpina*, which in retrospect I think must have been *P. alba*. Certainly *P. rubra* was here, in deep glowing brown-red, and also beautiful white violas, *Dactylorhiza sambucina*, *Lathyrus vernus*, and a puzzle which in my diary appears as 'a white broom.'

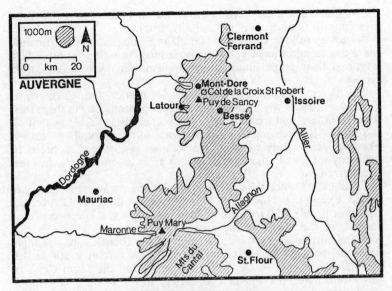

THE FRENCH ALPS

The great mass of the French Alps runs from the lake of Geneva in the north to the Mediterranean in the south, and from the Rhône valley in the west to the Italian frontier in the east. There is a great confusion of names, some relating to Departments of Provinces, some to mountain ranges, and some to individual mountain massifs. The main mountain ranges, which however are not clearly separated, are, from north to south, the High Savoy, the Graians, the Cottians and the Maritimes. The whole area is highly developed both for summer tourists and for winter sports; consequently there is a large choice of possible centres at which one can stay.

There are many approaches to the area—from Geneva or Martigny in the north, from various points on the Lyon-Marseille motorway, or across country from the Auvergne into Provence. The motorway from Paris is now very fast and easy, but there are tolls to pay. A good, relatively low-level road, the Route Napoléon, runs from Geneva via Grenoble to Cannes, and the high-level Route des Alpes pursues an erratic course, running more or less parallel with the Italian frontier from Geneva to Nice. It is a wonderful road, and most of the centres here chosen lie on or near to it. Many smaller roads connect these two main routes, and in addition there is a large number of roads running into inhabited valleys or across high passes—in fact the whole area is very well served for the motorist, who can drive to levels as high as about 2760 m. on the Col de Restefond. There are also roads over the frontier into Italy, and at times it is more convenient to cross over, and back by another route, rather than to make a longer détour within France. Such frontier-crossings do not normally present any problems.

A railway follows the Route Napoléon throughout its length, and there are in addition a good many railways running more or less west-east through the mountains, supplemented by bus and coach services.

The high mountains are mainly of igneous rock, though there are limestone areas as well. Limestone tends to predominate in the rather lower southern and western hills. The scenery is as varied as that of the Swiss Alps, ranging from the pastoral to the stark. The weather likewise is as moody as mountain weather is expected to be; it is distinctly warmer in the more southern areas as one approaches the Mediterranean.

Taking the French Alps as a whole, the flowers are abundant and varied. Except in the lower hills of the Alpes Maritimes and Provence, the 'basic flora' is still to be found, and in some places is very profuse. Indeed, in the north of the area, around Chamonix, this is the predominant flora and the dullest part of the French Alps—though scenically perhaps the most impressive. A little further south, in the Graians, additional species begin to appear and the Mont Cenis is justly famed for the wealth and variety of its flowers. This more specialised flora continues and abounds throughout the Cottian Alps, and in the high Maritimes new species appear, perhaps with some falling-off in the luxuriance of the more usual species, and there is a change-over to the more Mediterranean type of flora (though with some distinct and local plants) as one descends into the Maritime foothills. The eastern slopes of the Alps, in Piemonte (Piedmont) in Italy, are conveniently considered with the French Alps in this chapter.

The selection of convenient centres presents a problem—not merely because there are so many to choose from but also because the availability of a car and personal preference as between a lower town or a higher village very much affect the choice. So the reader will be conducted on a rapid tour through the French Alps, proceeding from north to south, and pausing at a number of centres suitable for different purposes on the way.

THE HIGH SAVOY

Chamonix, the main centre in the great mountains of the Haute Savoie, is easily reached from either Geneva or Basel, but if time allows there is much to be said for approaching it from the west and staying a day or two on the Lac d'Anneçy. We stayed in a very pleasant hotel in Talloires, on the eastern side of the lake. The hills and woods immediately behind the village are readily accessible to the walker, as are two low passes, the Col des Nantets and the Col de la Forclaz. For those with a car, the Chaîne des Aravis, with superb views across to the Mt. Blanc range, is easily reached. In early May the woods were interesting, with masses of lady orchids (*O. purpurea*)

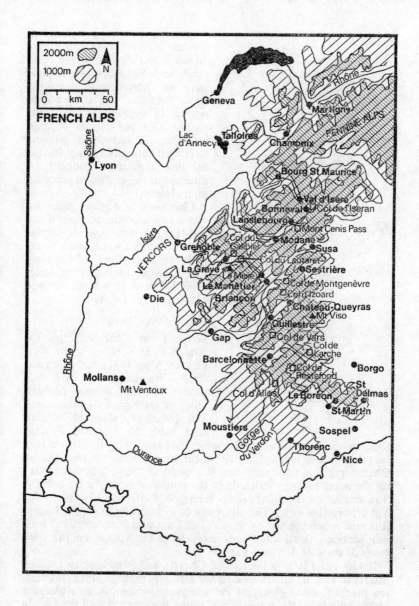

as well as many other species of orchid, *Lathyrus vernus*, *Trollius europaeus*, excellent and distinct forms of *Vinca minor*, *Cardamine pentaphyllos*, *Maianthemum bifolium* and *Convallaria majalis*. On the Chaîne des Aravis at this time the snows were only just receding;

Globularia nudicaulis

crocuses (*C. vernus*) abounded; *Soldanella alpina, Primula auricula, Draba aizoides, Globularia nudicaulis* and *Saxifraga oppositifolia* were in flower—and beautiful white forms of the early purple orchid, *O. mascula*. In early July on the Col des Aravis orchids, including *Traunsteinera globosa*, were still an outstanding feature of this limestone country. A pleasant area—but not a place for high alpines.

Chamonix is a great place for views and mountains, even if not outstanding for special alpine plants, but the whole area is gay with the 'basic flora' of the alps. **Les Houches,** some four miles away to the west, is a smaller and pleasant place to stay.

THE GRAIAN ALPS

South from Chamonix lies the Massif de la Vanoise, in the West Graian Alps. It is reached by car (from Chamonix) only by a wide détour through France (Albert-ville) or through Switzerland and Italy (Martigny, Great St. Bernard and Little St. Bernard Passes), these two routes meeting at Bourg-St. Maurice. This little town is in fact more easily reached, by either car or rail, from the west (Lyon, Chambéry) than via Chamonix. The question then is whether to stay on the north or the south side of the massif: if possible, do both. A 'low centre' on the north side is **Bourg-St. Maurice** and a 'high' one **Val d'Isère** (1840 m.). The latter can be reached by bus from Bourg; it is now much uglified by 'le ski', but I am told that there is at least one pleasant small hotel well away from the village on the road towards the Col de l'Iseran.

Below Val d'Isère is the Lac du Chevril, and from here an exciting little road runs up into the Val de Sassière, where among other interest-ing plants there is plenty of *Primula pedemontana*. A very pleasant uphill walk from Val d'Isère leads round the south side of the Lac du

An A.G.S. party in the Alps.

Photo: Mrs. D. A. Anderson ▷

Cicerbita alpina,
near Mürren, Switzerland

Photo: W. M. M. Baron

82

Primula minima and *P. glutinosa,*
above Hintertux, Austria

Photo: Miss D. M. P. Holford

Papaver kerneri and the Marmolada,
The Dolomites, Italy

Photo: *Miss M. G. Hodgman*

Viola eugeniae,
in the Abruzzi, Italy (p. 70)

Photo: *R. D. Nutt*

Asphodelus albus, Paradisea liliastrum etc.,
and La Meije, France (p. 100)

Photo: Miss D. M. P. Holford

84

Rhodothamnus chamaecistus,
The Dolomites, Italy (p. 57)

Photo: Miss M. G. Hodgman

Paeonia mascula subsp. *russii*,
white form, Sicily (p. 73)

Photo: F. F. H. Charlton

85

Convolvulus boissieri,
in the Sa. Cazorla, Spain (p. 148)

Photo: B. E. Smythies

Asphodelus aestivus, Lesbos

Photo: I. B. Barton

Geum coccineum, Bulgaria (p. 240)

Photo: G. E. Barrett

Rhododendron myrtifolium, Romania (p. 250)

Photos: G. E. Barrett

Campanula carpatica, Romania (p. 252)

Diapensia lapponica, Arctic Europe (p. 264)   *Photo: Prof. G. Pontecorvo*

Cassiope hypnoides at the North Cape,
Norway (p. 267)   *Photo: H. Taylor*

Pulsatilla vernalis,
in the Valais, Switzerland (p. 18)

89

Photos: Mrs. C. Greenfield

Ranunculus glacialis, Androsace alpina,
Gentiana bavarica, etc., Switzerland

Geum reptans,
on the Stelvio Pass, Italy (p. 53)

Photos: L. J. Bacon

Pulsatilla alpina subsp. *apiifolia,*
in the Engadine, Switzerland (p. 15)

Gentiana verna subsp. *tergestina* and *Androcase alpina*,   Photo: *L. J. Bacon*
above the Grossglockner Pass, Austria (p. 169)

91

Silene acaulis subsp. *longiscapa*,
France (p. 98)   Photo: *Mrs. C. Greenfield*

Saxifraga longifolia,
The Pyrenees (p. 116)

Lilium pyrenaicum and *Paradisia liliastrum,*
The Pyrenees (p. 120)

Saxifraga canaliculata in the Picos de Europa, Spain (p. 135)

Photo: Miss M. G. Hodgman

93

Teesdaliopsis conferta in the Picos de Europa, Spain (p. 134)

Photo: L. J. Bacon

Digitalis obscura in the Montes Universales, Spain (p. 143)

Photos: L. J. Bacon

Characteristic roadside flowers, including *Iris spuria*, in northern Spain (p. 139)

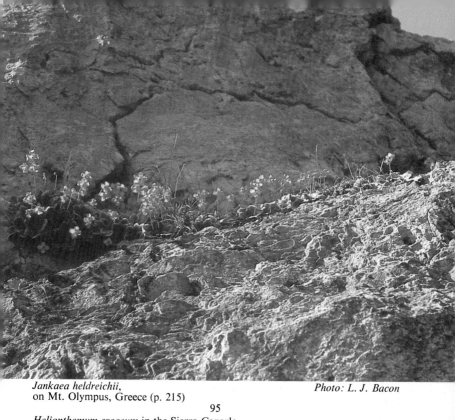

Jankaea heldreichii,
on Mt. Olympus, Greece (p. 215)

Photo: *L. J. Bacon*

95

Helianthemum croceum in the Sierra Cazorla,
Spain (p. !48)

Photo: *H. L. Crook*

Onosma erecta,
in the White Mountains, Crete (p. 237)

Photos: L. J. Bacon

Euphorbia characias subsp. *wulfenii* at Mistras,
in the Peloponnese, Greece (p. 222)

Chevril to Lac de Tignes (2100 m.). Among the flowers we found by and above this lake at the end of June were a fine form of *Corydalis solida*, *Campanula thyrsoides*, *C. rhomboidalis*, *Arnica montana*, and *Callianthemum coriandrifolium*. It was (in 1962) a beautiful spot, but I am told that it is now very built up. From Val d'Isère there are two cable railways to take you up to the Rocher de Bellevarde (2826 m.) and the Tête de Solaise (2551 m.), fine high points in the mountains on the south side of the valley. But the great merit of Val d'Isère is that it lies just below the north side of the Col de l'Iseran (2770 m.). Whether you visit this pass by bus or by car it is a wonderful drive, leading (when the pass is open, from late June till mid-October) to Lanslebourg and the southern side of the Massif de la Vanoise. The Col can be a bleak place, with a howling gale of bitter wind blowing across it, or it can be a sunny upland turf studded with neatly dwarfed forms of *Silene acaulis*, *Leontopodium alpinum*, *Erigeron uniflorus*, *Androsace obtusifolia*, *Phyteuma globulariifolium* (*pauciflorum*), and *Petrocallis pyrenaica* among many others. Rising steeply above the west side of the pass is the Pointe des Lessières (3041 m.), and an easy and well-defined (though steep) path leads up to this point—very well worth the scramble. I found here, as on some other occasions, that only a short way up the path I was out of the bitter gale blowing across the col, where the wind seems to rush in a shallow torrent. The rock here is acid, and among the plants by the path are *Campanula cenisia*, *Androsace pubescens* and *A. alpina* and the view from the top was, in all directions, among the finest I have ever seen.

And so down to Lanslebourg. The road drops steeply through screes running with snow-water, and the typical snow valley flowers are outstandingly fine and brilliant here. As you drop into the valley above Bonneval (1835 m.) and Lanslebourg the lower alpine flowers too are lush and beautiful, and if you are there in September (or are clever enough to spot the leaves) you will find among them *Colchicum alpinum*, a delicate miniature of the common *C. autumnale*. There are hotels in **Bonneval**, and it is perhaps quieter than Lanslebourg, but further from Mont Cenis.

Lanslebourg (1399 m.) is a good 'low' centre, with at least one very comfortable hotel. It is on the main road carrying traffic from France into Italy over the Mont Cenis Pass, but the main street and the hotel are by-passed by the heavy traffic. There is a railway to Modane, 25 km. away, and a bus service from there. Apart from the easy access that it gives the motorist to the Col de l'Iseran and beyond, it lies immediately below the north side of the Col du Mont Cenis, acclaimed for its flowers by Farrer and many after him.

Mont Cenis is a frontier area, with a fine lake between the pass and the frontier. The pass (2083 m.) is said to be closed from late November till late May, but we crossed it without difficulty on May 3rd, 1964. The level of the lake has been raised in recent years, to the detriment of the lakeside flora. The old hospice at the southern end of the lake is drowned, and commemorated by a new church, but I believe the hotel remains. It is a convenient place to stay for exploring the area, but the motorist may well prefer to stay at Lanslebourg, only 14 km. from the pass.

At the col itself, among the brilliant array of flowers, two stand out—*Silene acaulis longiscapa*, smothered with flowers a full 17 mm. across and looking like a very aristocratic dianthus, and *Viola calcarata* in incredible profusion and variety of colour, including beautiful clear whites. The road used to run along the north-east side of the lake at a lower level than it does now, and by the road there were curious deep potholes in which the flowers (protected from grazing) were especially beautiful. The same species are of course still to be found there, though the potholes are largely submerged. *Pulsatilla alpina* here is exceptionally robust—great wide ferny plants, 70 cm. or more high, with huge flowers. *Clematis alpina* used to trail down the potholes. *Erysimum helveticum* of a wonderfully fresh cool yellow grows with *Alyssum serpyllifolium*, *Androsace obtusifolia* and *A. carnea*. At the beginning of May we found the lake frozen, an impressive sight but a chilly one, and through the thawing turf myriads of *Crocus vernus* in white and purple were mingled with the rather wispy, pinky-purple *Bulbocodium vernum*. Above the road the turf merges into scree, and higher still there are impressive slabs of rock. *Viola cenisia* is here, with *Petrocallis pyrenaica* and *Anemone baldensis*, and others have reported *Campanula cenisia* and *C. alpestris*.

Campanula cenisia

An old military road, rough but drivable, runs from near the pass along the western end of the lake to the Col du Petit Mont Cenis, through rich turf where, in September, *Dianthus pavonius* (*neglectus*) in plenty was struggling up through the spent grass (quite out of character), and in moister and more low-lying turf there was *Colchicum alpinum*. As one reaches the rocks about the rather ill-defined 'col' *Primula pedemontana* grows with *P. hirsuta* (or so it seemed from the September foliage) and *Saponaria lutea* is plentiful in the crevices. Others, following Farrer, have proceeded further and found *Saxifraga diapensioides*, *Campanula alpestris*, *Bupleurum stellatum* and *Eritrichium nanum*. Back at the lake, at its southern end there used to be an alder grove where, wrote Farrer, *Cortusa matthioli* grew; we searched for it unsuccessfully, and now I believe the alders are gone too.

THE COTTIAN ALPS

To travel south from Mont Cenis into the Cottian Alps one must either drive down to Susa in Italy and re-enter France by the Col de Montgenèvre and so to Briançon or make a big sweep through France from Lanslebourg via Modane and St. Michel over the Col du Galibier and the Col du Lautaret, to Briançon.

The journey to Susa is a pleasant one, steeply down into the sunshine of Italy. Even at the beginning of May we soon left the snow and ran by a bank smothered with *Hepatica nobilis* in red, white, violet and blue. Later in the year by the roadside here are to be found *Dianthus sylvestris*, *D. carthusianorum*, *Campanula spicata*, and *Gentiana cruciata*. The drive up from Susa, where there is a very ruined Roman arena, to Montgenèvre is also very pleasant, and indeed in places, such as Exilles, spectacular.

The main road from Susa to Montgenèvre is not the only road. Mr. H. Taylor writes: "In Piedmont, between the Italian ski-resort of Sestrière and the town of Susa, there is a questionably motorable dirt-track (*Muri pericolanti su tutta la strada*) which teeters along the crest of a 2500 m. ridge; obviously just the place for plant-hunting. Towards the top of the tree-line are great drifts of *Primula latifolia*, and pink and yellow forms of *Dactylorhiza sambucina*, and *Pulsatilla vernalis*. On the loose shaly summit ridge there is a very compact form of *Alyssum serpyllifolium*, *Petrocallis pyrenaica*, *Campanula alpestris*, *Dianthus pavonius*, *Linaria alpina*, *Vitaliana primuliflora*, and *Viola calcarata* in a gorgeous variety of colours. The star plants of this ridge are that showiest of alpines *Geum reptans* and compact hairy clumps of *Androsace villosa* with rosy-centred flowers."

Montgenèvre itself, sitting on its col (1830 m.), is a winter sports centre, with most of the hotels closed in the summer, but we found one open and in a pleasant short stay found there, among the usual abundance of 'ordinary' flowers, the three garden-worthy species of *Ononis*; *O. rotundifolia*, *O. cristata* and *O. fruticosa*—the last a beautiful and by no means common shrub. However, Briançon is really a better centre.

The alternative route from Mont Cenis to Briançon takes one over two passes particularly famed for their plants as well as their scenery— the Col du Galibier and the Col du Lautaret. For the car-driver **Briançon** (1321 m.) is excellently placed as a 'low' centre. As already mentioned the Col de Montgenèvre is readily accessible from it, and the Col du Lautaret is only some 27 km. away along a very pleasant road. But **Lautaret** itself, where there is a hotel, has much to commend it as a high centre for two or three days for those who are active enough to spend time up in the mountains. On the pass, at 2058 m., is the Jardin Alpin of the University of Grenoble, formerly under the care of the late M. Ruffier-Lanche, who was always welcoming to A.G.S. Members—a welcome which still continues. In the turf around the hotel *Dianthus pavonius* and *Bulbocodium vernum* grow, and on the rock faces to the south of the col, *Lloydia serotina*, *Primula hirsuta* and *Eritrichium nanum* are to be found. As usual in the French Alps the higher rocks appear to be non-calcareous.

Along the Briançon road, to the east of the col, the famous larch-copse still contains a wealth of flowers, though partly destroyed by road-reconstruction. It is well-known as a site for *Campanula alpestris*, a somewhat inconspicuous plant which is in fact quite widespread in the Cottian Alps. Here, within a very small area, are

Ononis rotundifolia

Veronica allionii, Vitaliana prim-uliflora, Alyssum serpyllifolium, Dactylorhiza sambucina, Ononis cristata, O. rotundifolia, and an amusing little cerinthe (*C. glabra* or *C. minor*) and beautiful *Globularia cordifolia*. The pass is dominated on the south-west side by the great mass of Roc Noir (the north-eastern buttress of the Massif du Pelvoux), among whose rocks are *Eritrichium nanum, Androsace pubescens, Primula hirsuta, Primula latifolia* (and, it is said, hybrids between the two), *Saxifraga retusa* and *S. bryoides*.

Lautaret is a road-junction, and from the north side of the col a road rises steeply to the Col du Galibier (2545 m.). When the pass is open, a coach runs between St. Michel and Briançon. It is not usually open until late June. The road up from St. Michel is beautiful; nowhere have we seen richer alpine meadows. The pass is an exhilarating place. From the gentle saddle of Lautaret one looks up into the mountains, but from the heights of Galibier there is a view far in all directions. The Galibier road just above Lautaret is relatively sheltered, and here are *Daphne striata, Dianthus carthusianorum, Scutellaria alpina* and *Veronica aphylla* among a hundred others. Higher up are *Androsace obtusifolia, Gagea fistulosa, Leucanthemopsis alpina*, and as fine a display of good forms of *Ranunculus pyrenaeus* as we have seen anywhere except on the Col de Restefond. White *Androsace carnea* is the rule here, and *Callianthemum coriandrifolium* is reported from near the summit of the pass.

From the Col du Lautaret the Grenoble road drops steeply to the west through rich meadows where *Asphodelus albus* and *Geranium sylvaticum rivulare* are conspicuous, to **La Grave** (1526 m.) which has also been recommended as a centre for the areas of La Meije and the two cols, while on the Briançon road **Le Monetier-les-Bains** (1470 m.) has good hotels and is suitably placed for those who do not wish to stay either up on the col or down in Briançon.

From Briançon one may drive to Les Vigneaux and up the Gyr valley to Ailefroide and the Refuge Cézanne (1874 m.) on the south side of the Massif du Pelvoux. This is marked on the map as a 'scenic route' and Mr. W. M. M. Baron (*Bulletin* Vol. 23, p. 373) found it beautiful and rewarding. The other main excursion, by no means to be missed, from Briançon is to the Col d'Izoard (2300 m.), some ten miles to the south-west of the town. It is quite different from any other of the cols we have visited—a stark, startling, stony moonscape of a place, with fantastic pinnacles of rock soaring skyward from steep yellow screes. On the north side of the col, before the final pull-up, are little woods and valleys, where we found *Soldanella alpina, Saxifraga diapensioides, Daphne cneorum, Anemone baldensis, Moneses uniflora, Polygala chamaebuxus, Veronica allionii* and a white pulsatilla of endearing minuteness—a single stem with a leaf or two and a single flower hardly more than 17 mm. across, violet on the reverse of the petals. At the time we supposed it to be an exceedingly small form of *P. alpina*—but perhaps it was *P. alba*. Not far away was *Campanula alpestris*, growing happily in a heap of roadman's grit. So up to the col, passing the Refuge Napoléon, where you may lunch. The lifeless screes (like most lifeless screes) are very much alive when you climb to them. I recall a delicious scent here, which seemed to emanate from two plants—*Valeriana saliunca* and that most improbable cabbage *Brassica repanda*—neither of great beauty. *Linaria alpina* was in fine form here, and *Viola cenisia* and *Thlaspi rotundifolium limosellifolium* were present; not, truth to tell, a very rich haul. The views from the top, however, are stupendous, and as to the pass itself you can only look and look again and rub your eyes.

Beyond the Col d'Izoard the road drops to Château-Queyras and Ville-Vieille. From here you may drive by a small road up to St. Véran (2040 m.), locally, and doubtfully, acclaimed as the highest European village with a church, and said too to be well-flowered. By driving on through Abriès and beyond l'Échalp you can approach, as nearly as is possible by car from France, the remarkable Monte Viso. It is distinguished by its conical shape and by the way it stands out from its neighbours in the frontier mountains, particularly from the Italian side. At 3841 m. it is not the highest mountain in the western alps—several in the Massif du Pelvoux are higher—but it has a quality of its own, and the fact that it cannot be approached very closely by any road perhaps explains why it has received little mention in the *Bulletin*. There is indeed an account (Vol. 23, p. 372) by Mr. Baron of a stay in the Guil valley that leads towards the mountain, and we ourselves drove as far as we could up the valley one late September afternoon. It is certainly a beautiful valley, and plants described there include *Astragalus alopecuroides, Gentiana cruciata, Dianthus pavonius, Campanula alpestris, Primula latifolia, P. marginata, Petrocallis pyrenaica, Fritillaria tubiformis delphinensis* and white as well as typical forms of *Dianthus sylvestris*.

From Briançon the Route des Alpes continues southward through Guillestre to **Barcelonnette** (1132 m.), a little town whose merit, for us, lies in its proximity to no fewer than five mountain passes.

The Col de Vars (2109 m.) is on the main road south of Guillestre. It is an attractive rather than a spectacular pass. The mountain flowers are abundant, and we were pleased to find *Ononis fruticosa* again, and in the screes a yellow onosma (probably *O. helvetica*), and *Silene vulgaris prostrata*, a montane form of the bladder campion.

A little further south the road from Cuneo in Italy crosses into France by the Col de Larche (alias La Madeleine) (1997 m.). Though a little lower, it is rather more exciting than the Col de Vars. There is plenty of *Primula marginata* here, variable and some of it very lovely, *Tulipa sylvestris australis*, and that same yellow onosma. But for a richer flora it is worth dropping over onto the Italian side (or indeed approaching the pass from Cuneo). Here below the pass is a fine gorge where *Saxifraga callosa* is splendid on the cliff-face, and just beyond are rich meadows running up into hillsides where *Viola cenisia*, *Linum suffruticosum salsoloides* and *Hypericum coris* grow, for here we are entering the Alpes Maritimes.

From Jausiers, east of Barcelonnette, a magnificent road climbs steeply to the Col de Restefond (2802 m.), now the highest road-pass in Europe and not normally open till late in June—though here, as on so many other passes, if it is the flowers you are after rather than getting to the other side, it is of course worth while to drive up as high as you can, even when the pass is closed. On June 20th we found the pass just open, but there was so much snow about that there were few flowers to be seen at the top, and the views were limited by cloud, but there was still a wonderful sense of wild remoteness about the place, and on the journey up to the snow there was a fine variety of flowers that indicated a very mixed geology. *Daphne cneorum* was here, *Gagea fistulosa*, *Primula marginata* and *Anemone baldensis* and at the higher levels, where the screes began just below the snow, *Brassica repanda*, *Silene acaulis longiscapa*, *Vitaliana primuliflora*, *Ranunculus glacialis*, and also *R. seguieri*. But perhaps the most remarkable, as well as one of the most abundant, of the plants here was *Ranunculus pyrenaeus*—variable, but much of it with large full flowers, the whole plant being somewhat robust and very broad-leaved and generally conforming with what has been called subsp. *plantagineus*, a taxon which *Flora Europaea* is reluctant to recognise. Mr. H. Taylor, writing of this fine pass (also known as the Col de la Bonette) mentions *Bulbocodium vernum* by the stream at the start of the climb, *Campanula alpestris* on gravel banks by the road, *Dryas octopetala* and *Berardia subacaulis* in limestone areas, *Phyteuma globulariifolium pedemontanum* on granite, and *Viola cenisia* in the slaty summit screes.

Two more cols are reached by roads running south from Barcelonette; the Col d'Allos (2250 m.) on the Colmars road, and the Col de la Cayolle (2326 m.) on the road to Guillaume. There is an account of the former by the late Eliot Hodgkin in the *Bulletin* (Vol. 22, p. 238) and of both of them by Mr. C. A. Gibson (Vol. 24, p. 345). Both, especially the Cayolle, sound interesting and attractive, the flowers including many of those already encountered. In addition Mr. Hodgkin, whose visit was in August, found *Swertia perennis* below the Allos, and on the Cayolle Mr. Gibson found an aquilegia which was probably *A. bertolonii*, a beautiful species close to *A. pyrenaica*.

The Maritime Alps*

Behind the French and Italian Riviera lie the Maritime Alps, a southern extension of the Western Alps forming the border between France and Italy. They constitute an irregular mass of mountains, the highest of them projecting northward into Piedmont in Italy, and to the south they drop as progressively lower and hotter hills towards the Mediterranean coast. For our purposes the Maritime Alps can conveniently be divided into the high mountains of the north and the lower south-facing slopes, although there is of course no sharp dividing line. Only 25 miles inland, granitic peaks approaching 3000 m. soar upward through the crust of Jurassic limestone. On the limestone the river gorges and cliff-faces house numerous exciting endemic plants.

So far south the snows melt earlier than in the high alps, and the Maritimes are at their best in late May and early June when the rocks are sheeted with primulas and silver saxifrages. Although the high screes will not be uncovered for a further month the classic plants of the high granite cliffs are reasonably accessible at this time.

Striking inland from Nice, the road runs along the Var valley and then north-east along the Vésubie valley to **St. Martin-Vésubie**. Here the steep limestone cliffs of the gorges are a wonderful sight in late May and June; a mass of waving white plumes of *Saxifraga callosa* in its lovely form *lantoscana*, intermingled with the blue *Campanula macrorrhiza*. St. Martin makes an excellent centre from which to explore the higher peaks, with good hotels and camp-sites. You do not however have to go to Nice to reach St. Martin. It can be approached from the north, from Barcelonette, by the Col de Restefond and the Tinée valley, a wonderful drive but of course only when the Restefond is open. The main, and faster, approach for a visitor from England going straight to St. Martin would be down the Route Napoléon from Grenoble to Plan du Var.

The flora of the limestone region can be seen along the D31 to Venanson, with the yellow *Hypericum coris*, white *Linum suffruticosum salsoloides*, rose-flowered *Ononis fruticosa*, the endemic *Potentilla saxifraga*, *Geranium macrorrhizum*, and the occasional pure sealing-wax red of *Lilium pomponium*.

St. Martin is at no great height (960 m.), and the real mountains lie to the north and east. There are three motor roads into them, one running along the Vallon de la Madone de Fenestre, one to Le Boréon, and one along the Vallon de la Gordolasque. The D94 to La Madone de Fenestre is usually passable by the end of May, and gives easy access to the high alps. There can be few finer sights than the sheets of *Primula marginata* and *P. latifolia* which festoon the rocks. Both primulas occur in particularly fine forms, and rare hybrids between the two are recorded. Climbing higher towards the granite peaks, the beautifully symmetrical, brilliant green rosettes of *Saxifraga florulenta* may be seen occasionally sharing their home with *Androsace vandellii*, *Eritrichium nanum* and *Globularia repens*.

The famous cascade at **Le Boréon** (1500 m.) can be reached via the D89. For those with a car this is an alternative centre to St. Martin and is higher, smaller and quieter. The Boréon valley, a small high hanging valley, is lightly wooded and pleasant, and *Astrantia minor* and *Viola valderia* are to be found there. It is a good walking centre, and the special excursion is up to the Col des Cerises (Colle di Ciriegia) at 2551 m., on the Italian frontier. This is a beautiful place, despite the works of war—fortifications, dug-outs, wire netting, spent shells and bullets. The flowers here include the cool lavender *Viola nummulariifolia*—Farrer's tiny 'Queen Violet'—*V. valderia*, *Campanula alpestris* and *Thlaspi rotundifolium limosellifolium*.

The Vallon de la Gordolasque runs north-eastward from the Vésubie valley some six miles below St. Martin, and first one must climb by a twisting road up to **Belvedere** (830 m.) at the top of its little hill in the mouth of the Gordolasque valley. We found a very pleasant little hotel here. The road up the valley runs to 1702 m. The flowers are similar to those of the Vallon de la Madone de Fenestre and the charming *Hyacinthoides* (*Scilla*) *italica* is to be found on the hillsides in late May.

The high mountains of the Maritime Alps are well worth exploration from the northern (Italian) side too. From Borgo San Dalmazzo, south of Cuneo, two roads run westward into the mountains. Borgo can be reached either from the north, via Turin, or less directly from Tende in the south. There are hotels in Cuneo and also in Borgo, but this is an industrial valley. An alternative is to take the road leading to the Col de Larche and stay in **Vinadio**, an interesting little fortified town with a comfortable hotel; with a car it is sufficiently close to the mountains. We have already in this account visited the Col de Larche from the French side, and I will add only that the lower part of the valley, around Vinadio, is rich with flowers among which we saw *Lychnis flos-jovis*, well-known in our gardens, by the roadside, and the lovely *Vicia onobrychioides*.

The other road from Borgo runs along the Valdieri valley to Terme di Valdieri, of which Farrer had much to say. The vast hotel of which he wrote still stands, but now seems to be a hospital giving spa treatment. The road as far as the spa is reasonable, though cluttered with workings in connection with a new tunnel to be driven through the frontier mountains towards Nice. It is possible to drive well beyond Terme di Valdieri, up the Valle della Valletta, though the road is very rough indeed, then to climb by a good path high up into the face of Argentera (3297 m.), the highest in the

Maritime Alps. This climb is a very fine one. *Achillea erba-rotta rupestris* grows by the path, with *Androsace carnea*, *A. vandellii*, *Dianthus pavonius* and the beautiful *Minuartia laricifolia*. On rocks higher up in late June *Primula marginata* was magnificent, and there was a real abundance of *Saxifraga florulenta*. In mid-September plenty of the plants of the saxifrage were in flower, just beginning to set seed, but the pale pinkish flowers are not very impressive.

Returning to the Vésubie valley in France, a small road (D70) starting near Lantosque wriggles and twists its way eastward up to the Col des Turini. This is a beautiful drive, and here we are in the lower, south-facing hills of the Alpes Maritimes. From the col the road continues southward through hotter gorges and valleys to reach Sospel on the main road from Nice to Turin. Now we are among the west Mediterranean flora—the brilliant *Aphyllanthes monspeliensis* (in our gardens it is usually but a shadow of itself), rock roses—white (*Helianthemum apenninum*), yellow and sometimes rose or orange—cistuses (white or rosy purple), *Coris monspeliensis*, *Orchis tridentata*, *Linum suffruticosum* ranging from some 30 cm. high to the creeping form *salsoloides*, *Thymus vulgaris*, which can be a lovely plant (sometimes white), lilac-flowered *Lathyrus filiformis* among a vast range of peas, vetches, brooms and gorses, lavender (*Lavandula angustifolia*—sometimes grown as a crop), purple-blue *Catananche coerulea*, yellow *Antirrhinum latifolium*, stately *Euphorbia*

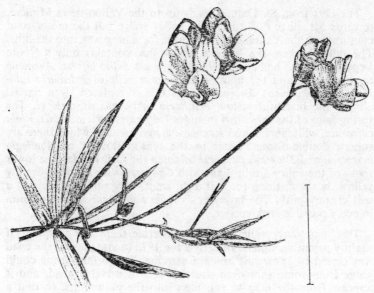

Lathyrus filiformis

characias, rosy drifts of *Saponaria ocymoides*, deliciously scented bushes of *Spartium junceum*, and—one of the loveliest and most widespread of them all—a gentian-blue milkwort, probably *Polygala nicaeensis*.

From Sospel (where we are not far from the Mediterranean, and in the June dusk there are fireflies) we turn northward along the main road up the Roya valley, and come at last to **St. Dalmas-de-Tende**. This region is the only home of the classic alpine-house plant *Primula allionii*, long since out of flower in May. This grows as tight wads in exposed crevices in the limestone cliffs, and as looser mats in the roofs of shallow caves protected from rain and sun. The limestone crevices provide a foothold for the hardy maidenhair fern, a pretty little moehringia (probably *M. sedifolia*) with white flowers and bright green foliage, and cushions of *Potentilla saxifraga*. The limestone cliffs on the west side of the valley above Tende are spectacular in May with the superb flowering spikes of *Saxifraga callosa*, while on the shadier aspects hard, warty cushions of *Saxifraga diapensioides* may be found. The eastern side of the Roya around La Bergue is the classic site for *Saxifraga cochlearis*, found in sizes ranging from the 'Major' to the 'Minor' forms of horticulture. Here a diligent search may reveal the local form of that spectacular butterwort *Pinguicula longifolia reichenbachiana*. Tende is a convenient centre for this area, but it is a busy little town and on the main road.

The D91 from St. Dalmas leads up to the Vallon de la Minière, towards Mt. Bego (2872 m.). The valley splits, but the motor-road continues up the Vallon de la Casterine for a long way into the hills. The other branch, the Val des Merveilles, contains only a 'route jeepable'. In the higher woodland there are *Scilla bifolia*, *Anemone ranunculoides*, and the maroon chequered bells of *Fritillaria tubiformis* (*delphinensis*). In some areas this is replaced by a partial albino, the beautiful yellow *Fritillaria tubiformis moggridgei*. The spring flora of the short turf includes *Tulipa sylvestris australis*, *Viola calcarata*, white iberis, and *Ranunculus pyrenaeus* of which there are superb double forms. Later in the season flowers of *Aquilegia bertolonii* and *Dianthus pavonius* brighten the turf. In May the lower rocks of the valley are brilliant with *Chamaecytisus hirsutus*, usually yellow, but sometimes (or is it a different, very similar, species?) a soft creamy pink. The lavender *Primula marginata* is in profusion in every possible rock-crevice.

This is a lovely valley, and at **Casterine** there are adequate, if slightly primitive, hotels. In early June 1978 (a late season) the road was closed by snow just above Casterine, but so far as one could judge from some snow-free stretches it is a drivable road, and it appears from the map to run high into the mountains, so that a visit in late June seems to have great possibilities.

Finally, the pleasures of any visit to the Maritimes will be markedly enhanced if you can obtain a copy of Farrer's *Among the Hills*, surely one of the finest books on plant-hunting.

THE WESTERN FRENCH ALPS AND PROVENCE

So far this account of the French Alps has concentrated upon the higher mountains to the eastern side, and their Mediterranean slopes, but it would be quite wrong to leave the reader with the impression that the mountains nearer to the Rhône valley are without interest. Eliot Hodgkin wrote (*Bulletin*, Vol. 22, p. 238) of two limestone areas in the western Dauphiné which even in August were interesting, and we found them delightful in early June. One is the Vercors, a National Park to the south-west of Grenoble, where the plants he recorded included *Allium narcissiflorum, Androsace villosa, Ranunculus seguieri, Primula auricula, Erysimum decumbens, Campanula alpestris* and the uncommon little white-woolly dwarf 'hardhead' *Berardia subacaulis*. The scenery is outstanding; an area of vast steep wooded hillsides, cliffs, and gorges, where in June the most impressive flowers were the vast array of orchids. The other area to which Mr. Hodgkin refers is the Montagne d'Aurouze, north-west of Gap. It is in marked contrast to the Vercors, a country of unwooded peaks and ridges and screes, limy, with a flora to match. All the 'usuals' were there in early June, and we were specially pleased to find *Daphne cneorum* in a very dwarf form, *Ranunculus seguieri*, and *Pulsatilla halleri*. For the motorist both these areas are accessible from the N93 between Gap and Die. There are many small hotels, of which three, at **Beaurières**, the **Col de Cabre** and **La Beaume,** are very conveniently placed between the two areas.

Still further south and west, on the northern fringes of Provence, is Mt. Ventoux (1912 m.). It is a fine mountain in a fine area, and it has the special merit (for the less spry) that a road runs right across the top of it. It is very much a tourist area, so that there are many hotels in the villages that surround the mountain, and there is a series of beautiful valleys, with small roads, especially to the north of the peak, so that a stay of two or three days is not wasted. We stayed at **Mollans,** on the north side, and found this convenient. The special feature of the mountain is the vast areas of wild scree round the summit, and here at the end of May we found many interesting plants breaking into flower at the edges of the receding snow. *Vitaliana primuliflora* was more abundant than we have seen it anywhere else. *Saxifraga oppositifolia, Draba aizoides, Androsace villosa* and *Papaver rhaeticum* are of course widespread scree plants, but with them were masses of a little viola (probably *V. cenisia*), *Globularia repens*, leaves of *Eryngium spinalba*, and a very compact little white or pink candytuft, the form '*candolleana*' of *Iberis pruitii*. At the summit this is exceedingly compact; lower down the mountain rather less so, but still a neat and tidy plant. A curiously incongruous plant in snow-gullies near the summit was a small form of *Helleborus foetidus*, whose flowers were very pale yellow with a deep purple rim. The flora lower down is interesting too for here, if one is travelling from the north, one begins to meet elements of the Mediterranean flora, so that one finds curious associations, such as *Vitaliana primuliflora* and lavender (*Lavandula angustifolia*) growing side by side. At lower levels there is *Globularia punctata*, the lovely 'vetches' *Vicia onobrychioides*, *Astragalus monspessulanus*, *Hedysarum hedysaroides* and *Lathyrus filiformis*, the yellow *Antirrhinum latifolium*, *Aquilegia vulgaris*, *Aethionema saxatile*, *Anthericum liliago*, *Catananche coerulea*, *Allium roseum*, and military and lady orchids, all set among box scrub, and the white-flowered *Amelanchier ovalis*. Mr. H. Taylor mentions *Campanula alpestris* (apparently not the calciphobe plant that I had thought it to be), *Aquilegia alpina*, *Crepis pygmaea*, *Ononis cristata* and *Centaurea uniflora* on Mt. Ventoux. It is altogether a remarkable mountain.

Lastly, but by no means to be overlooked, there is beautiful Provence, essentially a limestone plateau at an altitude of 1000 to 1500 m., but a warm country of hills and woods and rivers threading their way through spectacular gorges. An excellent approach to the French Alps (if you are willing to traverse them from south to north) is to cross the Auvergne and the Cévennes and enter Provence at Avignon. On the Montagne du Lubéron (one of a series of east-west ridges) there are to be found all, or nearly all, of the Mediterranean flowers listed on pp. 75 and 105. This is very much the flora of Provence; the 'basic alpine' flora is no longer with us in this southerly sunny part of France. Among the scrub of cistus and lavender, and the slender plumes of *Stipa pennata*, can be found the incomparable *Ophrys bertolonii*. Proceeding eastwards (and ensuring that you have plenty of time to spurn the main roads and take the small roads slowly) you will come in due course to the Grand Canyon du Verdon, flanked on its southern side by the Corniche Sublime. Proud names! It really is, however, something very out of the ordinary. *Fritillaria involucrata* is here, the leaves of *Crocus versicolor*, white and rose helleborines among many other orchids, paeonies (*P. mascula* or *P. officinalis*), *Convolvulus cantabrica*—and you may happen upon *Lilium pomponium*. A day can be well spent in the Gorge du Verdon, and there are hotels at **Moustiers-Ste.-Marie**.

Eastward again, and we come back to the Alpes Maritimes, now at their south-western end. This too is a fine and interesting area, and a good centre from which to visit it is **Thorenc**, set at 1250 m. on the south side of the Montagne de Thorenc, whose ridge reaches 1606 m. It is again a limestone area, with orchids in vast quantity and variety and where small roads in all directions provide an almost endless choice of hills and valleys and gorges to visit. Among the special plants of the area are *Fritillaria tubiformis* (*delphinensis*),

Crocus versicolor, Lilium pomponium (surprisingly common hereabouts), *Iberis pruitii candolleana*, the very pretty rosy-flowered annual *Androsace chaixii*, and the effective white mounds of *Ptilotrichum macrocarpum*.

France in the *Bulletin*:

5, 208 Fisher, F. H. Lautaret
13, 197 Branch, H. Maritimes
17, 315 Ferns, F. E. B. Alps
18, 269 Wells, E. D. Lautaret
& Montgenèvre
19, 341 Lowndes, T. H.
Maritimes
20, 150 Cadney, G. Alps
21, 127 Corley, R. S. Champex

22, 238 Hodgkin, E. Dauphiné
23, 372 Baron, W. M. M. Alps
24, 345 Gibson, G. C.
Barcelonnette
27, 162 Wacher, H. S.
Cottians
32, 173 Bacon, L. J. Alps
36, 66 Coxhead, E. Vercors

Other reading:

Farrer, R. *Among the Hills* Black (out of print)

*The section on the Maritime Alps
was contributed in part by Drs. P. and P. Watt.

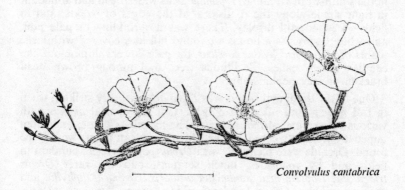

Convolvulus cantabrica

CORSICA*

The French rightly call Corsica 'the mountain rising from the Mediterranean.' It is some 160 km. long by 80 broad, and there are six peaks over about 2350 m., with Mont Cinto the highest point at 2710 m. Wherever you look there are tall jagged mountains, and there is a honeycomb of roads along the internal valleys.

The way to reach Corsica is by 'Fly-drive' to Ajaccio or Bastia. A small car is best to cope with the narrow, winding and undulating roads, which are nevertheless well-surfaced and breathtakingly scenic. It is possible to bring a car over by sea from Nice, Marseilles, Genoa or Leghorn, but Corsica is a favourite of French holiday-makers and booking in advance is advisable for both outward and return journeys. There are good hotels all over the island, and self-catering accommodation, but there is great pressure on all the facilities in the summer. In April we had no difficulty except in Ajaccio, and some of the large mountain hotels were understandably closed at that time. Good centres are **Ajaccio** and **Calvi** on the coast and **Corti** in the centre. Almost any of the valleys into the mountains are good hunting-ground, such as the Asco and Restonica valleys from Corte, and the Fango and Figarella valleys from Calvi. The scenery on all the roads is magnificent: one of the best is the main road from Ajaccio to Corte, and the secondary road from Vivario south through the centre of the island to Sartene is high, wild and grand.

We went from April 4th to 27th, and found *Crocus corsicus* abundant on all the high passes just below the snow in the north and east of the island, while *Crocus minimus* was flowering at lower levels in the south-west. *Cyclamen repandum* was widespread and abundant in light shade along the roadsides, at the edges of woods, and in fields—a wonderful display. There was a sprinkling of pale pink and white forms. As a bonus we found hillsides covered with large plants of *Helleborus lividus corsicus*, the pale flowers shining out like candles under leafless deciduous trees and among brown dead bracken—a spectacular sight.

One of the dominant plants was *Erica arborea*, very striking when in full flower, and often forming part of the coastal *maquis* with various cituses and *Arbutus unedo*. The *maquis* is dense, and often impenetrable, but where it opened Mediterranean plants were to be found. Orchids were plentiful, with *Orchis papilionacea* abundant in fields and by roadsides, much serapias, and the rarer *Orchis tridentata, Dactylorhiza sambucina insularis, Gennaria diphylla*, and various ophrys. Other low-level plants were *Narcissus tazetta, Matthiola tricuspidata, Asphodelus albus villarsii, Astragalus massiliensis, Thymelaea hirsuta, Ornithogalum exscapum, Morisia monanthos, Erodium corsicum*, and *Polygala nicaeensis corsica*. Going up the mountain valleys we found *Leucojum longifolium, Gagea neva-*

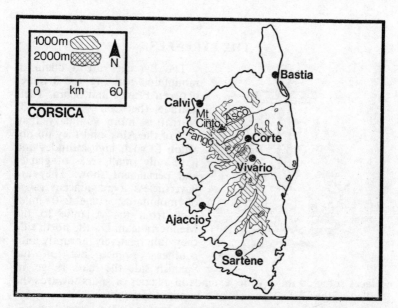

CORSICA

densis, a large sweet violet which we thought was *Viola suavis,* *Thymelaea tartonraira thomasii* (very different from the Greek form and confined to one small area), and the very showy white *Pancratium illyricum,* with *Brimeura fastigiata* in blue and white. *Anemone apennina* was about, often mixed with cyclamen, and *Arenaria balearica* grew on damp rocks in the gorges.

In April the snow was down to about 1200 m. on the passes, and we were unable to get up to the true alpines. Another time we hope to go in June; there was evidence that there would still be cyclamen and crocus in flower at greater heights, but one would miss those gorgeous hellebores.

Borago pygmaea

Others (writing in the *Bulletin*) have visited Corsica as early as March and as late as May, and other good plants recorded from this island include *Sedum caeruleum, Helichrysum frigidum, Leucojum roseum, Mentha requienii, Anthyllis hermanniae* and *Borago pygmaea (laxiflora).*

* Contributed by Mr. and Mrs. H. L. Crook

111

6

THE PYRENEES

Mt. Canigou

The Pyrenees are a chain of mountains forming the frontier between France and Spain. Their latitude (between 42° and 43° North) is more southerly than that of the Alps, and they do not attain to such high altitudes and have only small areas of glacier and permanent snow. They are nevertheless a magnificent range of mountains, some 270 miles long from the Atlantic to the Mediterranean. On the north side they fall relatively abruptly into southern France but on the Spanish side the main range, in places some 30 miles wide, extends in a series of spurs towards the valley of the Ebro, upwards of a hundred miles away.

Geologically the Pyrenees are a confused jumble, with primary rocks predominating but with frequent overlays of limestone. Climatically there is of course the gradation from low to high level to be expected in any mountains, but in addition at the two ends of the range, particularly at the Mediterranean end, the climate is milder, with hotter summers and wetter winters, than in the centre of the range. These climatic differences affect the flora, and also there are differences between the steeper and cooler northern French side and the hotter southern Spanish side. There is a useful note on Pyrenean geology by Col. Meadows in the *Bulletin* (Vol. 38, p. 323).

On the French side a good main road, the Route des Pyrénées, runs the length of the chain from St. Jean-de-Luz to Perpignan. For much of its course it is well away from the mountains and is a route from which to view them rather than enter them but this is not wholly true, for here and there, as for instance at the Col d'Aubisque and Col du Tourmalet, it traverses high passes over spurs from the main range. Many branches from the Route des Pyrénées run southward along deep valleys cut into the hills, and at six or seven places they cross the Pyrenees into Spain. On the Spanish side, the road from San Sebastian via Huesca to Barcelona is to a limited extent comparable with the Route des Pyrénées, but it is for the most part considerably poorer in quality, and rather further away from the main range. It receives the pass roads from France and like the Route des Pyrénées sends a number of small branches up into the hills, although some of these are very poorly surfaced indeed. To summarise, there are relatively few (perhaps ten) places where you can go by car right up among the high flowers, but there are numerous points of access where you can leave your car and walk.

The access by rail is reasonably good on the French side, poor on the Spanish. As with the roads, lines run part-way up the valleys leading into the mountains, and there are two routes crossing respectively the Col du Somport and Puigcerdá into Spain. Apart from these two crossings, there do not appear to be railways on the Spanish side.

Winter sports centres are developing throughout the Pyrenees, and the areas where ski-lifts are available are rapidly increasing.

French and Spanish are of course the native languages on the respective sides of the Pyrenees, but in the more easterly areas on the southern side the dialect is distinctively Catalonian. Generally, on either side, someone can be found who speaks English.

The flowers are outstandingly beautiful and interesting. The number of endemics is not so great as might be suggested by the frequency of the epithets "*pyrenaeus*" and "*pyrenaicus*" (or by Roger-Smith), but this is largely because the majority of Pyrenean plants are also found in the Picos de Europa, which Roger-Smith had not visited, and a smaller number, while mainly centred in the Pyrenees, are also found in the sierras of north-east Spain or in the Corbières. A few species (*Gentiana pyrenaica* springs to mind) are found in the Pyrenees and in the Balkans, but not between them. The effect however is that an English visitor entering the Pyrenees from France for the first time is likely to find a large number of beautiful plants which are quite new to him in the wild. The majority of these (there are exceptions, such as some of the aretian androsaces) are furthermore locally abundant. There are substantial differences in the predominant plants in different parts of the range, particularly as between the east and the west. Apart from the two extremes, where the lower levels and the maritime climates affect the flora, the Pyrenees are usefully considered in two areas; a more westerly zone running from the Col du Somport to Gavarnie and Bielsa, and a more easterly one from Andorra to Mt. Canigou. This is not to imply that the central area, round Bagnères de Luchon and the Val d'Aran, is not worth visiting: very much the contrary; it is scenically and florally a most beautiful area, with an abundance of the flowers that are found throughout the range, but those relatively few plants which are distinctive of the more easterly and westerly areas respectively are scarcer or lacking in the central zone. In selecting a few sample centres in which to stay account has been taken of these differences.

Hotels do not abound in the Pyrenees, though they are becoming more frequent. Nevertheless, most villages on through roads have at least one inn or hotel, and in the bigger townships (there are no large towns in the mountains) there is a choice of accommodation. Big hotels are few, but they exist in some spa towns and they are appearing in winter sports centres. Other examples are the Grand Hotel at Superbagnères and the Government Parador at Bielsa. In several visits to the Pyrenees we have yet to encounter a hotel that was either dirty or unwelcoming. 'The fleas that tease in the High Pyrenees' appear to be a thing of the past. There are useful lists of hotels in some areas in Col. Meadows' articles in the *Bulletin*.

The best time to visit the Pyrenees is hard to specify. In a typical year one can travel freely on the French side in mid-June, and from then to early July is a good time to see the flowers, but in a late year we have found the Route des Pyrénées blocked by snow at the Col du Tourmalet as late as the 4th July. There can be fine flowers on the Col du Somport (and snow too) on the 30th May and at the other end of the season to see the display of *Colchicum autumnale, Merendera pyrenaica* and *Crocus nudiflorus* one should go in early September. In a given year the mountain flowers are at their best a few weeks earlier on the Spanish side than on the French, and also the season is likely to be somewhat advanced eastward of Andorra as compared with, say, Gavarnie.

THE CENTRAL PYRENEES

Bagnères de Luchon (623 m.) lies on the Route des Pyrénées at about the central point of the range. It is a spa town, as well as a tourist and winter sports centre. Michelin will tell you which of your maladies you may hope to cure with its hot sulphurous radio-active waters, and the loquacious may hope to ease *leurs cordes vocales fatiguées*. In addition to its east-west links on the Route des Pyrenees, it is approached by main road from the north and also by rail. It is well supplied with hotels and guest-houses. There are several roads into the hills, a mountain railway up to the hotel at Superbagnères on a hill which dominates the town on its southern side, and many footpaths. The following places of floral interest can be reached, or at least closely approached, by car.

The road to Superbagnères traverses a beautiful hillside where much of the typical lower-level flora of the Pyrenees grows abundantly. *Viola cornuta* and *Prunella grandiflora* give a good show and *Asperula cynanchica* is in far finer form than our native squinancy-wort. We found a beautiful campanula which we made out to be *C. recta, Teucrium pyrenaicum, Ranunculus amplexicaulis, Saxifraga media, Dianthus barbatus* (Sweet William) and abundant leaves of the dog-tooth violet (*Erythronium dens-canis*).

The short drive up the Vallée d'Oô to the Lac d'Oô (with more of the low-level plants such as *Campanula patula, Eryngium bourgatii, Reseda glauca* and *Astragalus monspessulanus*) enables one to walk to the Val d'Esquierry. Roger-Smith found the track difficult to locate but if you leave your car at Granges d'Astau you will see the track running steeply up into the woods that clothe the entrance to the high-hanging valley. It is in these woods that the attractive parasitic *Lathraea clandestina* is to be found in early June and here too is *Ramonda myconi*, one of the loveliest Pyrenean flowers and almost a true endemic, growing here near its eastern limit. It notoriously shuns dryness and full sun, and here is in light woodland. The Val d'Esquierry is, truth to tell, rather dull scenically till you reach the head of the valley, but the flowers are a good sample of the Pyrenean flora. They include *Ranunculus amplexicaulis, Aster pyrenaeus* (like a taller *A. alpinus*) and *Potentilla alchemilloides*. Perhaps I should add that here, as throughout the Pyrenees, there are plenty of the lovely mountain flowers that one associates with the Alps, such as *Pulsatilla alpina* and *P.a. apiifolia, Anemone narcissiflora, Gentiana lutea, Scilla verna* and *Globularia repens*.

A rather longer drive of some miles takes one to an especially fine area—the lakes of Cap de Long and Orédon, at the head of the valley of the Neste d'Aure. It is reached from Luchon by following the Route des Pyrénées over the Port (or Col) de Peyresourde to Arreau, and then turning southward into a valley which steadily becomes steeper, finer and rockier. Here is *Ramonda myconi* again,

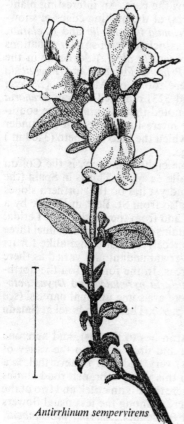

Antirrhinum sempervirens

and on the sunny rocks the pretty purple *Chaenorhinum origanifolium* and, an especial favourite, the white *Antirrhinum sempervirens*, with a purple tache on its lip—neat, charming, and an excellent and enduring rock-garden plant. The scenery in the upper valley is stupendous. One drives into a great amphitheatre of fantastically ridged and pointed hills, with several small glaciers, which are rare in the Pyrenees. The road will bring you to the Lac de Cap de Long (you look down upon beautiful wooded Lac d'Orédon on your way), and I believe that it has now been extended along the lakeside. In 1960 we had to walk, and very fine it was. In early July there were still snow-patches and between them grew *Gentiana alpina* (commoner further east), *Pinguicula grandiflora*, and the beautiful and deliciously fragrant *Daphne cneorum* in its prostrate form (*D.c. pygmaea* of gardens) creeping among the grass. This form of *D. cneorum* is widespread in the Pyrenees, although not confined to them, and references by Roger-Smith and others to *D. verlotii* were later corrected. Here too we found the fine *Iris latifolia*

115

(*xiphioides*) just coming into flower at the beginning of July at these upper levels and there were great sprays of *Saxifraga longifolia* high in the rock-crevices. Both these plants become commoner as one moves towards the west.

Another fine excursion from Luchon is to the Port de Vénasque (Puerto de Benasque), reached by driving southward along the valley of the Pique to the Hospice de France and walking from there. The hospice is an auberge at 1385 m., in a beautiful setting. Here at the time of our visit were huge Pyrenean Mountain puppies and enormous horse-flies. The meadows here are rich with orchids of the 'marsh' and 'spotted' varieties and with the lovely form of *Aquilegia vulgaris* which abounds in the Pyrenees and has sometimes been mistaken for *A. alpina*, which does not grow in these mountains. The Port de Vénasque is on the frontier, and the climb up to it is strenuous and exhilarating but not difficult. There is a delightful group of little lakes, the Boums de Port, just below the pass. An interesting plant-association (common in the Pyrenees) at the melting edges of snow-patches is *Ranunculus pyrenaeus*, *Primula integrifolia* and *P. elatior*. The two plants that one especially associates with similar situations in the Alps (*Crocus vernus* and *Soldanella alpina*) do occur in the Pyrenees, but are much scarcer. *Primula farinosa* and *Pinguicula grandiflora* are in fine form up here too. Col. Meadows (*Bulletin* Vols. 37, p. 66 and 38, pp. 183 and 323) reported finding *Arenaria tetraquetra* near the pass, and also noted that the area to the south-west of the pass, in Spain, is very interesting. Indeed it lies under Maladetta, the mountain block in which the Pico de Aneto (3404 m.) is the highest mountain in the range.

To the east of Luchon, only some eight km. away, is the Col du Portillon, leading down into the Valle de Arán. This is in Spain (the frontier has a big kink in it here) and yet lies on the northern slopes of the Pyrenees. It can be reached also from St. Béat in France by a road following the Garonne valley, and from the south, from Lerida, by a road that runs under the mountains in a rather grim tunnel three miles long. The Valle de Arán has received high praise alike for its scenery and its flowers, which are very abundant and varied as there are both calcareous and granitic areas. In the former (on the north-east side) *Aquilegia pyrenaica*, *Fritillaria pyrenaica* and *Dryas octopetala* are to be found, and also there are some unusual narcissi (see *Bulletin* Vol. 33, p. 68 and Vol. 40, p. 98). There is an hotel at **Saladu** and an hosteria at **Artiés**.

The upper end of the Valle de Arán lies to the east, and here one may cross the Puerto de Bonaigua and drop down to the valley of the Pallaresa. The road is (or was) very bad, but is nevertheless a regular bus-route. Some way down this valley a branch road climbs westward to the village of Espot, where there is an hotel, and two of the Society's Tours have been based here. Among the less usual flowers reported are *Pedicularis pyrenaica* (endemic), *Asarina procumbens*, and *Antirrhinum molle*.

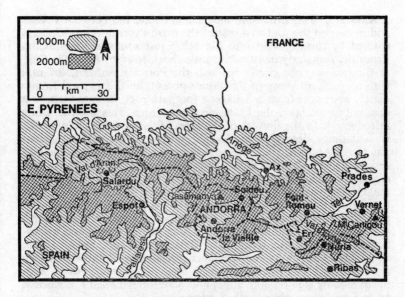

THE EASTERN PYRENEES

The traveller from England by road to the Eastern Pyrenees is likely to go via Toulouse, and from here the main road is the N20 to Ax-les-Thermes and Bourg-Madame. But if time allows take instead the road from Toulouse to Carcassonne (well worth visiting in its own right, and by the old battlements you may find that odd little primula-relative *Coris monspeliensis*) and then turn south and go via Limoux and Quillan to Axat and Formiguères. This is a beautiful road, skirting the Corbières, and running through the Gorges de St. Georges and the Gorges de l'Aude, among plants with a Mediterranean flavour, with the Pyrenees building up ahead. If it is Mt. Canigou that calls you take the tiny but perfectly negotiable road from near Axat over the Col de Jau to Prades, crossing the hills that lie between the Corbières and the Pyrenees proper. There are interesting 'hot hill' plants here—*Lavandula stoechas*, *Cistus crispus*, *C. monspeliensis*, *Antirrhinum majus*, *Asarina procumbens* and the magnificent *Campanula speciosa*.

THE CORBIERES are a group of predominantly limestone mountains lying to the north of the eastern Pyrenees and rising in places to just over 1000 m. The flowers are at their best in late April and early May. While most of the area is too infertile to display a rich array of vegetation there is both novelty and variety and one can find here dwarf narcissi, muscari, *Iris lutescens*, *Tulipa sylvestris australis* and a fair number of orchids and ophrys in open areas amongst the low scrub. However, other than bulbous and Mediterranean plants the subjects of rock-garden interest will be comparatively few.

ANDORRA. This little semi-independent state lies between France and Spain, on the southern side of the main Pyrenean slopes, and is entered by turning right into the N20b just south of l'Hospitalet. From the singularly unattractive little shack town of Pas de la Case at the frontier, one climbs towards the Port d'Envalira (2407 m.), with magnificent views (if the clouds permit) all the way up. Immediately above the frontier village, a footpath goes off to the left, to a charming little lake, the Etang de Font-Nègre. This walk is a fine introduction to the flowers of Andorra. *Primula integrifolia*, which is sometimes described in derogatory terms, makes magnificent patches in Andorra, and here as so often it grows with *P. elatior* and *Soldanella alpina*. The three gentians (*GG. verna, pyrenaica* and *alpina*) compete in intensity and brilliance of colour. They are a magnificent trio, all intermingled here—*G. verna* sometimes varying from its royal blue to mauve or dove-grey, *G. pyrenaica* (very much a plant of the eastern Pyrenees, but turning up again in the Balkans) varying in colour but always on the blue side of purple and magnificently distinct with its seemingly 10-petalled flowers, and *G. alpina*, tubby-belled and of its own special coerulean blue. *Pulsatilla apiifolia* is outstanding here (there were fresh huge flowers and tousled seed-heads side by side on 30th June) and here too is *Lilium pyrenaicum*, to be found more abundantly further east.

The Port d'Envalira used to be a wonderful place, alike for its views and its flowers: now, alas, there is a large radio station there, and all the clutter that goes with it. There is still, however, the fine view of the Cirque des Pessons, and you do not have to wander far from the road up the slopes of the Pic Mata (2640 m.) to be right away from the fuss and the people. A few miles down the road from the Port d'Envalira lies **Soldeu**, where there is a good hotel, and this is an excellent centre from which to see the mountain flowers of Andorra, for although the greater part of Andorra including its capital, Andorra la Vieille, lies to the south and west, this is the hotter, lower end and will make little appeal to those who are happy in the hills. It is true that you must go down almost to the town in order to reach the roads that run northward via Ordino and Arinsal to reach (on foot) the high mountains of north-west Andorra, and perhaps this area merits more exploration than has been reported, using Ordino as a centre.

Above Soldeu is a fine line of hills centred upon the Cap del Port (2682 m.) which are most easily reached from the Pic Mata. This is a most rewarding walk, among crags set in alpine turf. The fine saxifrage *S. geranioides* grows among these rocks, and in the turf are *Loiseleuria procumbens* (indicating its acidity), *Gagea nevadensis*, *Lychnis alpina* (with white forms), *Erysimum helveticum*, *Saxifraga bryoides*, delicately rose-tinged forms of *Leucanthemopsis* (*Leucanthemum*) *alpina*, and, one of the loveliest of all Pyrenean plants, *Androsace carnea laggeri*. All these abound—unless the sheep have been there just before you.

Just below Soldeu a track, drivable for a little way, leads up into the Vallon d'Inclès. This is a fine wild valley, surrounded by high crags, where *Androsace vandellii* grows abundantly. There is a much-publicised boulder in the stream at a low level with the androsace on it, but to see it at its best you must clamber up to the higher levels. Lower down, the leaves, often very beautifully marked, of *Hepatica nobilis* are to be found; you would have to come early to see the flowers, which in the Pyrenees tend to be white. I once found *Androsace vandellii* at its lower limit and the hepatica at its upper limit sharing the same crevice—odd bedfellows! *Chamaespartium* (*Genista*) *sagittale* grows low down in the Vallon d'Inclès. The Eastern Pyrenees abound in gorses and brooms, but this one, with its winged stems, is very distinct. In the moister places by the stream there are also *Saxifraga aquatica* and *Iris latifolia*, and higher up the valley a few flowers of *Narcissus pseudonarcissus* are still to be found at the end of June.

As one drives down the valley from Soldeu past Canillo to Encamp, the great limestone mountain of Casamanya lies on the right. It is a drive to take slowly, studying the roadside flowers before taking the path up into the mountain. The neat little *Ononis cristata* is here, as well as the larger yellow-flowered *Ononis natrix*, a good form of *Paronychia capitata*, *Arenaria aggregata*, *Minuartia laricifolia*, *Erodium petraeum glandulosum* (*macradenum*), and the beautiful and very garden-worthy *Vicia onobrychioides*. All these are to be found by the roadside, as well as by the path leading up to Casamanya and here too, higher up, are *Veronica nummularia*, a distinct and beautiful little plant, *Dryas octopetala*, *Valeriana globulariifolia*, and *Iberis spathulata*.

Leaving Andorra by the way we came in, let us follow the N20 eastward, crossing first the Col de Puymorens which is beautiful, magnificently flowered, but notoriously cloudy, down to **Porté**, which has been described (*Bulletin* Vol. 36, p. 233) as a good centre, with a good hotel. A small road from here is one of the approaches to the Pic Carlit (2921 m.). At Bourg-Madame the road skirts the Spanish frontier, leaving on the north a small Spanish enclave around Llivia to confuse the unwary, and between here and Mont-Louis it runs between areas, both to the north and the south, where the Eastern Pyrenean flora abounds. It is true that we have met most of the plants in Andorra, but here they are more profuse, and, because we are on the northern slopes of the Pyrenees, the terrain in late June and early July is less arid.

To the north of the road is the beautiful lake-strewn area leading up to the Pic Carlit. Font-Romeu, on its southern edge, has been used by the A.G.S. as a centre for its Tours, but it is now a much-developed and expensive winter sports centre and spa. From Mont-Louis a small road runs up to la Bouillouse, the largest of a great group of mountain lakes below Pic Carlit. It is a beautiful drive, through wooded crags where grow *Lilium pyrenaicum*, *Paradisea*

119

liliastrum, *Lathyrus laevigatus occidentalis* and *Chamaespartium* (*Genista*) *sagittale* in its neater and smaller form *delphinense*. The area above la Bouillouse is full of lakes and streams, so that the Pic Carlit is not easily reached, but it is a wonderful area for flowers. Nothing not already mentioned, except *Crocus vernus*, uncommon in the Pyrenees, grows here, but the whole hill-side is patched, starred and scented with *Trifolium alpinum*, *Gentiana verna*, *G. alpina* and *G. pyrenaica*, *Genista hispanica*, *Cytisus purgans* and the leaves of *Erythronium dens-canis*.

On the south side of the road, from Bourg-Madame to Olette, a series of valleys run more or less southward into the hills that form the frontier with Spain. Two of these, the Val d'Eyne and the Val du Sègre, are particularly fine and interesting for their flowers. At the little village of **Err**, south of Saillagouse, there is a pleasant small hotel, which forms an excellent centre for the whole area. Mr. Barrett (*Bulletin* Vol. 36, p. 233) mentions hotels at Fontpédrouse and Col de la Perche and also gives valuable information as to local transport for the traveller without a car.

The Val d'Eyne is an exceedingly beautiful valley, where the flowers are unbelievably abundant, varied and colourful. *Lilium pyrenaicum* is magnificent here. The hillsides are blue-hazed with *Linum perenne alpinum* (and there are white ones too), and *Aster alpinus*, *Rhododen-*

Ranunculus parnassifolius

dron ferrugineum, Potentilla fruticosa, Oxytropis halleri, Nigritella nigra (angustifolia), Iberis saxatilis and Delphinium elatum all contribute to the brilliant display. The special plant of the valley, however, although it is not confined to it, is the beautiful Adonis pyrenaica. Higher up, among the crags before the frontier ridge, Primula latifolia and Potentilla rupestris are to be found, and in the grit screes at the frontier itself there is a superbly beautiful form of Ranunculus parnassifolius, with great cup-shaped, semi-double, rose-veined flowers. Ranunculus pyrenaeus is here too, and there are fine robust hybrids between the two plants. A third ranunculus, R. glacialis, which is scarce in the Pyrenees, has been reported here. Beautiful Iberis spathulata, with tiny, plump, shiny, spoon-shaped leaves and large domes of rosy-pink flowers on inch-high stems, grows among the ranunculus. It seems (pace Flora Europaea) to be an annual here. There are orange-flowered forms of Papaver rhaeticum.

The Val du Sègre, a little further to the west, is entered near Llo by a small road which passes through the Gorges du Sègre. Here Saxifraga media is especially abundant, among many of the flowers already noted in the Val d'Eyne and elsewhere. Vicia pyrenaica is an attractive low-growing large-flowered vetch which is fairly widespread in the Pyrenees. Typically it is a rather plummy purple, but there is a good white form near the Gorges du Sègre. Unlike the Val d'Eyne, this valley is wooded beyond the gorge, but from the end of the road, where there is a meadow packed with thousands of Pyrenean lilies, it is a fairly short climb along a good path to the Pic de Sègre (2795 m.). Here are the same flowers as at the head of the Val d'Eyne, with Vitaliana primuliflora, and Myosotis alpestris in its particularly compact and beautiful form known to gardeners as rupicola.

The area just described is la Cerdagne, which has its Spanish counterpart, Cerdaña, to the south. This is undergoing development as a winter sports and holiday area, and is more approachable than many parts of the Spanish Pyrenees. It is entered from Puigcerda (across the frontier from Bourg-Madame), which is on both the main road and the railway from Toulouse to Barcelona. Some thirty miles from Puigcerda is Ribas, and from here a rack railway runs up to **Nuria** (2000 m.), now a winter sports centre with a hotel, as well as a monastery and centre of pilgrimage. The flora here (Bulletin Vol. 33, p. 72) is similar to that of the Val d'Eyne, including Adonis pyrenaica, but Cerdaña is, season for season, hotter and drier than the north-facing French Cerdagne. At Camprodon, to the east of Nuria, one of the rarer Pyrenean gentians, G. pumila delphinensis, has been reported, and Mr. H. Taylor mentions also Senecio leucophyllus, Oxytropis pyrenaica, and the endemic Cerastium pyrenaicum.

Returning to Mont-Louis in France, if we travel further eastward on the N116 we come to Villefranche-de-Conflent, and it is here that we turn south to Vernet-les-Bains in order to visit Mont Canigou. There are hotels at **Villefranche** and at **Prades** but it can be hot here in the valley in late June, for these towns are quite near to the Mediterranean. **Vernet** is a spa town full of hotels, catering expensively for invalids, but in the village of **Sahorre**, three miles away, there is, or was, a pleasant and unassuming little hotel. From here one may visit the Col de Mantet and thence walk into the frontier hills—the Mort de l'Escoula and the rocky cliff of the Esquerdes de Routja—or sample the Mediterranean flora by driving over the hills to Amélie-les-Bains but the main visit to be made from Sahorre is to Mont Canigou (2785 m.), a mountain the more impressive for its relative isolation.

The drive to the Hotel des Cortalets on Canigou is a somewhat gruelling experience for man and car alike—'*impraticable de novembre à juin, elle demeure, pendant l'été, dure difficile . . .*'—16 km. of it, with forty-three hairpin bends. So perhaps it is better to take a jeep from Vernet. The hotel belongs to the French Alpine Club, and you can stay there but members have priority. From the hotel it is not a difficult climb to the summit. It is a fine mountain, with beautiful flowers. Most of them are those we have met before, but the local speciality is *Senecio leucophyllus*, a delightful plant which is abundant here.

THE WESTERN PYRENEES

The most direct route from England to the Western Pyrenees by car or rail is via Bordeaux and Pau, and from here the main road and rail continue into Spain over the Col du Somport (1631 m.), which is normally open throughout the year. It lies too far to the west to provide a good centre for exploring the Western Pyrenees, but anyone travelling by car over the Somport into Spain is recommended to allow plenty of time for it, for the flowers, on both sides of the pass, are delightful. Three pretty little plants, *Hypericum nummularium*, *Petrocoptis pyrenaica* and *Asperula hirta* (the last two are Pyrenean endemics) are common in the rocks on the French side, and I have never seen *Saxifraga longifolia* so abundant and spectacular as here. There are two charming shrubs, *Amelanchier ovalis* and *Lonicera pyrenaica*, and *Chaenorhinum origanifolium* with *Erinus alpinus* in the rocks. On the pass itself, at the end of May, there is a wonderful display between the snow patches—*Dactylorhiza sambucina* in both colour-forms, *Fritillaria pyrenaica*, and *Primula columnae* in a carpet of *Androsace villosa*, *Anthyllis montana*, *Gentiana verna* (including white forms), *Valeriana globulariifolia*, *Vicia pyrenaica*, and a charming little veronica, *V. austriaca teucrium*.

Descending the slopes towards Jaca on the Spanish side one soon meets *Brimeura* (*Hyacinthus*) *amethystina*, a small and delicate china blue bluebell, then lovely ivory-flowered (sometimes pink-tinged) *Thalictrum tuberosum*, and *Aphyllanthes monspeliensis*. A journey to take slowly, and a fine introduction to the flowers of the Western Pyrenees.

122

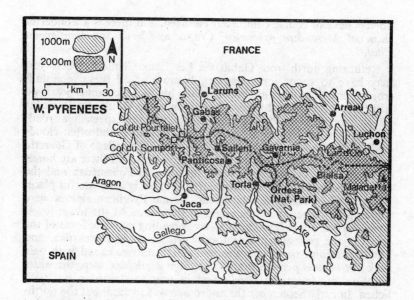

South of Pau is Gan, and from here a road runs due south through Laruns to **Gabas**, where there is a hotel, and it well merits a few days' stay. From just above the village an aerial railway sweeps up to the Pic de la Sagette (2054 m.) and this is an opportunity to be seized to reach the fine and abundant flowers. As the little carriage climbs steeply, the dammed lake below (the Barrage de Fabreges) dwindles fast, and across the valley the huge spectacular tooth of the Pic du Midi d'Ossou (2885 m.) rears up like a piece of stage scenery. The flowers up here, particularly on the north side of the Pic de la Sagette, are a fine assemblage of the best of the Pyrenean alpines, and one outstanding plant here is *Rosa pendulina* (*alpina*) *pyrenaica*—surely the best (some might say the only) rose for the rock garden, a neat, creeping, large-flowered, well-coloured 'dog rose' which later has most attractive fruits. A miniature railway runs from Sagette to the Lac d'Artouste, but unfortunately only from July to September, and the timing of the trains does not leave much opportunity to investigate the screes round the lake.

The other main excursion to be made from Gabas is to the frontier pass, the Col du Pourtalet. This is a wonderful drive, for plants as well as for scenery. There is *Anemone ranunculoides* with *Scilla liliohyacinthus* in the woods, and the roadside flowers include *Arenaria montana*, *Globularia repens* (*nana*), *Anthyllis montana*, *Asperula hirta* and *Pinguicula grandiflora*. On the rocks above the pass itself, on the French side, are *Vitaliana primuliflora*, *Fritillaria pyrenaica* (with bright yellow forms), *Ranunculus amplexicaulis*, *Tulipa sylvestris australis*, *Eryngium bourgatii* and *Gentiana nivalis*. By late August the

123

flowers have of course completely changed, and there is a wonderful show of *Merendera pyrenaica*, *Crocus nudiflorus* and *Gentianella ciliata*.

Returning north from Gabas via Les Eaux Chaudes, where you may have to show your passport, because at all these mountain frontier crossings there are low-level and high-level customs posts, we will turn eastward just before Laruns into the Route des Pyrénées which here, and indeed for 60 miles or so, is a most spectacular road, twisting and turning, rising and falling, unfenced and often cloud-covered, among the northern foothills. The little village of **Gourette** is now a winter sports centre, jumbled and ugly, but there are hotels here, and a path running steeply up towards Penemedaa and the spectacular black ridge of Pène Sarrière. This is a wonderful place. At the end of June, in a late year, all the Pyrenean alpines were bursting out together at the edges of the snow. At the lower levels were *Daphne laureola philippi* (a low spreading endemic form of the species), the parasitic purple toothwort, *Lathraea clandestina*, and odd *Ranunculus thora*. On the rocks high above, mixed with pale pink *Petrocoptis pyrenaica* and *Saxifraga aretioides*, were the white cushions of *Androsace hirtella*, set in granite stained russet with lichen. In early September the androsace was in seed, but the north-facing turf slope below was still a mass of flowers. Edelweiss abounded here, and there was *Geranium cinereum*, but the loveliest flower was the true *Aquilegia pyrenaica*, some 25 cm. in height, with small neat leaves and large clear blue flat-faced flowers; quite unmistakable in the Pyrenees though very close indeed to *A. bertolonii* of the Maritime Alps.

Continuing along the Route des Pyrénées one soon reaches the spectacular Col d'Aubisque, with magnificent views, if you are lucky, and with *Thymelaea (Passerina) dioica* in the roadside turf. And so at last to Luz, and the road that runs south to **Gèdre** and **Gavarnie**. There are hotels in both these places, and for the motorist either is a suitable centre for this wonderful area. Gavarnie is better situated for the purpose, but suffers daily invasion by coach-loads of tourists from Lourdes and emits its own distinctive aroma of horse-dung. For the pedestrian, Gavarnie gives nearer access to the Cirque, the Vallée d'Ossoue, etc., while Gèdre is more convenient for the Val d'Héas.

The Val d'Héas is a beautiful valley full of flowers, and nowadays the road is extended (there is a small toll to pay) right up into the screes below the Cirque de Troumouse, and you could not have a better 3 francs' worth! In the lower part of the valley, not far from Gèdre, *Ramonda myconi* grows by the stream, with *Hypericum nummularium* and the very effective *Saxifraga cotyledon pyramidalis*. *Paradisea liliastrum*, widespread throughout the Pyrenees, is in fine form in this valley, and in the turf leading up to the Cirque, *Daphne cneorum* f. *pygmaea* is profuse and delightful. The Cirque itself is perhaps less spectacular than the Cirque de Gavarnie, because it is too magnificently large to see all at once; a vast amphitheatre facing westward with a crest some eight miles long. The road finishes at around 2200 m., under the very crest of the Cirque. The rock here appears to be non-calcareous, and *Gentiana alpina, Lychnis alpina* and *Primula hirsuta* are in the turf and screes—yet one of the finest plants there is *Dryas octopetala*, and growing through its mats, their flowers intermingling, is a beautiful form of *Geranium cinereum*, indistinguishable from the 'Ballerina' of gardens. A side-branch of the Val d'Héas is the Val d'Estaoubé: *Silene pusilla* grows here.

From Gavarnie it is of course imperative to visit the Cirque. If you are unable to resist the pressures and blandishments of the cowboy-hatted muleteers you will be carried by pony or mule, but to see the flowers you will do far better to rise up early enough in the morning to have left Gavarnie before the Lourdes tourists arrive, or alter-natively go late in the afternoon after they have left. The walk up the valley is pleasant and easy, among the meadow flowers with which we are familiar in the Pyrenees. The upper part of the valley, near the Cirque, is dramatically beautiful, and the fine flowers—*Saxifraga longifolia, Lilium martagon, Geranium cinereum, Scilla lilio-hyacinthus, Asperula hirta* and *Lonicera pyrenaica* among them—contribute to this beauty. On the right hand of the Cirque, as one faces it, is a ridge called les Sarradets, traversed by a path of sorts. *Potentilla alchi-milloides* grows up here, and *Saponaria caespitosa* and *Aquilegia pyrenaica*, and one can scramble down to the Port de Gavarnie (a track across the frontier) though this is more easily reached by a separate path from Gavarnie. It is an interesting area, where *Ranun-culus parnassifolius* (a very poor form), *Veronica nummularia, Aren-aria purpurascens* and *Dryas octo-petala* grow. Back at the Cirque, *Pinguicula longifolia* (rather less attractive than the commoner *P. grandiflora*) grows in the damp rocks, and a footpath leads up to the Brèche de Roland on the crest. One of the reputed sites of the rare *Androsace pyrenaica* and *A. ciliata* is also in this area. There are paths leading up to the eastern shoulder of the Cirque, and from the brief accounts that have appeared it would seem to be an area meriting further exploration.

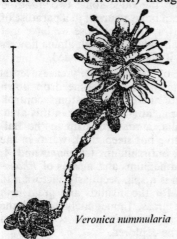

Veronica nummularia

Extending westward from Gavarnie is the Vallée d'Ossoue, a most pleasant and rewarding valley some five miles long, negotiable by car in its earlier part, and leading at its head to the mountains and glaciers of Vignemale. Many of the Pyrenean flowers abound here, including *Ramonda myconi*, which indeed plasters shaded rocks all around Gavarnie, *Saponaria caespitosa*, *Saxifraga longifolia* and the charming, sweet-scented *Narcissus requienii* (*juncifolius*).

A new pass-road from Gavarnie into Spain, following the Vallée des Especières to the Puerto de Bujaruelo, should further enhance the attractions of Gavarnie.

One further, and outstanding, visit to be made by car from Gavarnie is to the Col du Tourmalet and the Pic du Midi de Bigorre. Returning to Luz, and travelling eastward along the Route des Pyrénées, one passes through Barèges, where there are hotels, and after a magnificent drive of some twelve miles from Luz one reaches the Col du Tourmalet (2114 m.). This, the highest point on the Route des Pyrénées, can be closed by snow even in early July. Old friends abound here—*Iris latifolia*, *Arenaria purpurascens*, *Saxifraga longifolia*, *Linaria supina* (or one of its allies), *Saxifraga aretioides*, *Fritillaria pyrenaica*, and the sweet-scented *Petrocallis pyrenaica* (Heaven's answer to those who "can't stand crucifers"!). From the Col a little road runs northward to the Pic du Midi de Bigorre. It is a controlled toll-road, carrying traffic in only one direction at a time. The Pic du Midi (2877 m.) stands away from the main Pyrenean mass, and the views from it (there is an observatory and a *Table d'Orientation* there) are breath-taking. The Pyrenees are spread out before one, range upon range, thirty miles deep, to the south, and as far as the eye can see to the east and west. It is a popular centre for visitors, but you have only to climb the ridge some two hundred yards or so from the road, and you can be by yourself in a paradise of flowers. A list would be repetitive, for they are those we have met before, but for sheer brilliance and abundance of high alpine flowers the ridge below the Pic du Midi de Bigorre is unsurpassed.

Turning now to the Spanish side of the Western Pyrenees, let us visit once again the Col du Pourtalet, and this time drop down through Formigal to Sallent, where there is a Customs control. There is much winter sports development (with hotels) in this area. Beyond Sallent, just below Escarrilla, a road runs up to the **Balneario de Panticosa**. It is an attractive but steep road, warm in the June sun, with *Saxifraga longifolia*, antirrhinums (*A. majus* and *A. sempervirens*), pink and white helianthemums and masses of *Rhododendron ferrugineum*. The little town is a spa, peculiarly Victorian in atmosphere, with parks and walks for the invalids and great lush butterfly and burnt orchids in the grass. Immediately behind the town the mountains rise steeply to the Brèche de Roland and Gavarnie beyond—another area to be explored.

A few miles south of Escarrilla there is another road to the east, to Broto and Torla, and beside the road, within a stone's throw of one another, were four beautiful flaxes—blue *Linum narbonense*, white *L. suffruticosum*, rosy *L. viscosum* and yellow *L. campanulatum*. The Torla road leads to the National Park of Ordesa. There used to be a

Parador here; now there is no hotel, but I believe one can stay in Torla. The Park is scenically outstanding, though tending to be crowded, at least at a summer week-end, but as always one does not have to walk far to be at peace among the flowers. *Pinguicula longifolia* is in the damp rocks by the road, there are hepaticas and helleborines in the woods, and in the turf masses of leaves of *Crocus nudiflorus*. A path runs steeply up through the woods to arrive at last at the Circo de Cotatuero, a south-facing amphitheatre of cliffs, the counterpart of the north-facing Cirque de Gavarnie lying a mile or two away behind it in France.

Not far away to the east, but the other side of Monte Perdido, is the Valle de Pineta, and at its head is the Parador Monte Perdido. To reach it one has to make quite a big detour, starting southward from Broto. Again there are beautiful flowers along the road, in particular *Campanula speciosa* (both blue and white), *C. persicifolia* or one of its near allies, and later in the year *Catananche coerulea*, *Nigella hispanica*, the blue *Anagallis arvensis* and on the higher turf, *Colchicum autumnale* and *Merendera pyrenaica*. The road, though recently improved in parts, does not permit high-speed driving, but at last one reaches Ainsa and turns northward into the mountains again to enter the spectacular Desfiladero de las Devotas. *Saxifraga longifolia* and *Ramonda myconi* are with us again, and tucked away in the shaded ditch under the cliffs the distinctive leaves and purplish red flowers of *Petrocoptis glaucifolia*. At Salinas the road to the east (to Plan) is said to be well worth pursuing for the flowers, but proceeding northward one comes to Bielsa and the Valle de Pineta, and so at last to the Parador, a rather expensive establishment. It is a beautiful valley, with great walls of rock on either side, and Monte Perdido (3352 m.) at its head. Near the stream are fine colour-forms of *Erinus alpinus*, from near-blue to near-crimson. A road, negotiable by car, leads round the head of the valley to a waterfall, among masses of *Ramonda myconi*, showy *Asphodelus albus*, and a concentration of many of the best Pyrenean plants. From this road a track leads up over the shoulder of Monte Perdido to passes leading across the frontier to Gavarnie. *Lilium pyrenaicum* is here, and beautiful daffodils, and a charming little campanula in the rock crevices which has been identified (rather questionably) as *C. hispanica*. There was still a great deal of snow only a little above the Parador on the 25th June in 1972, but the season was exceptionally late, and in most years a slightly earlier visit would probably be better except for the highest flowers.

To complete this survey of the Pyrenees, brief mention should be made of the Basses-Pyrénées, the area roughly between the Atlantic coast and the Pau to Somport road. It does not seem to have been visited much by A.G.S. members, and our own experience of it is limited to a short stay in Ascain, near St.-Jean-de-Luz, in late August, and a subsequent journey from there to Gabas. Seen in this way it was a rather dry but attractive rolling, wooded countryside with low hills, and among the flowers we saw were *Erica vagans, Daboecia cantabrica, Wahlenbergia hederacea, Anagallis tenella, Lithodora (Lithospermum) diffusa* and *Gentiana pneumonanthe.* It probably warrants more exploration. Two plants—no doubt there are many others—occurring in this area but not further eastward are *Soldanella villosa* and the rare and beautiful *Buglossoides (Lithospermum) gastonii.*

The Pyrenees in the *Bulletin:*

Other reading:
Taylor, A. W., *Wild Flowers of the Pyrenees* Chatto & Windus

7

SPAIN

The Iberian Peninsula (Spain and Portugal) is a little larger than France, with an enormous flora, much of it very appropriate to the garden or alpine house. So it is not surprising that as Spain has become increasingly accessible more and more members of the Society have travelled there to see the flowers.

Spain is an upland country, practically without low-lying areas apart from a narrow coastal strip and the delta of the Guadalquivir below Seville. It is a vast plateau from which arise a great many blocks or ranges of mountains—the sierras. It is upon the sierras that most of the plants of interest to us are found, and this chapter will be based upon visits to a selection of them. The Balearic Islands in the Mediterranean off Spain's eastern coast are a province of Spain and will be considered separately in this chapter.

Scenically much of Spain is very beautiful, though there are vast areas of plateau which are relatively level, cultivated, and dull. Many of the sierras present grand outlines but nevertheless an impression of aridity arising from a sparseness of grass and turf. Frequently, however, the seemingly barren rocks are full of interesting plants, just as the screes so often are in the Alps.

The climate of central Spain is continental in type, with hot summers and cold winters, but not so the coastal areas. Northern Spain, fronting the Bay of Biscay, has less extremes of temperature and is a high rainfall area and consequently less arid in summer than central Spain. Eastern and southern Spain are mild and wetter in winter, though tending to be hot and dry in the summer—Mediterranean in fact. As always such generalisations are subject to considerable local variation, particularly in the mountains where altitude very much affects climate.

The geology is very mixed and some reference will be made to it in each of the sierras we visit.

Spain is developing rapidly in its provision for tourists. Much of this development is uncontrolled and ugly, though fortunately most of this is along the coastal strip and need not concern us. Inland, provision for the traveller is varied and unpredictable, but we have found the people helpful and have encountered no major problems. The roads vary from excellent to execrable, sometimes with startling suddenness, but in general the main roads are good and the side-roads readily negotiable. Distances in Spain are somehow longer than one expects, and it is as well to allow plenty of time. The secondary roads, though slower, are often much more peaceful, and much better for seeing both the scenery and the flowers, as well as the hundreds of places of historical and architectural interest, to some of which Col. Meadows alludes in his series of interesting articles in the *Bulletin*. But if you travel on second-class roads make sure that you start with a full petrol tank in the morning.

There is an extensive network of railways, consisting of two main components—lines radiating from Madrid, which is right at the centre of the country, and a line running along or near the Mediterranean coast from France to Portugal—and these, with other lines, connect all the main towns. In general there are local bus services connecting the towns and villages.

Access to Spain for the motorist driving his own car is from France over the Pyrenees (q.v.), the main point of access to all but the most easterly sierras being the Col du Somport, which is usually open. There is a car-ferry service from Plymouth to Santander. The quickest way to Spain is of course by air; there are services from London to more than a score of Spanish cities.

Hotels are less abundant than in France, and variable in standard. There are three types of government-sponsored hotel—the parador, the albergue and the refugio, in diminishing order of luxury and cost. We have found the paradores excellent, and some of them are delightfully situated or housed, in old castles and other buildings of historic interest, but they vary in their standards (1 to 5-star), and are by no means cheap. The only albergue in which we have stayed (in Antequera) was very comfortable. They are intended for only two nights' stay, but do not rigidly enforce this rule. The refugios are mountain huts. Privately run hotels can be very pleasant, comfortable, friendly and inexpensive, but are not always so. Many hill-villages have small inns (see *Bulletin*, Vol. 41, p. 307). In a few areas, such as the Guadarramas and the Sierra Nevada, as well as the Pyrenees, there is winter sports development which, as elsewhere, can be helpful to the summer visitor. In popular areas, and especially at week-ends, the hotels and paradores are liable to be booked up, and it is as well to 'phone ahead. We have found hotel staff very willing to do this for us. We have also found on more than one occasion that a parador may be unable to offer a room, particularly at the week-end, but that if one 'phones again, or calls, early on the day of arrival a room is found to be available.

Language can be a problem if you have no Spanish, but in the paradores and larger hotels there is frequently a member of the staff who speaks English. The menus, in the paradores, contain an English translation. Shopping for food in the smaller villages can be something of a guessing game, as there is a tendency for the shops to have screened or shuttered doors and little external evidence of their existence. The people are helpful and friendly once you speak to them, though till you do so they may appear to glower upon you.

As to the flowers, one cannot generalise. In the Pyrenees, as we have seen, there is still a large component of the 'basic flora' of the Alps, though with an added local flora of great interest, and more drought-resistant plants on the southern slopes. This same pattern continues westwards into the Cordillera Cantabrica, which in many respects can be thought of as a continuation of the Pyrenees. The Mediterranean flora which we met at the eastern end of the Pyrenees continues along the whole south-east seaboard of Spain, extending to some degree inland. Many of the plants listed on pp. 75 and 105 are found throughout this area. At Gibraltar, and inland through Andalusia, this flora is supplemented by interesting plants found also in north-west Africa—a mere 12 km. away across the Straits—of which those at the lower levels tend not to be hardy in English gardens. The Sierra Nevada, reaching 3478 m. at a latitude around 37°N, is a law unto itself, and the sierras of central Spain also have their special characteristics.

THE PICOS DE EUROPA

The northern rim of the Spanish plateau is formed by the Cordillera Cantabrica, running from Galicia in North-West Spain to Navarra, where a partial and ill-defined break separates it from the western Pyrenees. Around the centre of the Cordillera it rises to its greatest height in a dramatic block of mountains, the Picos de Europa. Few Members of our Society seem to have travelled far towards Galicia, but the Picos are more accessible by car (whether over the Col du Somport or following the coast of France through Biarritz), by sea to Santander, or by plane to Bilbao or Santander.

The Picos are close-knit, spectacular mountains, reaching 2648 m. in the Torre Cerredo, and to gain their very heart one must go on foot. Nevertheless, there is an exciting road that encircles the block (I will call it the 'ring road', but it is more of an erratic triangle than a circle) and from it a number of branch roads of varying negotiability seek to penetrate the massif. Let us approach the Picos from the north-east, coming via Bilbao and Santander and branching from the main road to Santillana for, anxious though we are to reach the hills and the flowers, there are two things here to detain us. One is the ancient little town itself, Sancta Juliana, picturesque and smelly, with a IXth century church and monastery whose cloisters and carved pillars are overgrown with *Erigeron karvinskianus*, a little Mexican daisy well-known in our gardens (as *E. mucronatus*) and widely naturalised in Southern and Western Europe. We could well spend the night here at the Parador de Gil Blas in a XIV-XVth Century mansion. The other great attraction here is at nearby Altemira, where the pre-historic cave drawings are (we thought) not very impressive, but it would be a pity to pass them by. And anyway the small coast road via Comillas runs through chalky heath where fields are dark with myriads of large-flowered deep maroon *Serapias cordigera*, and the bee orchids (*Ophrys apifera*), hardly less

131

abundant, have sepals ranging from a deep glowing ruby-red, with mahogany 'bees', to clear white with lemon-yellow 'bees'. *Teucrium pyrenaicum* grows here too by the roadside, and we saw a picked flower of *Lilium pyrenaicum*.

At Unquera a road branches off to the south and winds its way along the banks and gorges of the Rio Deva. At Pañes the road divides, one branch following the Rio Cares to the west, along the northern side of the Picos to Las Arenas and Cangas de Onis, and the other continuing southward (for now we have entered the 'ring road') through the magnificent Desfiladero de la Hermida to Potes. This is a fine place to be. Fifteen miles of dramatic limestone gorge, with the Rio Deva boiling along at its base. *Erigeron karvinskianus* seemed natural enough among the ancient man-made stonework of Santillana, but in the wild rocks of the defile it seems quite unnaturally naturalised. On damp faces of these same rocks are magnificent and abundant purple flowers of *Pinguicula grandiflora*. Among the boulders by the stream is *Petrocoptis glaucifolia*, with flowers of a deep strong purple-tinged rose—a much more powerful colour than those of the several other species of petrocoptis in northern Spain; and near by, and almost matching the colour, is the slightly sticky-leaved 'flax', *Linum viscosum*, a beautiful and excellent garden plant. The orchids are still with us; *Ophrys apifera* is joined by *O. scolopax* and various species of orchis. The startling thing is to find in this fairly frangible limestone, and cheek by jowl with the orchids, deep blue *Lithodora diffusa*. This is usually accepted as a calciphobe plant (though some say "not very") but this form is unquestionably lime-tolerant.

At **Potes** there is at least one pleasant and comfortable hotel, and this is a very suitable centre from which the motorist may explore the eastern side of the Picos. A road runs westward from here, still following the Deva valley, through Espinama to **Fuente Dé**, where there is a small parador, and this, for the walker who will climb into the high peaks, is a better centre than Potes. For the motorist it is a dead-end, easily reached from Potes. The Espinama valley is attractive, though rather shut-in, with a lush growth in June of geraniums, mallows, etc., butterworts on the rocks, and a pale-flowered petrocoptis which may be *P. viscosa*.

Fuente Dé is finely placed at the foot of a 'cirque' of high cliffs. A *teleferico* rises from near the parador in one magnificent steep sweep northward to the crest of the cirque, and from here there are paths leading up to Peña Vieja, one of the highest peaks of the Picos. We were there on June 14th, and found the snow only just leaving the hillside at the top of the *teleferico*. One of the problems of the Picos, as with so many other mountains, is to know just when to visit. Northern Spain is great country for narcissi, and those with a special interest in this genus will wish to go early, perhaps in May, though we found several species in fine form in mid-June.

Clearly for the highest alpines the appropriate season is much the same as in the Alps, late June and early July.

In the cable-car, as one nears the top, the little cabin seems to ascend almost vertically up the cliff face, and here are brilliant yellow patches of *Saxifraga aretioides*, and also firm clear blue domes of *Lithodora diffusa*, belying its name and solid with bloom on the limestone. The saxifrage here is a much finer plant than the same species as we had seen it in the Pyrenees. At the top, in patches left bare by the receding snow, was *Narcissus asturiensis*, its trumpets almost touching the ground. Here too were two special plants of the Picos, *Anemone pavoniana* and *Campanula arvatica*. The former (not to be confused with *A. pavonina* of the Eastern Mediterranean) is a beautiful plant, rather like a large *A. baldensis*: the campanula was not yet in flower. Spring and bell gentians and spring squills promised that in a day or two this would be a colourful alp, and a little stock, *Matthiola fruticulosa perennis*, was already in flower. Another special and beautiful flower of high levels in the Picos is *Aquilegia discolor*.

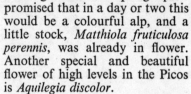

Aquilegia discolor

One of the tracks across the hills from the head of the teleferico leads to the Refugio de Aliva, an alternative pied-à-terre in the summer for the walker in these mountains. There is also a road leading up to it from Espinama. It is described on our map as 'Pista para Jeep', and in 1969 it defeated our car. It may however now be improved (*Bulletin*, Vol. 41, p. 307) and lead through not only to the Refugio but down the north side of the range to Sotres and perhaps to join the 'ring road' at Las Arenas.

Back at Fuente Dé, one can cross the alpine meadow, where there is *Androsace villosa* among many orchids, various ophrys, *Aquilegia vulgaris* and *Vicia pyrenaica*, and climb up the north-west corner of the cirque—not without difficulty, for the old steep zigzag mule track is largely broken away. *Anemone pavoniana* and *Saxifraga aretioides* are here too, and there should be fine walks high into the hills when the snow has cleared.

From Potes a road runs to the south-east, away from the main mass of the hills, to reach the Puerto de Piedras Luengas (1329 m.),

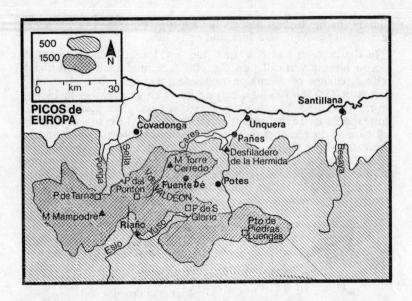

and this, even on a very wet day, is a wonderful drive. The twisting road follows the valley of the Rio Bullón among wooded hills, and lizard orchids (*Himantoglossum hircinum*) are massed by the road-side. The soil here is limestone, in vertical spikes and towers—the 'long stones' of the pass. *Asperula hirta* is here, and beautiful white *Draba dedeana*—a fine plant at its best, but some poor things seem to cower under its name. *Lithodora diffusa* (again here on the lime-stone) and *Anemone pavoniana* are by now old friends. A charming plant new to us was an attractive pansy with 2-3 cm. wide violet flowers, *Viola bubanii*. Perhaps the loveliest colour-show was given by two old acquaintances from the Alps—*Globularia repens* and *G. nudicaulis*, and their fine hybrid *G.* x *fuxeensis*.

The 'ring road' continues south-westward from Potes to the Puerto de San Glorio (1609 m.). This was a very pleasant journey, in spite of the bad road in 1969, but I believe it has been improved since. The scenery is magnificent, and in places we ran through meadows where there were extensive stands of the huge and magnificent *Narcissus pseudonarcissus nobilis*—well-named indeed. Among the rocks (a pebbly conglomerate) around the pass were *Erythronium dens-canis*, *Narcissus asturiensis* and fritillaries which we took to be *F. lusitanica*—though I now wonder whether they were *F. pyrenaica*, if indeed the two are different. A plant of special interest and beauty here is *Teesdaliopsis conferta*, a crucifer whose wide tussocks are smothered with white candytuft-like flowers. There were the leaves of a crocus, probably *C. serotinus salzmannii* (*asturicus*), on the pass, *Jasione crispa*, *Anthyllis montana*, and

134

Saxifraga pentadactylis, and along the road *Cistus salvifolius, Halimium alyssoides* and *Daboecia cantabrica.*

Westward the road runs through a short but impressive gorge down to Portilla de la Reina, and from here a branch road runs northward into the Valle de Valdeón, where you can walk to the great spiky ridge of Coriscao giving wonderful views into the heart of the Picos. The grey-leaved *Potentilla cinerea* is here.

Following the 'ring road' from Portilla, still south-westward, one comes to **Riaño**, which is, or was, an excellent centre from which to attack the southern side of the Picos. There was a parador here, but now the Rio Esla has been dammed, much of the area submerged, and the parador closed. There is, I believe, another hotel there, and Colonel Meadows mentions an inn at Portilla. The 'ring road' runs northward from Riaño, following the Rio Orña up to the Puerto del Pontón, and from this point a little road winds north-eastward into the mountains to a 'mirador'—a view-point—which is worth a visit not only for the view but also because many of the loveliest Picos flowers are gathered together here. Below the mirador the road runs through woodland where the wood anemones (*A. nemorosa*) are very large-flowered and many of them are in shades of soft violet and blue. There is a sweet-scented but untidy dianthus (*D. furcatus geminiflorus*), a neat spurge, also fragrant (*Euphorbia chamaebuxus*), *Linaria triornithophora* with large purple and yellow flowers and glaucous leaves on straggly stems, a 'mossy' saxifrage (*S. trifurcata* or *S. canaliculata*), *Sempervivum cantabricum,* and the largest *Ranunculus amplexicaulis* we have ever seen—great rounded plants, much branched, 45 cm. high and across and covered with large flowers.

Beyond the Puerto del Pontón the 'ring road' pursues its way northward towards Cangas de Onis and the valley of Covadonga. But before we quit Riaño let us follow the Oviedo road, running north-westerly along the upper valley of the Rio Esla. This is a lovely wide hummocky valley, separating the main block of the Picos from an outlying mass to the south-west in which the dominant mountain is Mampodre (2190 m.). Near La Uña there are limestone rocks, with spring gentians and orchids, *Campanula arvatica* and *Anemone pavoniana.* On the edges of woodland by the road on June 11th *Erythronium dens-canis* was already in pod. The road leads up to the Puerto de Tarna (1490 m.) and here a branch road to the left climbs steeply up to the Puerto de las Señales (1625 m.), where *Narcissus triandrus* f. *albus* grows by the roadside. From here it is easy to climb on to the slopes of Mampodre, and it quickly becomes apparent that its whiteness is due not to limestone but to a heavy encrustation with white lichen. Bilberry, heather and daboecia indicate that at least the top-soil is acid. There are sheets of a little thymelaea on the lines of *T. dioica.* The erythroniums here were flowering through the edges of the snow and the *Teesdaliopsis conferta* was superb.

In 1973 the Society ran a Tour centred on **Covadonga**, and the leader, Mr. T. L. Underhill, has kindly provided the following information. It is a small collection of houses with an hotel which is large and had a somewhat impersonal air, but provided excellent food. The countryside is good for walking, but steep. The bird and insect life are varied and interesting. An excellent excursion (by jeep) was to the Lakes Encina and Erol, with fine views and interesting flowers which included *Androsace villosa, Chaenorhinum origanifolium, Globularia nudicaulis, Hieraceum lanatum, Hutchinsia alpina auerswaldii, Narcissus bulbocodium, Pinguicula grandiflora, Scilla lilio-hyacinthus* and *Viola cornuta*. Other interesting plants seen near or from this centre were *Arenaria montana, A. tetraquetra, Astrantia minor, Bulbocodium vernum, Chamaespartium tridentatum, Draba dedeana, Erinacea anthyllis, Lilium pyrenaicum, Linaria triornithophora* and *Ornithogalum pyrenaicum*.

Those with cars can of course easily reach other parts of the Picos from Covadonga via the 'ring road', but it does not seem to offer substantial advantages as a centre.

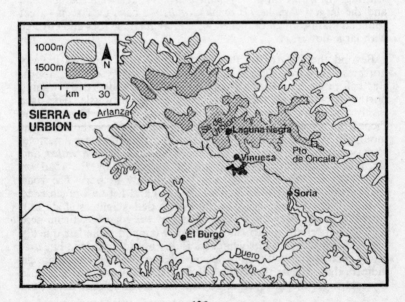

THE CENTRAL SIERRAS—URBION,* GUADARRAMA, AND GREDOS

Let us again enter Spain over the Col du Somport and travel across country to the mountains just north and west of Madrid—the Sierra de Guadarrama and the Sa. de Gredos, calling on the way upon the Sa. de Urbion.

South of the Somport is the little town of **Jaca**, fresh and pleasant, with at least one good hotel. From here, if you want to go fast to Madrid, you can follow the main road via Zaragoza, but if you want to see Spain and the flowers you will wander and dawdle along whatever smaller roads take your fancy to Soria. It is beautiful country, a complex of red rocky ridges and hills, clad here and there with groups of picturesque umbrella pines, and intersected by valleys green with scrub and rushes and willows. By the road-sides are flowers such as we have met on the southern side of the Pyrenees;

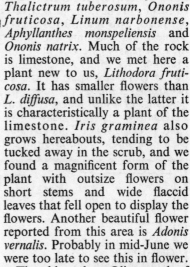

Iris graminea

Thalictrum tuberosum, Ononis fruticosa, Linum narbonense, Aphyllanthes monspeliensis and *Ononis natrix*. Much of the rock is limestone, and we met here a plant new to us, *Lithodora fruticosa*. It has smaller flowers than *L. diffusa*, and unlike the latter it is characteristically a plant of the limestone. *Iris graminea* also grows hereabouts, tending to be tucked away in the scrub, and we found a magnificent form of the plant with outsize flowers on short stems and wide flaccid leaves that fell open to display the flowers. Another beautiful flower reported from this area is *Adonis vernalis*. Probably in mid-June we were too late to see this in flower.

The old castle at Olite, south of Tafalla, is a parador. It has few rooms, but they were able to direct us to a private house nearby where we obtained a room for the night, and we dined in the parador —a very satisfactory arrangement.

The drive of 100 miles or so along the small road from Olite via Rincón to Soria is a pleasant one, and from Arnedillo very fine indeed. The Puerto de Oncala, some twenty miles to the north-east of Soria, is indeed a place to linger; a grassy upland jewelled with beautiful flowers—*Pulsatilla rubra hispanica, Leucanthemopsis pallida, Dianthus subacaulis brachyanthus*, and a very neat and beautiful little

* Contributed in part by Mr. I. B. Barton

veronica, probably *V. prostrata scheereri*—and with these ranunculus, sempervivum, orchids, linums and other more familiar species.

The parador at **Soria** is set attractively on a hill at the edge of the town, looking down upon the Rio Duero far below. This is no castle, but a good modern building. On the lower ground near the town, along the roadsides and the banks of small rivers, there is a great variety of orchids, including *Ophrys scolopax, Orchis coriophora* and some superb *O. militaris*, together with the Spanish form of *Iris spuria*, colourful *Erodium carvifolium*, and such old friends as *Anthericum liliago, Paradisea liliastrum* and *Cephalanthera rubra* to remind us that we have not entirely left the flora of the Alps behind us. Indeed around Soria there is to be found a mixture of typical Pyrenean plants, with a contingent from the Alps, and of species more often associated with central Spain.

Some fifty km. away to the north-west is a complex of mountains, collectively the Sierra de Urbion, reaching 2228 m. The road to them runs past the attractive Pantano (=reservoir) de la Cuerda del Pozo, with beautiful *Arenaria montana* growing by it. North of Vinuesa the road into the mountains becomes rougher, and leads up to a pass where our map indicated the existence of the Casa de Sta. Inez. We found no Casa, but the walk to the ridge of the Sierra de las Hormazas (part of the Urbion complex) was pleasant and rewarding, among myriads of small *Gagea nevadensis*, spring gentians, *Myosotis alpestris* f. *rupicola*, the yellow-flowered form of *Leucanthemopsis* (*Chrysanthemum, Tanacetum*) *pallida*, and *Ranunculus amplexicaulis*. This last was a stand of small-flowered plants, each of a single stem, and quite different from the beauties we had

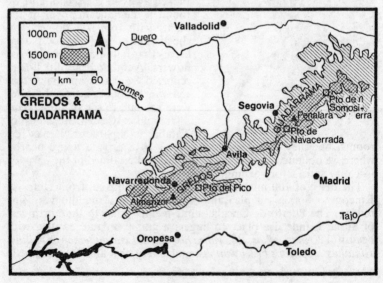

138

seen in the Picos. There were charming hoop-petticoat daffodils (*Narcissus bulbocodium*) at the edge of the snow. Another attractive little plant here was, I believe, *Viola montcaunica*, prettily marked in lighter and darker purples.

There is a side-road up to the Laguna Negra, a small brooding lake overshadowed by limestone cliffs. Just below this lake the open spaces between the trees were brilliant at the beginning of July with great bushes of *Erica australis* and *E. arborea*. Both these tree-heathers should be completely hardy forms, since even so late in the year there was still a lot of snow only a little higher, above the limestone cliffs. Under the trees by the lake were many typical woodlanders, including *Hepatica nobilis*, *Helleborus viridis* and *H. foetidus*, *Scilla lilio-hyacinthus*, and the rare *Streptopus amplexifolius*. The cliffs too were interesting, and here was *Sempervivum andreanum*, endemic to northern Spain. It was discovered by and named after Mrs. Giuseppi (see *Bulletin* Vol. 11, p. 109).

From Soria it is a drive of nearly 100 miles via El Burgo to reach Cerezo de Abajo on the Burgos-Madrid road, and there is no practical alternative to the main road, but it is interesting enough passing through wild eroded country among red hills and ridges, often with castles on

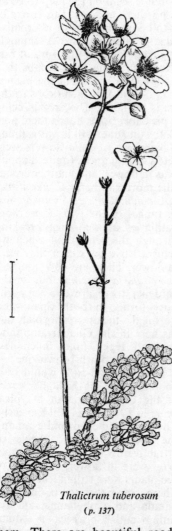

Thalictrum tuberosum
(*p. 137*)

them. There are beautiful road-side flowers including great violet patches of *Iris spuria*, and hills painted with *Lavandula stoechas pedunculata*, the 'long-eared' form of this plant, in which the rather insignificant little flowers are overtopped by exceptionally long upright bracts of a rich soft purple.

Running then southward through the Montes Carpetanos one reaches Cinco Villas, where a turning to the west leads into the Sierra de Guadarrama. This range runs from north-east to south-west just south of Segovia. The Montes Carpetanos seem on the map to be an extension of the Guadarrama at its northern end, but this is one of many instances where there appear to be overlapping or alternative names, and without local knowledge it is difficult to disentangle them. The road that we are following from Cinco Villas runs at first along the valley of the little Rio Angostura, but later climbs to a high pass, the Puerto de Los Cotos (1830 m.) between the highest peak (Penalara, 2430 m.) and Hierro (2376 m.). It then drops to the **Puerto de Navacerrada**, where there is an hotel. The area is being developed for ski-ing, and there are probably other hotels there now as well. When we first crossed the Cotos on June 18th it was running with snow-melt, and the beautiful *Narcissus rupicola* flowers were immersed, and sometimes completely submerged (quite happily it seemed) in it. *Crocus carpetanus* was in flower, and another crocus was in early fruit: whether it was the more southerly *C. nevadensis* or the more northerly *C. serotinus salzmannii* (*asturicus*) we were not sure—it seemed to fall between the ranges of the two. There were

Fritillaria lusitanica

fritillaries as well, just breaking through the scree, and when we returned five days later they were in flower. These are now 'lumped' as *Fritillaria lusitanica*, but for the gardener there are two very distinct forms in both Spain and Portugal—the dwarf chocolate one (as here in the Guadarrama) and the tall leggy (and much less attractive) reddish-brown one.

Probably mid-June would be a good time to visit the higher screes of the Guadarrama in a typical year: in 1972 it was still too early. There was much promise among the rocks and turf; sheets of attractive dwarf *Ranunculus gregarius* were in flower, but most of the plants were still in leaf or bud. There appeared to be a campanula and a phyteuma, an erysimum and a brassica, a sedum, and a linaria which was probably *L. nivea*.

There are delightful drives along tiny roads leading into the hills on both sides of the Angostura valley, from Lozoya northward to the Puerto del Lozoya and from Rascafria southward to the Puerto de la Morcuera. We found abundant and beautiful flowers at the lower levels, but they were the roadside flowers of central Spain. A special find however, above the Puerto del Lozoya, was *Armeria juniperifolia*, which was very neat and beautiful.

The high land of the Guadarrama is continued south-westward in a group of sierras of which the highest and most southerly is the Sa. de Gredos. Their northern side is reached via Avila. One may wish to make a detour to Segovia to see the impressive Roman aqueduct and the cathedral, beautiful from a distance, lowering and oppressive at close quarters but cheered by *Sarcocapnos enneaphylla* growing in its walls. But if Segovia does not call, there is a remarkable road leading straight across the Campo Azálvaro to Avila. It is a fine drive, at first alongside a stream and among great rosy clumps of paeony (*Paeonia broteroi*, probably). The Parador de Gredos is near **Navarredonda** and the road to it from Avila runs between the Sierra de Villafranca and the Sa. de la Paramera—a beautiful drive. The parador is very conveniently placed, since it is near the Puerto del Pico (1395 m.), giving access to the south side of the range as well. On the northern side the road runs between many-flowered banks, some of the brightest colour coming from *Erodium carvifolium*, an attractive species with finely-cut leaves and carmine, blotched flowers. On the south side of the pass, growing in the roadside grit, is a plant of singular beauty, *Polygala microphylla*, whose large flowers are of that intense saturated blue that one associates with the best forms of spring gentian, and borne abundantly on stems spread flat against the grit.

The valley that leads down from the Puerto del Pico to Arenas de S. Pedro, on the south side of the Gredos, is warm and sunny and beautiful with white, yellow and cream brooms. The white is *Cytisus multiflorus*, very variable and some of them looking just like Kew Broom. Among the shrubs there are many beautiful flowers; *Arenaria montana* and a cluster-headed arenaria which I think must be *A. aggregata erinacea*, gageas, *Crocus carpetanus*, spiked purple *Linaria elegans*, *Lithodora diffusa* (here on acid soil, and sprawling, with few and large flowers), *Linaria triornithophora*, *Halimium alyssoides* and *Cistus ladanifer*—a touch of the Mediterranean. A road runs along the south side of the sierra, and there are forest roads leading up into the woodlands. These we found a bit dark and dank, and it was interesting to see the same flowers—*Linaria triornithophora*, *Lithodora diffusa* and *Polygala microphylla* laxly clambering among the bracken.

On El Bierzo, the hill that rises above the Puerto del Pico, grew *Jasione crispa*, and at least two kinds of narcissus in seed (probably *N. requienii* and *N. bulbocodium*). A branch road from the south side of the pass leads across to Esteban, and from here one can turn northward again and cross the hills over the Puerto de Serranillo. The hill above this pass (it is in fact El Bierzo, which we have encircled) is a place of wild rocks and chasms. It is rather flowerless, but lilac

141

Erysimum linifolium grows at the foot of the cliffs and there is a linaria (I think *L. saxatilis*), *Dianthus langeanus, Saxifraga pentadactylis* var. *wilkommiana*, and *Antirrhinum grosii*. Never have we seen a plant looking more out of place than this last. It is a large-leaved, large-flowered, very soft, almost floppy snapdragon, and here it grew as a true fissure-plant, tenuously anchored (so it seemed) in soil-less hair-cracks in the vertical rock. The flowers are a very pale yellow.

The Parador de Gredos, lying between the Gredos and the Sa. de Villa Franca, is magnificently placed, overlooking the valley of the Tormes and hillsides where kites, which fly up to the hotel windows, and eagles soar over the pine-trees. A little road runs westward to Hoyos del Espino, and from here one can drive southward almost to a Spanish Alpine Club refugio on the slopes of Almanzor (2592 m.), the highest mountain in the sierra. It is a fine drive, at first by a streamside where the rather attractive dense-spiked, creamy-flowered *Ornithogalum concinnum* grows among an abundance of orchids. In drier areas, *Leucanthemopsis pallida* is common in both white and yellow forms, and the pretty little annual *Hispidella hispanica*, whose daisy-flowers are yellow with an inner zone of brownish purple.

Ranunculus abnormis

The road ends in a small parking area among rocks and turf, with snow-water running through the turf to the stream below. Here was a magnificent display of gold— *Ranunculus abnormis*, that beautiful and surprising buttercup with grassy leaves and large shining adonis-like flowers on stems up to 18-20 cm. On the other side of the stream there are fine daffodils. A path leads on across the rolling hills up to a rocky ridge which ultimately rises to Almanzor. Great areas of the hillside up here are golden too, with millions of *Narcissus bulbocodium nivalis* flowering in the soaking turf and particularly in the runnels where they are sometimes totally immersed in water. *Narcissus rupicola* is on rather drier slopes, so that it tends to be separate from the hoop-petticoats. Other great areas are lilac with the flowers of *Crocus carpetanus*. Much of the ridge above was covered with snow when we were there, and, as in the Guadarrama the day before, one could but guess at the tiny plants burgeoning in the screes between the snow-slopes. As far as I could judge (under the critical gaze of a herd of ibex—this is a National Park, where game is protected) there were leaves of colchicum and *Merendera pyrenaica*, fritillaries, a linaria, and many other plants just showing their first points of green. An interesting plant reported from here is *Aquilegia dichroa*.

SOME WESTERN SIERRAS*

THE SIERRA DE FRANCIA AND THE SIERRA DE GATA

These ranges form a connecting link between the Sierra da Estrêla in Portugal and the Sierra de Gredos in central Spain but are of sedimentary rocks. They lie south-west of Salamanca, and are centred on the Peña de Francia (1723 m.). There is a good hostel in **La Alberca**, a village which is a National Monument. Late May is a recommended time to visit. Special flowers of the area include the strongly scented *Linaria incarnata*, yellow *Allium scorzonerifolium*, *Chamaespartium tridentatum* and *Ornithogalum concinnum*.

THE SIERRA DE GUADALUPE

This is part of the Montes de Toledo in South-West Spain, half-way between Toledo and Badajoz. The hills lie behind the village of **Guadalupe**, where there is a parador and some accommodation available in the monastery. The hills are of sandstone and limestone and the flowers include *Narcissus triandrus* and *N. rupicola*, *Gagea nevadensis*, *Leucanthemopsis* (*Tanacetum*) *pallida* and *Linaria elegans*.

THE NORTH-EASTERN SIERRAS— MONTES UNIVERSALES AND JAVALAMBRE

Starting again from Somport, and perhaps again staying the night at Jaca, we will travel southwards through Zaragoza to Teruel and the Montes Universales. The road to Huesca is beautiful and indeed dramatic in places with fantastic rock formations. It is superficially arid, because of the lack of grass, but the rocks and the roadsides are filled with beautiful flowers such as we have met already in travelling across to the central sierras. The valley of the Rio Ebro is more dull, and Zaragoza we found something of a nightmare to drive through, but it is ringed by a motorway now, so perhaps it is easier. As one climbs away from the Ebro valley, the country becomes mountainous again and very similar to the Jaca-Huesca area, with similar flowers. One especially delightful plant that was new to us was *Digitalis obscura*, a perennial foxglove with large russet flowers. It is limestone country, and *Lithodora fruticosa* and the prettiest of the European asphodels, the pink-flowered *Asphodelus fistulosus*, occur.

At **Teruel** there is a parador, and this is a good centre for visiting both the Montes Universales, which lie to the west of Teruel, and the Sa. de Javalambre away to the south. These, particularly the former, are not very clear-cut mountain ranges. The land all around is high,

* Based on information contributed by Mr. and Mrs. B. E. Smythies

143

except where the rivers Guadalaviar and Turia cut through it, and the terrain is very much like the high land we have already driven through. The flowers, not surprisingly, are similar too. Nevertheless, it is a pleasant land, and among the rocks and ravines there are flowers to reward one's search. *Erinacea anthyllis* clothes the hillsides and is far more free-flowering than in most gardens, so that it conspires with *Lavandula stoechas pedunculata* to paint the hills a soft violet. *Tulipa sylvestris australis* is common, and we found plenty of a very nice dwarf blue centaurea (*C. triumfetti*). Inconspicuous among the rocks, but fascinating when you do spot it, is the near-black *Linaria aeruginea*. Ornithogalums (built on *O. umbellatum* lines) are frequent in damper areas together with a variety of ophrys, especially *O. scolopax*. In one gorge north of Salvacañete—the most exciting place we met in the Montes Universales—were two flowers growing in tight crevices in the rock, *Sarcocapnos enneaphylla* and *Antirrhinum pulverulentum*. The latter is reminiscent of *A. sempervirens* of the Pyrenees, but the flowers are yellowish and the whole plant a little softer. Another extremely beautiful plant here was *Ptilotrichum spinosum*, very clear white and very tight-cushioned on the rock. *Alyssum serpyllifolium*, *Chaenorhinum villosum* and *Saxifraga corbariensis valentina* were among the other attractive plants of this area, and in breaks between flower-seeking we watched hoopoes and a brilliant golden oriole.

The Sa. de Javalambre is a wide upland area reaching 2020 m. in Javalambre itself, but there is no clearly defined peak. At La Puebla de Valverde on the Valencia road from Teruel a little turning goes off to Camarena, a small village tucked down in a gulley by a stream. On the map the road ends here, but in fact the rocky track up the other side is negotiable by car and leads up to an outlying hill, S. Pablo, whence it is an easy and pleasant though unexciting walk across stony downland to Javalambre itself. We found vast flocks of sheep and goats here, so not surprisingly there was no abundance of flowers, but here and there, sometimes tucked down under the prickly erinacea bushes, we found tulips (*T. sylvestris australis*), *Dipcadi serotinum*, gageas, leaves of *Merendera pyrenaica*, muscari and *Ranunculus gramineus*. The last is easily missed, because the flower looks like a common meadow buttercup and the leaves like grass, but it is in fact an attractive plant, both in the wild and for the garden. Here and there were bushes of *Prunus prostrata* (not very prostrate here, in spite of the goats) and a pleasing find was *Thalictrum tuberosum* with rose-flushed flowers. This was the southernmost point at which we found this lovely plant.

Our next main port of call is the Sierra de Cazorla, but this is a long way to the south, and it would be a great pity to by-pass one of the most remarkable places to be seen in the whole of Spain, the Ciudad Encantada, in the Serrania de Cuenca. The drive from Teruel to Cuenca is pleasant and on a good road, and in **Cuenca** itself there are hotels. A road running north from the town follows the valley of the Rio Júcar, through a stupendous limestone gorge, where by the roadside we found blue pimpernel, a delightful bush smothered with creamy-yellow roses (presumably *Rosa pimpinellifolia*) and two beautiful alliums—*Allium moly* and *A. roseum*—well-known and sometimes reviled, but each of these was a particularly fine form, short-stemmed, large-flowered, small-leaved and the *A. roseum* without menacing bulbils among the flowers. A road climbs high above the gorge and, where the river makes a right-angled bend, there is a local show-piece, the Ventana del Diablo—'the Devil's window'—from which he keeps malevolent watch on the comings and goings in the gorge hundreds of feet below. Here the road tunnels through the limestone, with 'windows' facing in either direction. The horizontal roof is fairly dark, and receives no water except from seepage and in this roof there grows a remarkable and beautiful plant, *Moehringia intricata*. This little troglodyte is like a full-flowered, clear white arenaria, with little shining rounded leaves.

The valley of the Rio Júcar leads to the Ciudad Encantada, the Enchanted City, a place amazing, beautiful and fantastic, and florally interesting to boot. It is a vast area of sedimentary rock where, it seems, a sheet of hard surface limestone overlies several strata of softer rock and the hard layer has been cut through and undermined by water action leaving a group of fantastic formations—arches, bridges, narrow switch-back channels, and precarious-looking 'mushrooms' 40 or 50 feet high with flat tops and narrowing to a more or less pointed foot. Fritillaries, *Antirrhinum pulverulentum*, *Chaenorhinum villosum* and *Sarcocapnos enneaphylla* grow in the rocks, and there is cool lager at the little restaurant. Near by there are woodlands, and here is *Ophrys lutea* in an exceptionally fine form, and a very beautiful orchid—*Orchis patens*. There is *Convolvulus lineatus* by the roadside.

Mr. H. L. Crook adds that, further up the valley of the Júcar, **Tragacete** (with a hotel) is a good centre. He found by the roadside the attractive blue annual larkspur *Consolida orientalis*, and *Nepeta nepetella*. From Tragacete good forest roads go to Albarracín over an entrancing landscape of prostrate *Juniperus sabina*—an attractive alternative route between Cuenca and Teruel.

The long drive southward from Cuenca to Cazorla is sometimes dull, sometimes excitingly beautiful. If you need to spend a night on the way, where better than in the enthralling castle, now a parador, at **Alarcon,** at the southern end of the *pantano* of that name? Seen in the Spanish evening sunshine the castle is golden, and its setting is perfect, and you can probably have squid for dinner.

Of course one stops time and again on such a journey, and we found the delightful lilac-blue *Lathyrus filiformis* (a good garden plant), leaves of colchicum, *Convolvulus lineatus*, *Hypecoum imberbe*, *Ornithogalum narbonense*, *Dipcadi serotinum* and *Leuzea conifera*.

145

ANDALUSIA—THE SIERRA DE CAZORLA, SIERRA NEVADA AND SERRANIA DE RONDA

Andalusia is the southernmost region of Spain, stretching from the Portuguese frontier to beyond Almería, including almost all the southern coast, and extending northward to beyond Cordova. It is divided by the Guadalquivir valley into the Sierra Morena to the north and a wide mountainous area (collectively and historically the Cordillera Boetica) ranging from the Sierra de Cazorla in the north-east through the Sierra Nevada to the Serrania de Ronda in the west. It is a delightful area scenically, climatically and florally, though with marked contrasts between at the one extreme the high Sierra Nevada, and at the other the most southerly coastal areas around Gibraltar. There is a great deal of valuable information on the whole area in Lt. Cdr. Stocken's *Andalusian Flowers and Countryside*.

For our purposes it is convenient to consider separately the group of sierras around Cazorla, the Sierra Nevada, and a less clearly defined area, based on Malaga, roughly from Ronda to Granada.

THE SIERRA DE CAZORLA

As one travels southward from Cuenca, the Sierra de Cazorla builds up attractively. The road runs with the Rio de la Vega between limestone crags, with great bushes of *Ononis fruticosa* on the verges, and a lovely and unusual form of *Linum suffruticosum* with straw-yellow flowers. We never saw this anywhere else.

There is no doubt that the place to stay in the Sierra Cazorla is the parador. It is set up in the hills, twenty miles on from the village of Cazorla—exciting miles, sometimes through wild rock, sometimes through banks of lush scrub, with *Orchis coriophora fragrans* by the roadside, *Dictamnus albus*, *Iris xiphium* and, abundant on the rocks and in the ditches near the parador, the lovely local speciality, *Viola cazorlensis*. Dwight Ripley (*Bulletin* Vol. 12, p. 38) spends a paragraph on describing the colour of this viola, summing it up as 'the inspiration of poets and the despair of aunts with taste'. In truth it varies quite a lot, but then so I suppose do poets and aunts. The parador is a modern building most happily placed on the south-east slope of the Sierra de Cazorla. This, together with the Sierra del Pozo and the Sierra de Segura, forms a great U-shaped mass of mountains, opening to the north-east, from which run the headwaters of the Rio Guadalquivir, which surprisingly turns itself about and finally flows into the Atlantic in the Gulf of Cádiz. They are mountains of rugged white limestone, warm (they are a mere eighty

Viola cazorlensis

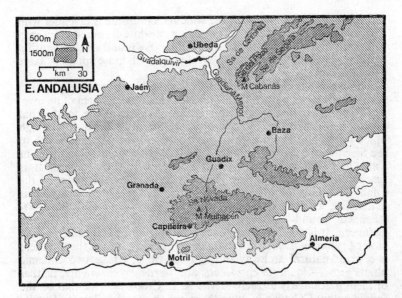

miles or so from the Mediterranean) yet sufficiently high (a little over 2000 m.) for some of the plants to be hardy even in cold English gardens, though others need the protection of an alpine house. There is snow on the higher hills for a few weeks in the winter. Between the hills there are deep wooded valleys; the upper slopes and screes and the high ridges are white bare rock from a distance, but full of flowers.

Behind the hotel the hill rises steeply to the Prado Redondo, a high crest beyond which the mountains drop sheer to Cazorla and the plain beyond. The lower parts of the hill above the parador are clothed with pines and, rather exceptionally for Spain, there are footpaths leading up through them. This is a most interesting area where within a short space one encounters many of the special plants of the southern sierras—large-flowered rose-pink *Polygala boissieri*, the charming sulphur-yellow daisies and neat silvery foliage of *Leucanthemopsis pallida spathulifolia*, *Erodium daucoides cazorlanum*, wholly charming and of a colour described by Dwight Ripley as 'like peach ice-cream'—and of course the viola, glowing in warm carmine with a touch of magenta, or cerise, or crimson, according to your fancy (or just 'intense pinkish purple' as *Flora Europaea* has it), narrow-petalled, long-spurred, neat and elegant on its tiny linear leaves. Other local plants are the mat-forming scabious *Pterocephalus spathulatus*, *Globularia spinosa* with close-packed tuffets of little prickly leaves and rather poor washy-blue flowers on long stems, and the very beautiful *Hyacinthoides (Scilla) reverchonii*, dwarf, with shiny leaves and large deep-blue flowers. There are leaves of *Crocus nevadensis* beside the woodland path, and those of the lovely mottled

147

Colchicum lusitanum. Higher, the wide rocky hillside is lavender with *Erinacea anthyllis*, and just here and there a white-flowered plant may be found. In a crevice between the boulders we found a very beautiful toadflax, *Linaria lilacina*, a delightful plant with loose spikes of large soft-lilac flowers.

Below the parador is *Narcissus hedraeanthus*, tiny, gawky, pallid with a distinctive, pathetic, not-long-for-this-world charm of its own.

The most exciting spot in this group of sierras is the saddle that separates the Sierra de Cazorla from the Sierra de Pozo. It is a high upland area of green turf, with views away to the west and south to the Sierra Nevada, and on its eastern side is the great white ridge of Cabañas (2306 m.), the highest mountain in these ranges. It is reached by a winding narrow road that runs along the ravine of the infant Rio Guadalquivir. In the grass on the saddle are *Crocus nevadensis*, an attractive gagea, *Colchicum lusitanum* and the short-stemmed, round-belled chocolate and green form of *Fritillaria lusitanica*. It is a short, steep, easy scramble up to Cabañas, passing violet *Erysimum linifolium cazorlense* on the way, and at the top there is a great natural archway through the ridge, where two endemic plants grow—*Aquilegia cazorlensis* and *Geranium cazorlense*, neither of them particularly attractive. Mr. H. L. Crook tells me that on the saddle below Cabañas in June there are sheets of yellow and white *Helianthemum croceum* and on the ridge, *Draba hispanica*, *Thymelaea granatensis* and the yellow *Anthyllis rupestris*. Up on the ridge the views are fine, and other interesting plants are *Arenaria tetraquetra granatensis*, *Narcissus rupicola* and *Convolvulus boissieri* (*nitidus*).

Driving down the valley from the parador one can cross over into the Sierra de Segura—a fine drive, slow, up-hill and down-dale, through magnificent scenery and fantastic rock formations. It is an area full of paeonies and lizard orchids and white-flowered *Saxifraga globulifera* and the allied *S. rigoi* which die down to attractive red resting buds in the summer. At the end of May Mr. Crook found here *Anemone palmata*, the rare endemic *Geranium cataractarum*, and *Cynoglossum cheirifolium*.

As to the best time to visit, we were there in early June and this proved a most rewarding time, but no one short visit can exhaust the flowers of the Sierra Cazorla. There are many more than I have mentioned. For instance, Dwight Ripley writes of *Hypericum ericoides*, *Anthyllis ramburii*, *Pinguicula vallisneriifolia* and *Ptilotrichum reverchonii* in this highly interesting area. Many of its flowers are, as one would expect, the same as those of the Sierra Nevada, only sixty miles away.

THE SIERRA NEVADA*

The Sierra Nevada, composed mainly of mica schist, rises to 3487 m. on its highest peak, Mulhacén. There is a good metalled road on the north side up to the 3392 m. summit of Veleta. There are good

* Contributed by Mr. and Mrs. H. L. Crook

hotels at the ski-centre at around 2400 m., and many of course in near-by **Granada**, where the Alhambra is a famous tourist attraction. It is advisable to book ahead in Granada.

Our visits were made in June, when the main road was blocked at about 2500 m. by a snow-drift in a deep north-facing gully and between the patches of snow there was apparently inhospitable black scree. However, when we climbed up we found a wonderful collection of true alpines, nearly all endemics of the southern mountains. *Ptilotrichum purpureum* made little rose-pink cushions amongst the dwarf junipers, in company with white *Thlaspi nevadense*, *Arenaria armerina*, *Vitaliana primuliflora assoana* (smaller and more compact than the northern forms), *Ranunculus acetosellifolius*, *Leucanthemopsis radicans*, *Saxifraga nevadensis*, *Anthyllis vulneraria atlantis* (a red-flowered form of our native kidney-vetch), and a rather small pansy, *Viola crassiuscula*. Lower down near the hotels a vertical cliff carried cushions of *Androsace vandellii*, much more silvery-leaved than in the Alps. At about 2000 m. there is an isolated limestone outcrop, the Cerro Dornajo. It was a veritable rock garden, covered with saxifrage, helianthemum, and *Cerastium boissieri*, and here too was beautiful *Convolvulus boissieri* (*nitidus*) with wide mats of silvery foliage and large stemless pink flowers.

Below this is a region of 'vegetable hedgehogs', characterised by a Sierra Nevada endemic, *Vella spinosa*, a pale yellow spiny crucifer making bushes up to a metre across. *Erinacea anthyllis* is here too, and in between the 'spiny horrors' are *Fritillaria lusitanica*, *Prunus prostrata*, *Bupleurum spinosum*, *Onosma tricerosperma granatensis*, *Paeonia broteroi* and the annual *Thymelaea sanamunda*. By the roadside were clumps of *Orchis coriophora fragrans*, the sweetly scented southern form of the bug orchid, so named from the characteristic stink of the typical form, and a small antirrhinum (*A. hispanicum*) with a striped upper lip, *Digitalis obscura* and *Salvia blancoana*. *Polygala boissieri*, both white and pink, was on the grassy slopes.

By July or early August it should be possible to get higher, and *Gentiana verna*, *Ranunculus glacialis*, *Saxifraga oppositifolia* and *Draba aizoides* are found at these higher levels and are an interesting link with the flora of the Alps. More special and local are *Eryngium glaciale*, *Linaria glacialis*, *Senecio boissieri* and *Biscutella glacialis*. Conversely late March or early April is the time to see the spring

Colchicum triphyllum

bulbs, *Crocus nevadensis*, *Colchicum triphyllum*, gageas, and *Narcissus triandrus pallidulus* (*concolor*).

From the village of Zubia a good dirt road leads towards another isolated limestone outcrop, the Cerro Trevenque, home of *Erodium boissieri* and the rare *Scabiosa pulsatilloides* so rapturously described by Ripley, but the gem of our visit was another anthyllis, *A. tejedensis*, white-woolly with yellow flowers.

The south side of the range is not so easy of access. The metalled road to Veleta from the north does in fact continue down on the map as a dirt road, probably negotiable only in the most favourable weather conditions. However, there are plants of interest around the little Moorish village of Capileira, reached from the Granada-Motril road. The endemic broom *Adenocarpus decorticans*, with golden flowers over soft silvery foliage, is there, and another handsome broom, *Lygos sphaerocarpa*.

Though we have come to the Sierra Nevada from the north by road, it is in fact reached much more quickly and easily by flying either to Granada or to Malaga and hiring a car. If the Sierra Nevada is the main objective then Granada is of course the nearest approach but Malaga is within easy driving of the Sierra Nevada and is a more convenient centre for South-Central Andalusia, the next area to be considered.

MALAGA TO RONDA

There are hotels in **Malaga**, including a parador. The town itself, while it has features of interest, is a congested place, and the coastal strip for miles in either direction is made ugly with concrete boxes. Nevertheless it is a centre of communications, and so a very convenient starting-point. Southern Andalusia contains some very beautiful country and is full of interesting flowers over a long period. Our own visit in mid-March was very rewarding. A visit at the end of April, reported in the *Bulletin* (Vol. 45, p. 308), added many new flowers to the list—*Romulea clusiana*, *Viola arborescens*, *Scilla peruviana*, *Convolvulus lanuginosus*, *Iris xiphium*, and *Psoralea bituminosa*, which we did not find in flower in March, while Mr. and Mrs. Crook found a number of additional interesting plants, some of which are mentioned below, as late as the first half of June.

A fine road, but congested at the week-end, runs northward from the town over the Puerto del León, and just north of Colmenar a small road branches to the east towards the Sierra Tejeda. It is lovely country, rolling, much cultivated, with rocky outcrops, spinneys of cork-oaks, and distant views of high mountains. We saw especially fine forms of the Mediterranean butterfly orchid *Orchis papilionacea* here, and beautiful white narcissi (*N. papyraceus*) growing in thick glutinous mud. There are tall pink antirrhinums, masses of *Vinca difformis*, *Convolvulus althaeoides tenuissimus*, leaves of a colchicum, and a very attractive saxifrage in the style of *S. granulata*, but taller and with pink-tinged flowers—perhaps *S. carpetana*. Later the road,

150

joining that from Torre del Mar, turns northward, climbs spectacularly and runs through the gap between two bold mountain masses. This is the Ventas de Zafarraya, the entry to a great high-level plain, and a most exciting place. *Iris planifolia* grows here—that isolated outlier of the Juno irises. It is common and widespread through South-Central Andalusia, but in most areas by mid-March it had finished flowering, and only on these colder and windy heights around Zafarraya did we find it still in flower, including white forms. Mrs. P. Warburg writes that the iris was in full flower along the roadsides in mid-January, and *Narcissus papyraceus* was also coming into flower at that time. There are many interesting plants in the rocks of the Ventas, but they were mostly not in flower in mid-March. Those that we could recognize included *Campanula mollis* and *Lapiedra martinezii*. The latter is a daffodil-relative with very distinctive narrow strap-shaped leaves and rarely-produced, rather unimpressive flowers. A little further north is an easily accessible mountain, La Torca (1497 m.), where we found exceedingly beautiful forms of the somewhat variable *Crocus nevadensis*. Another fine plant here, and widespread throughout the Mediterranean, is the large orchid, *Barlaea robertiana* (*longibracteata*).

Some forty miles north of Malaga is the delightful little town of **Antequera**. It can be reached either by the main road over the Puerto del León or by a smaller road through Almogia and past the Sierra del Torcal. There is a pleasant albergue, and Antequera is an excellent centre for a short stay. The town itself is most attractive, and the Zona Monumenta and the dolmens outside the town are by no means to be missed. But for our purposes interest centres upon El Torcal, a vast area of grey-white limestone, weathered into fantastic formations, in the Sierra del Torcal. It is reminiscent of the Ciudad Encantada. Among the plants in this interesting and pleasant place are *Linaria anticaria*, *Crocus nevadensis*, *Chaenorhinum macropodum*, *Iris lutescens subbiflora*, *Narcissus papyraceus*, *Rupicapnos africana decipiens*, *Saxifraga biternata* and the big soft biennial *Saxifraga latepetiolata*. It is orchid country, with *Ophrys tenthredinifera* and *Orchis papilionacea* outstanding by the roadside and there is plenty of *Bellis rotundifolia*, like the rose-tipped daisies of our lawns but several sizes larger—a beautiful plant.

To the south-west of Antequera is an exciting area round the Pantano Conde de Guadalhorce. It is approached either from Antequera via Campillos or from Malaga via Alora. The small roads are lined with *Gynandriris sisyrinchium* and cheerful bright annuals such as *Convolvulus tricolor* and *Silene colorata*. There are groves of oranges and lemons as one approaches little Alora, remarkable on its hill. A narrow road twists its way across the hills from Alora to the Desfiladero de los Gaitanes, a most dramatic gorge where the Rio Guadalhorce cuts between enormous cliffs and opens into a shallow wide pool. We found beautiful flowers around here, some that we had met before, some that we could not name, such as a romulea (probably a form of *R. bulbocodium*), a pink astragalus, a beautiful deep-blue anchusa or pulmonaria, a brilliantly coloured annual linaria (probably *L. depauperata*) with purple, yellow-throated flowers and orchids galore. These included the four species of ophrys which so often occur together in the West Mediterranean—*OO. fusca, lutea, speculum* and *tenthredinifera*—and the not very pretty *Orchis saccata*. We found too, by the lake, yellow narcissi which were probably *N. rupicola*, but the yellow narcissi of Spain and Portugal are very confusing. The plant that delighted us most of all in this area was *Narcissus cantabricus*, like *N. bulbocodium* but pure white, with one or two very thin leaves.

Some forty miles to the west of Malaga is the remarkable little town of **Ronda**. It is well worth a stay of a few days. There are several hotels listed, most of which we could not find, but we landed up at a modern bed-and-breakfast establishment and dined out at a restau-

Iris filifolia

rant, and found this very satisfactory. One way from Malaga to Ronda is by the small cross-country road via Coin and Burgo. In the area of Alhaurin de la Torre there are plants of special interest. One of them is *Anemone palmata*, with clear golden, russet-backed flowers, beautiful as they open but becoming a little leggy later. In a woodland on a steep hillside here we found *Iris filifolia*, surely one of the most shapely of all irises, but in March still in bud, and with it the seed-pods of a leucojum which was probably *L. autumnale*. Near by, in an area marked out for building-plots, was a form of *Ophrys fusca* with brilliant iridescent peacock-blue lips to the flowers. On the Sierra Prieta, near Yunquera on this road, Dwight Ripley found *Sarcocapnos crassifolia* and violet *Linaria clementei*. It has been said that every Spanish sierra has its own linaria—certainly there are very many.

An alternative route from Malaga to Ronda is to follow the coast road, which is fast but ugly, to San Pedro Alcántara, west of Marbella, and then turn northward

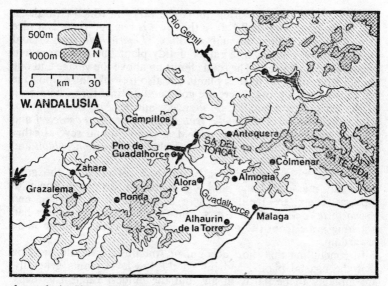

through the Sierra Bermeja and the Serrania de Ronda. This is a fine drive across the hills, though the southerly part is undergoing 'urbanisation'. Higher up it is wild and beautiful. The soil appears to be acid, with arbutus, heathers, *Lithodora diffusa* and again the beautiful white *Narcissus cantabricus*. Then, with startling suddenness, the rock is limestone and the whole scene changes colour and form.

Ronda is a fascinating town, perched on a high sheer cliff and cleft in twain by a deep ravine, magnificently bridged. To see it to best advantage one should take the little road that drops dizzily from near the Roman gateway down into the ravine through turf massed with *Iris planifolia*. There is a fine view too of the whole town from the road that drops down to it from the Serrania, and it is well worth going into these hills again and spending some time there. *Anemone palmata* is here, crocus leaves (probably one of the subspecies of *C. serotinus*), *Colchicum lusitanum*, a distinctive form (subsp. *laciniata*) of *Digitalis obscura* (not yet in flower in March), fritillaries, romuleas, *Hyacinthoides hispanica* and paeonies. Stocken mentions *Paeonia coriacea* as well as *P. broteroi*, and other interesting plants such as *Omphalodes linifolia*, *Jasminum fruticans*, *Clematis cirrhosa* and *Ranunculus rupestris*. A common plant by the roadside, not far from the town, is a delightful little rose-purple erodium, probably one of the *E. cicutarium* complex, perhaps annual but seeding itself about freely, a wonderful plant for the edge of a gravel drive.

To the east of Ronda is the little town, or large village, of Grazalema, reached by tiny roads through beautiful park and woodland, a softer and gentler terrain than is usual in Central Andalusia. But as one nears the town the scene changes suddenly, with fine pointed

153

limestone mountains towering above the valley in which Grazalema lies. On a great rock wall before the town is reached there is a nice large-flowered yellow annual toadflax, *Linaria platycalyx*, and *Ornithogalum reverchonii*, a rather untidy plant but with large and beautiful white flowers. The road climbs up above the village and one should stop not only to seek plants but also to look down upon the sea of red-brown roofs. There are good and distinct forms here both of the early purple orchid, *O. mascula*, and of *Narcissus rupicola*. Ripley wrote also of *Biscutella frutescens*, *Saxifraga haenseleri* and *Papaver rupifragum*, and Mr. and Mrs. Crook found several other interesting plants here in mid-June, including *Teucrium polium* and *Campanula mollis*.

The road climbs magnificently up to a col crossing the great mountain mass of Pinar and Coros before dropping down to Zahara. There are fritillaries here again, mossy saxifrages, and *Arenaria tetraquetra granatensis*—but in mid-March the snow had not long gone from the pass and a later visit could well be more rewarding.

In concluding this short account of Andalusia I should mention that the coastal plants, and indeed the low-level plants generally, are unlikely to be hardy in any but the mildest English gardens, though many are excellent alpine house plants.

MAJORCA

The Balearic Islands lie off the east coast of Spain. Of the three main islands—Majorca, Menorca and Ibiza—only the first has any considerable mountains or specialised flora.

Majorca is a diamond-shaped island, mainly low-lying but with a range of considerable mountains (reaching 1346 m. in Puig Mayor) along the north-west coast. The only large city is Palma, from which communications radiate. The island is usually reached from England by plane to Palma, where cars can be hired. There are railways serving the centre and east and bus services covering the whole island. Palma is a popular tourist centre, with plenty of hotels, but there are pleasanter places. We stayed at **Puerto de Andraitx**, near the western end and, with a car, this is not a bad place for reaching the mountains, though it is badly situated, because of the nightmare journeys through Palma, for exploring the rest of the island. The coastal areas are being extensively developed, often in what seems an unplanned and untidy way: the island is full of dumps and litter. For all this, it is still a beautiful place, with lovely plants including a number of endemics, some attractive architecture, interesting features such as a multiplicity of working windmills in one area, and you may even see a camel in a field.

People go to Majorca, especially in February and March, for the sunshine. We were there in early March in almost continuous rain. February, they assured us, was the best month. Part of the truth is that we drove into the rain because we drove into the hills; it seems that in the spring it is a sunny island with rainy hills. For the flowers, early March seemed to be quite a good time to visit, although Polunin and Smythies suggest later, even as late as May.

The flora is of course Mediterranean, with consequent reservations as to hardiness, but the mountains are subject to snow, and many plants from the higher levels are hardy in the open garden, at least in the south of England, and many more in the alpine house. The mountains are of limestone, and most of the plants are likely to be lime-tolerant. Beautiful orchids abound in the lower-lying parts of the island—*Ophrys tenthredinifera*, *O. fusca* (varying from dull to beautiful), *O. speculum*, and *O. bombyliflora*; the stately *Barlaea robertiana*, *O. italica*, and *O. longicornu*. Many of these are to be seen by the roadsides, with showy *Chrysanthemum coronarium*, *Asphodelus fistulosus*, *A. aestivus*, borage (*Borago officinalis*), blue 'scarlet pimpernel', delicate *Bellium bellidioides*, gageas, muscari and, quite unexpectedly, drifts of *Freesia refracta* and an occasional *Gladiolus tristis*. These two exotics are of course either garden-escapes or perhaps relics of a florists' trade, and a field of purple *Anemone coronaria* may have had a similar origin. Another exotic, unwelcome in the almond orchards and olive groves, is the yellow *Oxalis pes-caprae* from S. Africa.

The lower slopes of the hills are densely clothed with trees and shrubs, including the small palm (*Chamaerops humilis*), the endemic *Hypericum balearicum*, *Erica multiflora*, *Cistus albidus*, *C. monspeli-ensis*, *Globularia alypum*, *Daphne gnidium* and *Cneorum tricoccon*—daphne-like in its foliage and habit, but with the flower-parts in threes and 3-lobed berries ripening from green through yellow to red. The undergrowth can be very dense, and made more difficult to negotiate by the spiny climber *Smilax aspera*.

One of the loveliest shade-loving plants, under the shrubs or on the north side of walls and rocks, is the spring-flowering *Cyclamen balearicum*, and in similar situations are the greater periwinkle (*Vinca major*), *Viola arborescens* (more odd than beautiful), and *Euphorbia characias*. On sunnier walls and rocks *Clematis cirrhosa* grows, and in sandy places the tiny blue *Romulea columnae*.

And now into the mountains, which are very beautiful, and in many places fall as sheer cliffs into the sea. A road runs the length of them, though in its more northerly part it is on the inland side of the mountains: a road slow, twisting and beautiful and not to be rushed. Puerto Soller, due north of Palma and readily reached by road, is a popular resort, and not far away there grows one of the special endemics, *Helleborus lividus*. From here the coast road swerves inland behind Puig Mayor. A branch road runs up into the mountain, but it is unfortunately a prohibited area, with some sort of military installation at the top. It might be possible to obtain permission to visit the mountain for botanical purposes: we did not attempt this, but further along there is a branch road leading down to the sea at La Calobra, and from here it is possible to ascend the north side of Puig Mayor on foot.

The Calobra area, and the road leading to it, are strikingly beautiful. The road drops by steep hairpin bends between magnificent limestone peaks and caverns, and down gullies filled with great toothed and jagged pinnacles. La Calobra is an attractive little bay between colossal cliffs. Here are masses of *Allium triquetrum*, summer snowflake (*Leucojum aestivum*), the sole justification for whose name seems to be that it flowers just a little later than *L. vernum*, and, jammed into the rock-crevices, a pretty white narcissus which was presumably *N. tazetta*.

Cala Tuent is another little bay near to Calobra. Here we found two pretty little spiny plants of the Balearics, *Astragalus balearicus* and *Teucrium subspinosum*, and in the same place the well-named *Ononis minutissima*, yellow-flowered, and enchanting if your lens is powerful enough.

Puig Mayor is a pleasant hill to climb from the north side. There is no path, so that it is not fast going, and would need more than the three hours that I had for the return journey, to reach the top. I found an old garden favourite here, *Arenaria balearica*, as well as *A. grandiflora* and the rather coarse *Brassica balearica*, and *Helleborus foetidus* pretending from a distance to be *H. lividus*. Not a great haul—there must be much more of interest in the fine cluster of peaks and gullies higher up.

Crocus cambessedesii

The mountains are in fact very colourful in places, especially with *Rosmarinus officinalis*, which is specially beautiful here—not the rather straggly rosemary with wishy-washy lilac flowers of our herb-gardens, but prostrate, hugging the rocks, and massed with flowers of a strong glowing blue-purple, or sometimes clear white.

Widespread among the stones in the hills is *Crocus cambessedesii*. In March we found only the leaves and unripe fruits; the exquisite flowers are produced over a long period in the autumn and winter.

Still further to the north-east the road reaches Puerto Pollensa and the spectacular headland leading to Cabo Formentor. The road follows a great spiky ridge, and the scenery is magnificent. On the cliffs here is *Paeonia cambessedesii*, one of the loveliest of paeonies, and near it, *Erodium reichardii*, very attractive and very variable, the

156

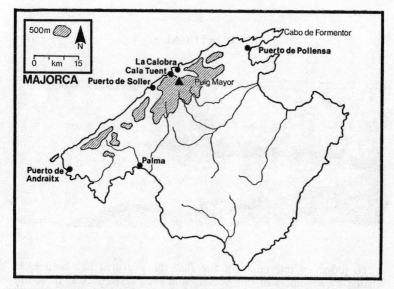

flowers ranging from a purple-veined white to a deep pink. By the shore is another delightful little plant, *Senecio rodriguezii*, small and sprawling, blue-grey leaved, with daisies of a subtle indefinable colour—pink, faintly tinged with salmon and lilac, and with it a neat dwarf sea-lavender, *Limonium minutiflorum*.

8

PORTUGAL

Cape St.Vincent

To judge by references in the *Bulletin*, Portugal has been little visited by Members of our Society and such references as there are relate to Central and Northern Portugal, notwithstanding that the south-facing coast, the Algarve, is a pleasant area for an early spring visit and has a flora of interest to the rock gardener.

There is a good network of roads (not always well-kept) and also of railways, and airports at Oporto, Lisbon and Faro. There is of course no direct approach by road from England, and the journey through France and Spain is a very long one. There are 'Fly-drive' arrangements available in Lisbon and Faro.

From 'negative information', i.e. a lack of information to the contrary, it would seem that hotel accommodation is adequate, and there are Government hotels (*pousadas*) corresponding to the Spanish *paradores*.

Language can be a problem. Portuguese has close affinities with Spanish, and the latter language is I believe widely understood. We met one or two French and English speaking people in outlying areas in the Algarve, but not many.

In Southern Portugal the countryside is pleasant and varied, much of it intensively cultivated, hilly rather than mountainous, and without the striking beauty of parts of Spain. The mountains are mostly in the north, are less high than those in Spain, and are mostly of primary and other acid rock. These facts, together with the very wet climate, were adduced by Dr. Giuseppi as the reasons why the flora is very different from that of Spain. It also appears from the written accounts to be very much more limited and there are few true alpines. There are some limestone ranges, such as the Serra da Arrabida, near Setubal, and the Barrocal in the Algarve.

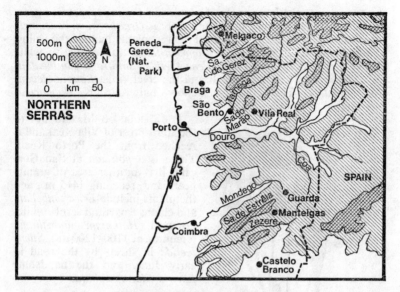

THE NORTHERN SERRAS*

THE SERRA DA ESTRELA

These granite mountains, to the south-west of Guarda, are the highest in Portugal (1991 m.), and form part of the Central Sierras of Iberia. Geologically and floristically they are related to the Sierras of Gredos and Guadarrama in Spain. Rounded slopes, strewn with granite blocks, alternate with steep rocky glens. The area is well served by roads, one of which traverses the summit. The snow-drifts blocking the highest part of the road may not be cleared before the first week in June, or it may be open in early April.

The ideal place to stay is the **Pousada de Sao Lourenco**, whence it is possible to walk all over the summit area. A suitable alternative is the hotel at **Penhas da Saúde** and at a lower altitude there is plenty of accommodation in Castelo Branco and Manteigas.

The flora is like that of other granite areas of north-west Iberia, an acid-tolerant mixture of heathers, brooms and Cistaceae (rock-roses and sunroses). The heathers are *Erica australis*, *E. arborea*, *E. lusitanica*, *E. umbellata* and *Calluna vulgaris*. The commonest brooms are *Cytisus purgans*, *C. scoparius* and *C. striatus*, while *Chamaespartium tridentatum* turns whole hillsides yellow. *Halimium alyssoides* covers extensive areas at the higher elevations, giving way to grassland above 1850 m. In April a number of bulbs are in flower. *Narcissus asturiensis* and *N. bulbocodium nivalis* cover the higher slopes in their thousands, while patches of *N. rupicola* may

* Contributed by Mr. and Mrs. B. E. Smythies

159

be found near the large rocks. Colonies of *Crocus carpetanus* grow in wet turf near melting snow, and there is *Ornithogalum concinnum* near the lakes. In late May special interest plants include the yellow *Viola langeana*, *Phalacrocarpum oppositifolium* (an attractive white 'daisy'), the sticky rosy-pink *Silene foetida*, *Saxifraga continentalis* (a white 'mossy'), *S. spathularis* and the erect violet *Linaria elegans* (*delphinoides*). The common yellow buttercup is *Ranunculus nigrescens*.

Linaria triornithophora

THE SERRA DO MARAO lies to the south-west of Vila Real and is reached from the Porto Road. There is a *pousada* at **Sao Gonçalo**. It is another area of granite heathland, reaching 1415 m., and the plants include *Erica umbellata* and chamaespartium scrub, white-flowered *Halimium umbellatum* (common at 1100–1200 m.), *Silene foetida* in sheets by the road in early June, and the handsome *Linaria triornithophora*.

THE SERRA DO GEREZ AND THE PENEDA-GEREZ NATIONAL PARK in the north-west corner of Portugal near Braga are more varied and interesting, and the National Park includes one of the least frequented and most beautiful areas in Portugal. There is a *pousada* at **Sao Bento** and a choice of accommodation in **Caldas do Geres**, and in the Minho valley in **Peso** and **Melgaco**, convenient for exploring the north side of the National Park. From Caldas, where there is an information office for the National Park, forest roads lead up into the mountains. The most famous plant of the area is *Iris boissieri*.

THE ALGARVE

This is the south-facing coast of South Portugal, from Cape St. Vincent to the Spanish frontier, backed by the Serra de Monchique and the Barrocal. It is a popular area for an early spring visit, somewhat comparable to Majorca and Andalusia, being mild with a good deal of sunshine from February to April. It is not however Mediterranean, but faces on to the Atlantic Ocean.

The Algarve is reached by flying to Lisbon, whence it is a day's drive, or to Faro. One can hire a car in either place. There are many small towns, some with hotels, and villages along the coast, and villas can be hired through British travel agents. We stayed at **Carvoeiro**, which is mid-way between Faro and Cape St. Vincent, and this proved a very satisfactory centre. Our visit was in mid-March, which was quite a good time to visit both for weather and for flowers. It was too late for the display of almond blossom, which is said to be a very fine sight in January, and was just a little early for the cistuses which are magnificent in April; they were just beginning to come into flower. Some of the characteristic Mediterranean plants are present, particularly along the coast and in the limestone band, the Barrocal, which runs parallel with the coast a few miles inland. Cistuses are especially abundant and conspicuous, including *C. ladanifer, C. salvifolius, C. monspeliensis, C. populifolius* and, at Cape St. Vincent, *C. palhinhae*—a large-flowered, dwarfed, super-sticky form of *C. ladanifer*.

Cape St. Vincent with its neighbouring stretches of coast, facing both south and west, is an area not only scenically outstanding but also full of interesting flowers. The rainfall is high, and the plants tend to be dwarfed by strong winds from the Atlantic. *Allium subvillosum* is here, *Armeria pungens* (a showy and superior sea-thrift with pointed leaves), and *Bellevalia hackelii*, a 'muscari' with large flowers in deep and bright blues. On the rocks are the perennial *Calendula suffruticosa* and *Asteriscus maritimus*, both at the border-line of hardiness, and *Hyacinthoides (Scilla) vicentina*, differing only slightly from *H. italica*, which is abundant in the Algarve. The air here is scented with sweet alison, *Lobularia maritima*. Under the cistuses there are the eye-catching little parasites *Cytinus hypocistis* and *C. ruber*, coral and yellow, *Romulea bulbocodium*, both purple and white, *Lavandula stoechas* and in the sand by the sea *Frankenia laevis*, *Silene colorata* and *Pancratium maritimum*—the last showing only its leaves in March. There are charming halimiums, both white and yellow, probably *H. verticillatum* and *H. commutatum* and on the cliffs we found *Jasminium fruticans* and the exotic 'apple of Sodom', *Solanum sodomeum*, a native of Africa, naturalised here.

A few kilometres inland from Carvoeiro is the little town of Silves, set on a hill, with a fine fort. The double form of *Oxalis pes-caprae* is common around its walls, but it is a shapeless monstrosity, and you will do better to admire the old town than spend time hunting for it. Far more attractive by the roadside, though a little gawky for the rock garden, is the rose-purple, yellow-centred *Centaurea pullata*. We are on the limestone here, and it is orchid country, with *Orchis italica, O. morio*, and species of *Ophrys*—*O. bombyliflora, O. lutea* and *O. speculum*, and the man orchid, *Aceras anthropophorum*.

We drove north from Silves to the Barragem de Arade, a large and beautiful reservoir. It was here that we saw our first *Narcissus bulbo-*

codium. N. bulbocodium obesus is said to grow hereabouts. In the ensuing days we found *N. bulbocodium* varying from dwarf and tiny to huge and gross, both in flower and in leaf, but—appropriate as the adjective 'obese' might be to the latter—there were none with the prostrate leaves that are supposed to characterise *N. obesus*. A plant here that was distinct, by its single rather broad leaf, was *Scilla monophyllos*, abundant among the *Hyacinthoides italica*, and another squill, also quite distinct, was *S. peruviana*, not yet in flower in March. This last is reputedly a plant of damp places, but we found it on the dry rocky hillsides, where its rosettes were barely distinguishable from those of the sea squill, *Urginea maritima*. One of the most beautiful roadside flowers is *Gynandriris sisyrinchium*, with small bright violet-blue iris flowers, white-centred, opening around mid-day, and very fleeting. A fine plant by the reservoir is *Lithodora diffusa lusitanica*, upright, much-branched but compact, and massed with deep blue flowers and very distinct from *L. diffusa* of Spain and our gardens.

Further west, inland from Lagos, is another reservoir, the Barragem de Odeáxere, where many of the same flowers are to be found,

Anemone palmata

and here also was the fine yellow *Anemone palmata* and the rather more delicate and less frequent white form; white versions of yellow flowers are somewhat unusual. *Fritillaria lusitanica* was there too, the tall form with rather narrow reddish-brown flowers, small for the height of the plant.

On the limestone hills (the Barrocal) between Benafim and Loulé many of the same plants abound, and with them we found *Paeonia broteroi* and more narcissi—the big 'paper-white' *N. papyraceus* in deep wet soil by streams, and on the stony hillsides a pretty dwarf jonquil like a tiny *N. requienii* but with a curved flower-tube, *N. gaditanus*. Small plants and minute plants were intermingled; the latter may have been the form *minutiflorus*, but, as so often with Iberian narcissi, giving names to different forms among an infinite variety seemed a useless exercise.

An area which is geologically and scenically distinct is the Serra de Monchique, some 24 km. inland from Portimao. The two peaks of this serra reach about 800 m., and there is a car road up one of them. The rock is noncalcareous, and a distinctive feature is the widespread plantings of eucalyptus trees, the first step I believe, in a reafforestation programme. The fallen leaves of these trees seem to allow little growth beneath them, and the flowers are dull and limited. Some of

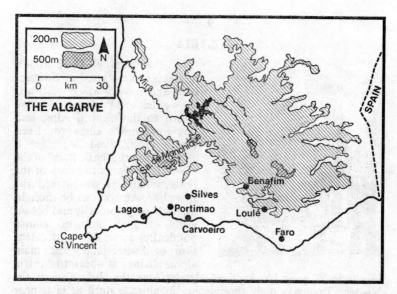

those previously mentioned were here, *Lithodora diffusa lusitanica*, *Scilla monophyllos*, *Romulea bulbocodium* and *Paeonia broteroi* but the only additional plant that we recorded was *Daphne gnidium*.

It would be wrong to leave the Algarve on a dull note. It is a beautiful tract of country, neat, clean and carefully tended, with a delightful mixture of cultivated and wild land. It is not very mountainous but is rarely flat and is decorated here and there with clumps of umbrella pines and of palms, with clean, beautiful and interesting small towns in the hinterland.

Portugal in the *Bulletin:*

14, 50 Giuseppi, P. L. Portugal and its Plants

24, 302 Wells, W. Q. Dwarf Narcissi in Portugal
28, 338 Waley, F. R. Spain and Portugal

Other reading:
McMurtrie, M., *Wild Flowers of the Algarve.* (Pub. by the author)
Taylor, A. W., *Wild Flowers of Spain and Portugal.* Chatto & Windus

9

AUSTRIA

Heiligenblut

In this survey of Europe's mountains we started in Switzerland and moved away westward till we reached Portugal. Now we return to the Central Alps, and this time move eastward. Even within Switzerland we saw a change from the 'basic flora' of the Oberland towards the flora of the Eastern Alps as we entered the Engadine. Austria can be thought of, both geographically and botanically (though not of course politically) as an eastward extension of Switzerland. The main alpine chain continues into Austria in a series of great blocks, the Oetztaler Alps, the Hohe Tauern, the Niedere Tauern, slowly diminishing in altitude until at last, near Vienna in extreme Eastern Austria, the Danube basin is reached.

Austria extends for some 350 miles from west to east, with the alpine chain as its back-bone. In the Austrian Tyrol, which is Western Austria, roughly to the west of Salzburg, the whole country is mountainous, though the mountains are split into northerly and southerly ranges by the valley of the Inn. Eastern Austria is mountainous too, apart from the extreme eastern tip, but the mountains do not reach such high altitudes as in the Tyrol. In the areas bounding the Danube valley (Upper and Lower Austria—lying roughly between Salzburg and Vienna), and also in South-Eastern Austria, the country is hilly rather than mountainous. The greater part of the country, therefore, is of interest to the searcher for mountain flowers. Some selection is necessary in this book, and the areas mainly to be considered are the Tyrol, the Hohe Tauern and Carinthia.

The country as a whole is, like Switzerland, well-attuned to tourism, and also to winter sports. Until recently this was certainly more true of the Tyrol than of Eastern Austria, where the facilities were more limited and the charges lower, but any such differences are diminished now. In general the roads are good along the main valleys and negotiable into the mountains and there are railways along the main valleys and connecting the towns.

The chief approaches from England are (i) through Switzerland via Basel and Zürich to Landeck, or along Lake Constance to Feldkirch and the Arlberg Pass (ii) by the German autobahn via Ulm to Füssen and Innsbruck (iii) by the autobahn via Munich to Innsbruck or to Kufstein, and (iv) by the autobahn to Salzburg or on to Vienna.

There is an abundance of hotels of varying standards as well as of rooms to let. Even so, in the more popular areas, and along the main roads, it is not always easy to secure accommodation in the height of the season, in August, and if one must go then it is well to book ahead. The language is German, but many people have some English.

THE TYROL

The Tyrol, occupying Western Austria, is still the most-visited part of the country for those who go to see the mountains, partly because of its relative proximity and partly because it is exceedingly beautiful and varied and has been long established as a tourist area. Nevertheless, its flora, approximating to that of the Engadine in Switzerland, is less specialised than that of Central and Eastern Austria.

The Tyrol is split lengthwise by the east-west valley of the River Inn. The long narrow strip lying to the north of this valley, running from extreme Western Austria (strictly the Vorarlberg, not the Tyrol) to around Kitzbühel and including the mountains that form the Bavarian frontier, is very beautiful, very popular and crowded, and rich in the 'basic flora'. An A.G.S. Tour in 1953 was based at **St. Christoph** on the Arlberg Pass and **Zurs** on the nearby Flexen Pass. In both places there were excellent walks, some assistance from funicular railways, and a juxtaposition of lime and granite formations so that the full range of plants as seen in Eastern Switzerland was reported, with the notable addition of *Cortusa matthioli*.

Of greater interest, as well as greater altitude, are the mountains that lie to the south of the Inn, and in particular the Oetztaler Alps that here form the frontier with Italy. Two long valleys, the Pitztal and the Oetztal, run southward from the Inn valley near Imst to penetrate these high frontier mountains. A good road runs up the Oetztal, a deep steep-sided very beautiful valley, reaching at last the village of **Sölden** (1362 m.), now very much a winter sports centre, with many paths and one or two small roads into the mountains on either side of the valley. This is a good centre for the motorist visiting the Oetztal, though our own preference is for the smaller village of Zwieselstein, some three miles further on. There is at least one good hotel here, and Zwieselstein lies at the point where the valley forks into the Ventertal and the more easterly Gurgltal. The main road continues up the latter as far as the village of Obergurgl (1910 m.), but a little before this a new road has been built through Hochgurgl up to the frontier at the Timmelsjoch (2497 m.)—a new pass over to Italy.

Let us then take **Zwieselstein** as our centre, though the walker may well prefer one of the higher villages such as **Obergurgl** or **Vent**, and he can reach either of these by post-coach. In 1975 we entered Austria by the Timmelsjoch from Merano in Italy. This was on 4th July, and I think we have never had a worse drive. The road on the Italian side is said to be bad at any time—narrow, twisting and badly surfaced.

On this occasion it was in addition in dense cloud-cover and cut through 3.5 metre vertical walls of snow, with the traffic head to tail but still barely visible, so we cannot speak of the flowers of the Timmelsjoch. On the Austrian side the toll road is good, and we broke free of the cloud into the beautiful Gurgltal; beautiful, that is, apart from the works of man, for here, as so often, ski-ing has taken over the once tiny and beautiful village of Obergurgl. But there are still paths into the alpine slopes above the village and though they were closely grazed by the time we were there, there were still

Primula glutinosa

interesting flowers to be seen. Outstanding among these was *Primula glutinosa*. At its best this is one of the loveliest of the European primulas, a deep blue-violet, with the tight-clustered flowers enhanced by the purplish-brown baggy calyces. But it varies a good deal, some of the flowers being rather small and pinkish mauve. It grew in turf, in both moist and dry areas, and in places flowered through sheets of pink-flowered *Loiseleuria procumbens*. *Androsace obtusifolia* was here, *Soldanella pusilla*, and *Gentiana brachyphylla*. An A.G.S. Tour in 1950 was based upon Obergurgl and Vent, and members walked higher up the valley to the Ramolhaus (3006 m.), an alpine club hut, and recorded among other plants *Soldanella minima, Campanula cenisia, Primula halleri, Aconitum vulparia, Senecio abrotanifolius*, and *Gentiana nivalis*.

The road from Zwieselstein up the Ventertal is rather a different affair, or at least it was in 1975. It is a small road, mostly in adequate condition, but in one part it is very narrow, so that traffic is regulated. It is a beautiful valley, a little lower (as far as Vent, 1896 m.) than the Gurgltal, wooded in places, with *Maianthemum bifolium, Convallaria majalis, Trientalis europaea*, pyrolas, moneses, *Linnaea borealis* and *Clematis alpina* in the rocky woods. Most of the flora here (as in the Gurgltal) seems to be calcifuge, but here and there on the hillsides an abundance of butterfly and scented orchids suggested that perhaps there were calcareous patches. *Linaria alpina* was here, and a very pretty little phyteuma (probably *P. hemisphaericum*). Above Vent the valley bifurcates again, into the Rofental and the Niedertal, and there are fine high-level paths making a round of several mountain club huts. There is a good path up to the Ramolhaus and so over into the Gurgltal. For the walker, therefore, **Vent** is an excellent centre, still relatively unspoilt.

Some years ago, in August, we visited the Pitztal, running parallel with and to the west of the Oetztal. At that time one could drive on a

166

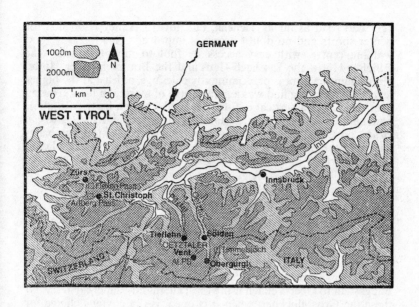

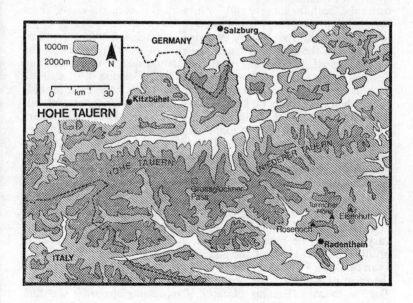

167

very bad road as far as **Tieflehn**, but now the valley is opened for winter sports and no doubt access is improved. This too is a good walking centre, with easy access by foot to mountain huts—the Riffelsee Hütte, the Taschach Haus and the Braunschweiger Hütte. Here again the flora is predominantly calcifuge, at least at the higher levels. A surprising find was a great fringe of martagon lilies growing near the top of a vertical cliff-face around 2234 m. by the Riffelsee, and another surprise was a stand of frog orchids (*Coeloglossum viride*) on the glacier moraine alongside a tongue of the Taschach-ferner. In the woods not far from Tieflehn there was a fine display of *Linnaea borealis* in flower.

THE HOHE TAUERN

THE GROSSGLOCKNER PASS

Eastward from the Tyrol the alpine chain continues as the Hohe Tauern, an awkward barrier across central Austria. There are now three routes by which the motorist can cross this great mountain barrier—(i) by the Felber road tunnel from Mittersill to Lienz (ii) by the Grossglockner Pass (2500 m.) from Bruck to Dölsach (iii) from Badgastein to Ober-Vellach using the Tauern rail-tunnel car-ferry. Of these the Grossglockner, when it is open, is the obvious choice for those who wish to see the flowers, and even if you do not want to travel on to South-East Austria the pass is well worth a visit for its own sake, both for scenery and for flowers. It is normally closed from November till late May. It is a good road, steep in places, carrying a lot of traffic and indeed very crowded in August. There is a toll to pay, so that the cost is the same as that of travelling through the Felber Tunnel. It is a long pass, and should not be rushed. A day devoted to the Grossglockner is not too long. Because of its altitude there is no one perfect season for visiting it. We have been in mid-June, when the flowers on both sides of the pass were wonderful, but the road at the higher levels ran through snow-fields with no flowers to see, and we have been in mid-August when the lower levels were sere and shorn, the road hot and crowded, but round and above the pass, a mere hundred yards from the road, one could be alone among flowers of exceptional interest and beauty. Mid-July might be an excellent compromise—or it might miss the best of both!

In June, below the snow, the upper Alps were massed with flower—the 'basic flora'—and on the wet short turf, whence the snow had just gone, were masses of *Primula minima*, fine and profuse in flower, varying from pale blue-mauve to deep magenta-pink: 'the smallest primula' is here at its best and larger-flowered than any other primula I can think of. The soil on the Glockner is clearly non-calcareous, for the most part at least, and *Loiseleuria procumbens, Lloydia serotina, Daphne striata, Dianthus glacialis, Phyteuma globulariifolium* and *Saxifraga oppositifolia* were among the many plants in flower in these upper Alps in June. On the south side of the pass, near Heiligenblut, we found plenty of the pretty, biennial *Campanula patula* and also *Dianthus sylvestris*, compact and with large and brilliant flowers.

In August, the same flowers were to be found at higher levels, and others as well. The gentians were particularly outstanding. *Gentiana verna* varied somewhat in colour, and we recall with particular affection flowers of a soft dove-grey—a most unusual colour for any flower. *G. nivalis* put on a good show, and the lovely biennial *Gentianella ciliata*, and the two little annuals, *Gentianella tenella* (usually calcicole, according to *Flora Europaea*) and *G. nana*. A thousand feet or so above the pass (there is a good path, and one is all alone) there are silty screes where the fine mica schist shines as though it were wet, and here was *Gentiana tergestina*, or one of its close allies, in finer form than I had ever seen, growing with white and pink *Androsace alpina* and another startlingly beautiful plant, *Saxifraga rudolphiana*. The precise status of this plant is uncertain: it is obviously allied to *S. oppositifolia*, perhaps a subspecies, perhaps only a form (*Flora Europaea* hedges its bets), but it is distinct and exceedingly beautiful—great ruby-red full cup-shaped flowers on the very minutest of foliage, smaller-leaved even than that of *S. retusa*. But one can sympathise with the taxonomists' predicament, for all round the pass *S. oppositifolia* grows in a wide variety of habit, leaf-form and colour—white, pale pink, carmine, salmon, purple, and everything in between. For good measure the allied *S. biflora* is there too, but we did not see *S. retusa*. Among the many other plants were *Campanula barbata* and a very fine form of *C. scheuch-zeri*, *Crepis aurea*, *Erigeron alpinus*, *Geum reptans*, *Helianthemum oelandicum*, masses of *Primula farinosa*, *Tofieldia calyculata*, *Silene pulsatilla*, *Saxifraga caesia* and *Leontopodium alpinum*.

Saxifraga biflora

CARINTHIA

Carinthia (Kärnten) is a large province of Southern Austria lying along the frontiers with Italy and Jugoslavia. These two frontiers are formed respectively by the Karnische Alpen and the Karanwanken mountains. North of these mountains is a series of lakes, and Carinthia's 'Lake District', centred upon Villach and Klagenfurt, is a popular tourist area, where it may be difficult to secure accommodation without advance booking in the high season.

The northern half of Carinthia is also mountainous, rising towards the Niedere Tauern in Styria, an eastern extension of the main alpine chain. So for our purposes there are two main areas to consider—the mountains in the north of the province and the Karawanken in the south-east.

THE EISENHUT GROUP

The alpine chain in Styria and Carinthia is wide from north to south, diffuse, and many are the names of 'tauern', 'gruppen', 'bergen' and 'alpen' that appear on the maps. We have followed Roger-Smith, who visited the Eisenhut (2441 m.), which stands near where the provinces of Salzburg, Styria and Carinthia all meet. He was staying at Klagenfurt, and was dependent upon public transport, so that he approached the mountain from the east (via Flattnitz) and did not have time to reach the summit of this 'not very imposing mountain that dominates the place'. We also approached it from Klagenfurt, in 1963 and 1966, travelling via Feldkirchen to the **Turracher Höhe** where, high in the hills, is a small and beautiful lake. This is a more direct approach than Roger-Smith's, but in 1963 not entirely a joy-ride, since the gradient reached 32% at one point, and was almost as steep for several miles of very rough track. However, in 1966 a new road was being made, and now the Turracher Höhe is readily accessible from the south. There is a very pleasant hotel by the lake, with some less attractive evidences that ski-ing has arrived. To the south-east of the lake, rising directly from it, is the Schoberriegl (2208 m.), and here are beautiful and interesting flowers—indeed everything reported from the less readily accessible Eisenhut. It is acid rock, and in late June the hillsides were carpeted with rosy-pink *Loiseleuria procumbens* through which grew a small neat form of *Pulsatilla alpina* whose white flowers were suffused on the outside with Prussian blue. *Primula minima* and *P. glutinosa* grew together, both in fine form and abundant, and with them another rosy primula, which may have been *P. hirsuta* but was probably *P. villosa*. Roger-Smith's hoped-for *P. carniolica* does not grow hereabouts. A special plant of this area, here abundant and tending to grow in turfy wads packed into rock-crevices, was *Androsace wulfeniana*, with beautiful deep rose flowers. *Campanula alpina* was also in flower, *Androsace chamaejasme*, *Lloydia serotina*, *Cerastium lanatum*, *Valeriana celtica*, abundant *Saponaria pumilio* carrying last year's seed, and, in a remarkable great cleft through the rocks at the summit, *Callianthemum coriandrifolium* and (most oddly) *Clematis alpina* sprawling over the high crags.

The road continuing northward from the Turracher Höhe runs under the western slopes of the Eisenhut, and at the beginning of July in 1966 we drove as far up the forested slopes as we could, and I went up. From this side the mountain is indeed imposing. It is an enormous horse-shoe round a fine wooded river valley. There are paths, but it is well to have a large-scale map. I did not, and realised

170

later that, like Roger-Smith, I had not reached the highest point. But all the flowers of the Schoberriegl were there, in even greater abundance, with magnificent ruby-red *Ranunculus glacialis*, and *Geum reptans*, a white cushion-androsace which I suppose must have been a compact form of *A. alpina*, and white *Silene acaulis*. *Androsace wulfeniana* here seemed to prefer the screes to the crevices. *Saponaria pumilio* was still in early bud.

Northward from Turrach the road continues to Salzburg, crossing the Schladminger Tauern at the Tauern Passhöhe. This is a fine drive, and there would be much to be said for approaching the Eisenhut from Salzburg and lingering in the Schladminger Tauern on the way. The Schoberriegl and the Eisenhut are but two of a range of peaks within easy reach of the Turracher Höhe, which would be a suitable centre for several days' stay.

In 1971 I visited the area in mid-August, travelling this time over the Grossglockner and via Lienz and Spittal to Radenthein. From here a small road runs northward up the Koflachgraben valley, whence it is not a difficult climb (though there is no clear path) to Rosennock (2434 m.). It is only some 17 km. as the eagle flies from the Eisenhut, and carries a similar flora. It is a magnificent mountain, with a great east-facing cirque and fine views in all directions. Here again *Androsace wulfeniana* was abundant, but this time growing in short level turf at the edge of the scree, among *Campanula alpina*, *Anemone baldensis*, *Senecio incanus carniolicus*, *Sempervivum wulfenii*, and above all *Saponaria pumilio*. This last was by now in flower, and the highest turf was rosy with its ragged flowers. *Primula minima* and *P. glutinosa* were here and, rather surprisingly, *Dryas octopetala*. On the lower slopes of the mountain was *Dianthus superbus carniolicus*, huge-flowered but rather lanky.

THE KARAWANKEN AND HOCH OBIR

The Karawanken mountains of glistening white limestone are an imposing chain, separating Austria from Jugoslavia. **Klagenfurt,** a town of some size, provides a possible centre for the motorist, and is also accessible by rail from Innsbruck, Salzburg and Vienna. **Ferlach,** some 10 miles to the south, is a smaller, quiet place, with an hotel, but we preferred to stay in the remote village of **Zell Pfarre** right under the northern slopes of the Karawanken.

A road from Klagenfurt, passing close to Ferlach, runs up to the frontier at the Loibl Pass, and this is the only place for several miles in either direction where a car can be taken to the crest of the Karawanken. In fact, the road now enters Jugoslavia through a fine tunnel, but it is still possible to drive up the old road, very steep and twisting, to the top of the pass. This is very well worth the effort. Our first visit was on midsummer day, and we saw plants of our well-loved rose helleborine, *Cephalanthera rubra*, and the fine yellow pea *Lathyrus laevigatus*. An exciting find was *Lilium carniolicum*: this was not yet in flower, but when we returned a few years later

171

on July 1st the fine red turk's-cap flowers were a joy to see. We made our first acquaintance here with *Hacquetia epipactis*, a jolly and improbable little member of the Umbelliferae. It flowers in March for us at home, and indeed here on the Loibl Pass on midsummer's day it was still early spring, and there was *Hepatica nobilis* in flower near the edges of some patches of snow alongside the woods. *Androsace villosa* was abundant. This is the reputed area for the specially hairy form *A. villosa arachnoidea*, but these were relatively hairless. Especially exciting and attractive was *Primula wulfeniana* in the turf and turf-packed crevices.

The road from Ferlach up to Zell Pfarre follows a beautiful narrow wooded valley, where we found *Linum viscosum, Astrantia bavarica*, fine huge purple *Lamium orvala, Gentiana asclepiadea*, blue and purple aquilegias (forms of *A. vulgaris*), a pretty rosy-pink form of *Aster bellidiastrum, Paederota lutea, Rhodothamnus chamaecistus, Erica herbacea* and *Aruncus dioicus*. Several of these plants were strongly reminiscent of the Dolomites, and it seems likely that there is at least a proportion of dolomite in these Carinthian limestones.

Zell Pfarre (948 m.) lies in a valley running parallel with the Karawanken, and is overhung on the north side by the Freiberg (1922m), an outlier from the main range. A path from the village leads up the wooded hillside, where we found orchids, *Daphne striata, Soldanella alpina* (or *S. montana*) and *S. pusilla, Anemone trifolia*, leaves of *Cyclamen purpurascens, Corydalis bulbosa*, and a superb display of *Helleborus niger*. Many of the flowers of this beautiful plant opened, and remained, a clear rose, and higher up the hill they were breaking through the edges of the retreating snow. Here, in midsummer, the Austrian name 'Schneerose' seemed far more appropriate than our 'Christmas rose'. It is not a difficult walk to the summit of the Freiberg, where there is a magnificent view across Carinthia—the Höhe Tauern and the lakes, the Eisenhut to the north, the great River Drau flowing away into misty distance in the north-east, to the south and west the Karawanken

Rhodothamnus chamaecistus

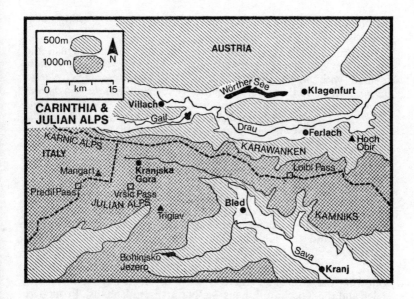

and the Carnics beyond, and nearby on the eastern side another even greater outlier of the Karawanken, the Hoch Obir.

The Hoch Obir (2142 m.) is a superb mountain, readily reached from Ferlach, but even closer to Zell Pfarre. There is now a road on its southern side as far as Kazmun, and from here a good footpath climbs through the woods to the summit ridge. In mid-June the flowers in these woods were much the same as those on the Freiberg. It was interesting to find *Anemone trifolia* on the lower slopes giving way to *A. nemorosa* higher up, but perhaps this is not so surprising when one recalls that the former plant flourishes also in warmer areas such as the northern Apennines. Above the woods, among turfy rock, were *Dryas octopetala* and cheerful orange *Senecio abrotanifolius,* and the path leads up to the edge of a great glistening white amphitheatre. It is here, in the limestone screes, that the real fun begins. The scree is packed with treasure; *Alyssum wulfenianum, Gentiana terglouensis, Petrocallis pyrenaica, Saxifraga caesia* and *S. squarrosa, Thlaspi alpinum,* and brilliant yellow *Papaver rhaeticum.* Among these were plants of even more special rarity and beauty, for here, though not yet in flower, was *Gentiana froelichii,* with an abundance of *Primula wulfeniana* interspersed with *Ranunculus traunfellneri*—a local close relative (or perhaps subspecies) of *R. alpestris* with deeply cut leaves—and another special glory, *Saxifraga burserana.* This neat and beautiful Kabschia is variable in the wild as in the garden. On the Hoch Obir you may find all the 'minors', 'majors', 'glorias', 'crenatas' and so on of nurserymen's lists, but not

173

'sulphurea', for this I believe is not to be found in the wild, and is suspected of being a hybrid.

I returned to the Hoch Obir some years later in mid-August, and all the fun and beauty were still there. This time the woods were scented with warm pine resin and the sweetness of *Cyclamen purpurascens* and there were *Dianthus sylvestris*, *Digitalis grandiflora*, *Epipactis atrorubens* and, on the rocks beyond the woods, *Gentiana cruciata*, *Campanula thyrsoides*, *Saxifraga crustata*, *Potentilla clusiana* and pink-tinged *Silene alpestris*. On the screes *Gentiana froelichii* was now in flower—a most beautiful plant with neat narrow shining leaves and flowers of soft diaphanous Cambridge blue, with a delicacy of appearance (and alas of constitution too) lacking in the great alpine bell-gentians. I found a campanula which I think was *C. pulla*. It is a wonderful mountain, in shape as well as in its flowers. Roger-Smith visited it from Klagenfurt, and it took him two days. He spent the night at the mountain hut between the Hoch and the Kleiner Obir—a hut which I believe is now destroyed.

The main Karawanken ridge is readily reached from Zell Pfarre by following the little road (there is a small toll to pay) to a hunting lodge and the Koschutnik-haus—a 'Natur-Fremdenhaus'. From here a path runs eastward under the Koschuta ridge, at first through spruce and a few pines where, in August, *Gentiana asclepiadea* was superb, then on to white north-facing screes where were *Papaver rhaeticum*, *Thlaspi rotundifolium* and *Hutchinsia alpina*. There are great boulders thrown down from above, and these carried *Rhodothamnus chamaecistus* and, on a north face, overhanging, with little if any direct sun at any time, the finest *Campanula zoysii* I have ever seen. Colossal domes and mats of *Potentilla clusiana* shone white with flower in the shade under the north-facing cliff where it joined the scree. To reach the crest, where the only evidence that it is a national frontier is a great sign saying '*Staatsgrensen*', it is necessary to climb a steep gully, probably 200 feet high. There is an abundance of red paint-blobs to show the way, but it is no walk. At one point I found a beautiful white *Campanula cochlearifolia* tickling my nose!

Up on the ridge, in the sunshine, there is *Androsace villosa*, *Dianthus monspessulanus sternbergii*, *Veronica aphylla* and, once again, lovely *Gentiana froelichii*. The peak of Koschutnikturm (2136 m.) is easily reached from here. The sheer drop is behind you as you look down upon the gentler slopes into Jugoslavia, and somehow you have to get down that gully again.

Around Vienna

A part of Austria which we have never visited is the extreme northeast, in the neighbourhood of Vienna. There is a most interesting account of this area by Roger Facer in *Bulletin* Vol. 44, p. 325. He writes of the coming together here of the flowers of the Alps, of

Eurasia, of Central Europe, and of South-East Europe; and mentions, among many other plants to be found in the area, *Iris pumila, Adonis vernalis, Pulsatilla pratensis, Campanula sibirica, C. pulla, Dianthus pontederae, Primula clusiana, Soldanella austriaca, Cortusa matthioli, Viola alpina* and *Dianthus alpinus*. It sounds a most rewarding area to visit, and any member thinking of doing so will do well to read Mr. Facer's account.

Austria in the *Bulletin:*

18, 315 Jukes, E. H. T.
   Oetztal
19, 89 Cadney, G. Oetztal
21, 93 Gibson, A. G. C.
   Zimba, Lünersee
21, 313 Wacher, H. S. Arlberg

25, 339 Comber, E. O.
   Vorarlberg
32, 260 Bacon, L. J. Carinthia
44, 325 Facer, R. North-East
   Austria

10

JUGOSLAVIA

In Jugoslavia we enter the Balkans—in many ways a new world for those whose explorations have hitherto been only in Western Europe. It is a federation of six Socialist Republics, but let it be said straight away that any apprehensions that Members may have about entering a Communist country can be dismissed. The people are as friendly and helpful in Jugoslavia as anywhere else. On the other hand there are probably more differences *within* Jugoslavia than within most European countries. This is partly a matter of geography. It is a country nearly 1000 km. long, bordering Italy and Austria in the north-west and Greece in the south-east. Many different races and cultures are brought together in the one state, and historical factors still exert their influence—Austrians and Italians, Bulgarians and Turks have all within fairly recent times been in political control of different parts of the country. Generalisations about Jugoslavia can easily be misleading.

It is a long and rather narrow country, running from north-west to south-east along the Adriatic sea, although in its most southerly part separated from that sea by Albania. Apart from the great plain to the north of Belgrade (Beograd) it is largely a mountainous country, and from these mountains three groups are selected for main consideration in this chapter; the Julian Alps in Slovenia, the mountains of Montenegro lying north of Albania, and the Macedonian mountains in the south.

The visitor from England has a choice of routes, all of which (apart from flying to Belgrade or sailing across the Adriatic from Italy) will take him first into Slovenia. The motorist is most likely to enter via Austria or Italy. The two most westerly passes from Austria are the Wurzen Pass, approached from Villach, and the Loibl tunnel from Klagenfurt, both routes converging on Ljubljana. The former is low and dull; the Loibl Pass is exciting and has been described from the Austrian side. There are at least three other frontier crossings from Austria further eastward. A traveller from Northern Italy, for instance from the Dolomites, may enter the Julian Alps (q.v.) from Tarvisio, or he may travel by the autostrada from Venice either to Gorizia, when the main road leads to Ljubljana, or through Trieste to reach the Dalmatian coast road. Another alternative for the motorist is to put his car on the train at Calais and travel with it to Villach or Ljubljana. Our own experience of this method of travel was that it was very slow, uncomfortable, expensive and left the car covered with an atrocious film of oil. Perhaps we were unlucky; it certainly saves a lot of driving. There are also car ferries from Ancona and Bari in Italy to Zadar, Split, Dubrovnik and Bar. The motorist wishing to visit Southern Jugoslavia may well prefer to fly to Beograd and hire a car there. We found this a very satisfactory arrangement for visiting Montenegro and Macedonia.

The main railway line entering Jugoslavia from the north-west runs from Villach under the Karawanken Mountains to Jesenice and Ljubljana, and there are also lines from Klagenfurt and Graz converging on Zagreb. From Italy there are railway entry points where the main roads are; from Tarvisio, Gorizia and via Trieste.

The Jugoslavian roads vary a great deal in quality. The main spinal road—the *autoput*—from Ljubljana via Belgrade, Niš and Skopje to the Greek frontier north of Thessaloníki must suffer in any comparison with European motorways. Indeed a few years ago it was atrocious, but a great deal of work has been done on it, and that small part of it on which we travelled in 1977 was of an excellent standard and this improvement is being steadily extended. There are plenty of other good roads and plenty of bad ones, particularly in the mountains. The bad ones can be very bad indeed, and it is worth making enquiries before you set out on a small mountain road (which may be the only more or less direct route through to your destination) to make sure that you will be able to get there. It should be added that there is some extremely bad driving, and road accidents seem to be commonplace.

There is an extensive network of railway lines in Northern Jugoslavia. The centre and south are rather less well-served, but nevertheless most of the main towns are connected by rail.

Language can be a problem, though (as always) less so than one might anticipate. Slovenian is the main language in the north and Macedonian in the south, and Serbo-Croat is generally understood throughout the country. In the south the Cyrillic alphabet tends to be used. English is taught as a second language in many schools, and it is always worthwhile, when any communication problems arise, to ask boldly and loudly, "Does anyone here speak English?". We have used this technique with success—and also without. In the Travel Bureaux (Kompas in the north, Putnik in the south) there may not be an English-speaking clerk, but it has been our experience that generally someone can be found who speaks English, French or German.

Hotels are less abundant in Southern than in Northern Jugoslavia, but lists are available from the Tourist Agencies and only once did we find the hotel of our choice full up. As with everything else in the country they seem to vary tremendously in their standards. Many hotels are described as 'motels', but this does not have the same significance as in England: it seems to mean little more than that there is accommodation for motorists. In some places, such as alongside the

177

lakes Ohrid and Prespa, there are large park-like areas containing a complex of hotels which are very pleasant and quiet. There are also 'Camping Hotels' which in addition to providing residential accommodation include a camp site and a restaurant.

Food, as provided in hotels, is sometimes surprising and not always in accordance with a conservative English taste. Apart from the problems of reading the menu, the dishes, so far as our experience goes, tend to be rather limited, but meat seems to be plentiful, and one certainly does not starve. We found the coffee atrocious, and it seems to be an acceptable practice to take your own dried milk and coffee powder into breakfast and ask for hot water! On one occasion we were presented with a rich soup for breakfast. Buying one's own food is always fun, and there are now self-service stores in most towns and large villages. One can run into difficulties, for example in buying bread, because the shops may be shuttered and not readily recognisable. Always, however, there is good humour, and willingness to help and oblige the visitor. One commodity which we did not succeed in obtaining was a small butane gas container for making roadside tea or coffee. One may not travel with a supply of these by plane.

Maps are a problem, in that there are not, so far as we have been able to discover, accurate large-scale maps, comparable to those of the U.K., Italy, Switzerland and Austria, for instance, to assist the walker. Small-scale motoring maps can be misleading, partly because of the rapid development of road-construction, partly because they cannot be expected to indicate the degree of negotiability of the smaller roads. We ran into trouble near the Albanian frontier because of the limitations of our map but I hasten to add that both the military and the police were very courteous and helpful. Place-names are liable to vary in their spelling on maps.

Petrol stations are sufficiently frequent on the main roads but it is as well to fill up before driving into the more remote areas. Petrol stations and car-servicing garages are two quite distinct things in Jugoslavia, and the latter are by no means frequent in the south.

In general, an awareness of the needs of tourists seems to be developing throughout the whole country and this of course especially so along the coast, in mountain areas of particular scenic beauty, in a few places where winter sports are developing, and where there are sites or buildings of special architectural or historic interest.

The flora is varied and exciting, changing dramatically as one proceeds from Slovenia, where, in the Julian Alps, there is a strong affinity with the Dolomitic flora and a considerable element of the 'basic alpine' flora, to Macedonia where the flowers are almost entirely different, resembling those of the Southern Balkans, with Asian, Caucasian and Mediterranean influences. The 'basic alpine' flora is largely lacking in Macedonia: there are plenty of flowers, but not the rich floral displays of the alpine meadows. The mountains of

Slovenia, the coastal ranges, Montenegro and Macedonia (though not, I believe, those of Bosnia) are predominantly limestone.

There are problems of plant identification in Central and Southern Jugoslavia. I know of no readily portable *Flora*, and many of the plants are not those seen in the Alps, nor indeed in our gardens. In particular we saw several beautiful blue Boraginaceous plants, probably species of anchusa, lithodora or pulmonaria, which we could not identify. They are of course in *Flora Europaea*, but that is hardly a *vade-mecum!*

Finally, in this general introduction to Jugoslavia, one should mention that it is a land of exciting birds and animals, of beautiful churches and monasteries, of Grecian and Roman sites, and of friendly people often still wearing, as their normal attire, the traditional costumes of their many races. Where but in Ohrid would you see an amiable old gentleman in Turkish dress ambling down the street fumbling his worry-beads, with a plucked rose sticking out of his mouth?

SLOVENIA

Slovenia is the most north-westerly of the six Socialist Republics of Jugoslavia. Most of it is more or less mountainous, but the highest mountains, and those which concern us here, lie to the west, north, and south-west of Ljubljana, and consist of the Julian Alps, the Kamniks and the Karst country behind Trieste. The north-westerly approaches to Jugoslavia already mentioned pass through Slovenia, and indeed mostly converge upon Ljubljana. It was at one time a part of the Austro-Hungarian Empire, and the north-west frontiers underwent change after both world wars, so that a considerable part of what is now Slovenia has within the present century been either Austrian or Italian. This is to some extent reflected in place-names (and there are some problems in localising the areas referred to by Roger-Smith and by early contributors to the *Bulletin*) as well as in culture, food and language. Slovenian is normally spoken, but some Italian and German still persist. Hotels are on the whole more frequent and better, or at any rate more akin to those of Western Europe, in Slovenia than further south. In particular in the Julian and Kamnik Alps there are many large mountain huts which are really hotels.

The flora is, as one would expect, very similar to that of the Dolomites and of Southern Carinthia, though the 'basic alpine' flora is rather less abundant. The area to be considered is almost entirely limestone, and probably largely dolomitic.

THE JULIAN ALPS (Map p. 173)

These mountains are bounded on the west by the Italian frontier and on the north by the upper valley of the Sava river, and are centred upon Triglav (2863 m.), the highest mountain in Jugoslavia, a great last outpost of the Eastern Alps.

A possible centre for visiting this area is **Bled**, which lies in the Sava valley near the main road and railway from Tarvisio to Ljubljana. It is on a lake, and is a popular tourist centre. From Bled there is fairly easy travel by road or rail to Mojstrana and to Zlatorog, which are two excellent points of attack upon the Julian Alps. Our own preference however was to get nearer in to the mountains, staying first at **Zlatorog**, a hotel (and little else) at the western end of a very beautiful lake, the Bohinjsko Jezero, lying to the south of Triglav. It is only some ten km. from the village of Bohinje Bistrica, on the railway line from Bled. The Julian Alps are a complex block, with Triglav on their northerly side, and south of Triglav there is a vast east-facing semicircle of mountains surrounding the Bohinjsko Jezero. This seems to have been the frontier with Italy at the time when Roger-Smith visited. There are wooded areas round the lake, and here in late June *Cyclamen purpurascens* abounded, and we found *Anemone trifolia*, a tiny astrantia (probably *A. carniolica*), *Cardamine kitaibelii, Epipactis atrorubens, Cephalanthera rubra*, and by the roadsides attractive *Scorzonera purpurea rosea* and *Dorycnium pentaphyllum germanicum*—and Roger-Smith reported *Hacquetia epipactis*.

South of Bohinje is Crna Prst (1844 m.), a mountain and pass on the old frontier, and this is one of the classical sites for beautiful silver-leaved *Geranium argenteum*. The great semicircle of the Julian Alps is in fact a double one, two more or less parallel curved ridges enclosing between them the high hanging valley of Komna, a National Park, containing a series of lakes (the Seven Lakes of Triglav) and also several mountain hotels. This is a fine area to visit, and it can be reached by a good, very steep, path from the Hotel Zlatorog. The path climbs through woods, where, in addition to the plants found lower down, there are *Cephalanthera longifolia, Cardamine trifolia, Clematis alpina* and abundant *Lilium carniolicum*. The Komna valley, like all the area, is of limestone, and on a sunny day it glows harshly white. Nevertheless there is plenty of vegetation. The two outstanding plants (by now old friends) are *Gentiana clusii*, in a superb form, and masses of the wholly charming rose-coloured *Rhodothamnus chamaecistus*. There are *Genista radiata* and, on the snow-patched screes, *Anemone baldensis* and *Ranunculus traunfellneri*.

The main peak of Triglav can be reached from Komna, but it is a long way from Zlatorog and one could not do it in a single day and look for flowers as well. The most direct approaches are from the north-east, from Mojstrana in the Sava valley. A better centre however is **Kranjska Gora**, higher up the valley and not far from the Italian frontier. Mojstrana is readily accessible by either road or rail from Kranjska Gora, and the latter place has the advantage of more hotels and of giving access to the Vršic Pass and thence to the Trenta valley and the Italian frontier mountains.

The Sava valley is beautiful and overhung by the fine Karawanken mountains on its northern flank and the even more spectacular mass of Triglav and the Julian Alps to its south. We stayed in a small modern hotel in Kranjska Gora—one which we later came to regard as rather typical of Jugoslavia, cheerful, fairly clean, well-equipped, but in poor repair.

From Mojstrana three more or less parallel valleys run up to Triglav. The Vrata valley carries a negotiable road to a mountain hotel, the Aljažev Dom (1015 m.), near the foot of the stupendous northern face of Triglav. It is a beautiful wooded valley, where we found abundant *Moneses uniflora*, and *Arctostaphylos uva-ursi*. In the stream-bed were masses of *Saxifraga squarrosa*, like an even more compact form of *S. caesia*, and the scented fringed pink *Dianthus monspessulanus sternbergii*, together with *Aster alpinus*, *Senecio abrotanifolius*, *Silene alpestris*, *Teucrium montanum*, and *Cyclamen purpurascens*. Some of these seemed oddly out of place in the shingle, and the cyclamen in particular produced odd irregular tubers (some deep, some on the surface) just as do potatoes grown in stony ground. A good path runs from the Dom, at first up the side of the stream-bed where in June there was only a small trickle, and *Campanula zoysii*, washed down from above, grew in the shingle. After crossing the valley the path climbs very steeply up to the Staniceva Koća (2332 m.), a mountain hut on the shoulder of Triglav. It is not as difficult as one might expect, looking at the great sheer wall, because there are steps cut in the rock, with pitons and wire ropes. There are plenty of lovely flowers, but I found no new ones apart from a white flax which was probably a form of *Linum perenne alpinum*. The summit on 27th June was completely under snow, but others, going later, have reported hybrids of *Saxifraga caesia* and *S. squarrosa*, *Ranunculus glacialis* growing in peat pockets over the dolomite, and *Eritrichium nanum*.

From Kranjska Gora a road runs southward to the Vršic Pass, crossing one of the main spurs of the Julian Alps and leading over and down to the Trenta valley (the valley of the River Soca). Above the pass there are great gaunt white screes where are beautiful *Thlaspi rotundifolium*, *Papaver rhaeticum*, *Petrocallis pyrenaica*, *Alyssum ovirense*, *Potentilla clusiana* and *P. nitida*. On the south side of the pass, above Na Logu, is the Alpinetum Julijanum, which at the time of our visit was well cared for and fairly well stocked, and from here there is a fine drive down the Trenta valley to Bovec. From this little town one may visit the frontier mountains north of the Predil Pass, and also drive southward to the Karst country behind Trieste. To do either of these things from Kranjska Gora involves a very long day, since the road over the Vršic Pass is rather slow, steep, twisting and poorly surfaced. Consequently we found it advantageous to stay on the south side of the pass at Na Logu, where there is a satisfactory hotel. Near here, on our way down to Bovec, we found *Aquilegia kitaibelii*, a charming plant closely similar to *A. einseleana*, and *Senecio integrifolia aurantiacus*.

From near Bovec, the main road runs north to the Predil (or Predel) Pass into Italy, and just below the pass a small road winds north-eastward, running under the frontier ridge, towards Mangart (2678 m.). This is a most rewarding drive. The road is steep and roughish, with magnificent scenery, and leads to an alpine hut at 2072 m., whence one can climb to the summit. When we were there, on 24th June, the road was still closed by snow, but we climbed up to the frontier ridge, where the views into Italy were stupendous, and the flowers on this wonderful limestone ridge included *Rhodothamnus*

Campanula cespitosa

chamaecistus, *Primula auricula*, *Linum perenne alpinum*, *Saxifraga burserana*, *Potentilla nitida* (one clump had edelweiss flowering through it), *Saxifraga caesia* and *S. crustata*, *Paederota bonarota* and *P. lutea* and the hybrid between them, *Petrocallis pyrenaica*, *Campanula zoysii* (not yet in flower), a beautiful dwarf form of *Dianthus sylvestris* (? subsp. *tergestinus*) and an abundance of *Eritrichium nanum*. Here, as in the Dolomites, the eritrichium grew in humus-packed crevices or in turf lying thinly over the limestone and was, I think, a little less intense in colour than on, for instance, the acid rocks of the Pordoi. I revisited the ridge some years later on 20th August. At this time *Campanula zoysii* was in fine and full flower, and also the rather attractive and distinct little *C. cespitosa*, widespread in scree and even in roadside grit, and looking like a *C. cochlearifolia* that had decided to take a tip from *C. zoysii* and shut its mouth —though in fact its basal leaves are quite distinct from either of those two species. *C. cochlearifolia* and *C. scheuchzeri* were also abundant here in August.

THE KARST COUNTRY

Along the east side of the Gulf of Trieste, a little inland from the coast, there is an interesting area of low limestone hills. Eliot Hodgkin visited these both in May and in early July (*Bulletin*

Vol. 22, p. 349 and 26, p. 9) making for Mt. Vremsica on the first occasion and Nanos the second time. He recorded here *Polygala nicaeensis* (probably subsp. *carniolica*), *Gentiana tergestina* (a large flowered subspecies of *G. verna* with winged calyces—the *G. verna angulosa* of gardens, but not the true *angulosa*, which is not European), *Chamaecytisus purpureus* including white-flowered forms, *Pulsatilla montana*, *Helleborus dumetorum*, two crocuses, *Chamaespartium sagittale* and *Lilium bulbiferum* among many other plants, Mrs. Hecker also visited Nanos (*Bulletin* Vol. 31, p. 238), in late July, and mentioned *Campanula versicolor*, *C. pyramidalis* and *Centaurea rupestris* among others. We went to the Karst in late June from Na Logu (rather a long day) travelling via Bovec, Tolmin, Lokve and Ajdovscina, and returning by the faster road through Nova Gorica. It is a pleasant journey, through interesting country. On the limestone ridges of Nanos we found three flaxes, *Linum tenuifolium*, *L. flavum* and *L. viscosum* all in the same vicinity, *Onosma echioides*, *Lilium carniolicum*, *Gladiolus illyricus*, *Gentiana lutea*, *G. utriculosa*, *Inula hirta* and *Scabiosa graminifolia*. This is a pleasant change from the high rugged mountains of the Julian Alps. A more direct approach would be from Ljubljana via Postojna, famed for its vast limestone caves.

THE KAMNIK ALPS

The Kamniks lie to the east of the Julian Alps, and between Ljubljana and the Karawanken Mountains. As would be expected, they carry a flora very similar to that of these two ranges, particularly the latter, but they are scenically attractive and are a popular tourist area, and there are several mountain hotels among them. There are accounts of visits to the Kamnik Alps in the *Bulletin* (Vol. 31, p. 238 and Vol. 32, p. 129), but neither these accounts nor our own brief visit there at the end of June suggest that as regards plants they have much to offer that is not to be found in the Julian Alps or the Karawanken. Our own visit took us from Ljubljana via Kamnik and the Crnilec Pass to the Savinja valley and thence to the alpine hut at **Logarska** where we stayed the night, and we also travelled northward from Kamnik to the Kamniško Sedlo (saddle). These two routes in fact converge upon the same point, close to the Austrian frontier. The journeys were (in 1966) along very narrow and badly surfaced roads, in wooded valleys, with pleasant scenery. At the Kamniško Sedlo the views are very fine, and here again *Eritrichium nanum* was abundant, growing on the limestone.

It would be wrong to leave the impression that the Kamniks are florally dull. As so often, it is a question of where you go first, and a visitor to this area who had not been previously among the flowers in the Julian or Karawanken mountains would indeed find the Kamniks exciting, as well as scenically beautiful.

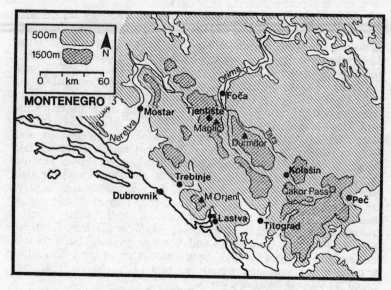

MONTENEGRO (CRNA GORA)

Montenegro lies immediately north of Albania, with a short stretch of Adriatic coast. One approach to it is from the north-west, along the Dalmatian coast—a route which passes the Velebit Mountains, north of Zadar. We have not travelled this way, but there is an interesting account by Brian Mathew and Christopher Grey-Wilson in the *Bulletin* (Vol. 39, p. 197). There seems to be an affinity between the Velebit plants and those of the Karst country further north (see p. 182), but in particular the climate and situation are such that it is a rich area for autumnal and early spring flowering bulbs, including *Colchicum bivonae, Crocus dalmaticus, C. reticulatus* and *C. cartwrightianus sativus.* Among other plants mentioned are *Iris pallida, Globularia meridionalis, Cyclamen repandum* and *Digitalis lanata.*

A little inland from the Montenegran coast is a ridge of limestone hills centred upon Orjen (1895 m.), and this is a most interesting area. The small road winding along the ridge from Trebinje to Risan is in places very rough going indeed. This ridge road can be reached from the coast road at Gruda, south of **Dubrovnik**. The latter is a fascinating town, and would be a good base from which to visit these hills. We ourselves stayed at **Lastva**, a few miles east of Trebinje, in a delightful and fascinating old country house. One of the most brilliant flowers in the roadside cliffs at lower levels in May in this area is *Moltkia petraea*, putting up a far better show than it usually manages in an English garden. In the hills we found *Anemone apennina* in flower, a beautiful yellow flax (probably one

184

of the *Linum flavum* complex), an abundance of orchids, including *Ophrys scolopax cornuta, Orchis morio, O. pallens* and *Traunsteinera globosa*, and a fine display of delightful *Scilla litardierei* (*pratensis*). There were leaves of crocuses (Mathew and Grey-Wilson mention that *C. malyi* and *C. vernus montenegrinus* grow here), of colchicum (probably *C. hungaricum*), of iris (*I.? pumila*), of *Cyclamen hederifolium* and, just past flowering, *Helleborus multifidus*.

If one travels to Montenegro from Beograd one drives through a magnificent land of woodlands and river gorges, passing between high mountains and among fantastic limestone ridges and *causses*. At Foca the main road divides, one branch going on to Dubrovnik and one to Titograd. The former traverses a National Park containing the mountains of Maglić and Volujak, the road running through a gorge, the Sutjeska-Schlucht. There are hotels at **Foca**, and one at **Tjentiste**. Most of the Park lies to the south-east of the main road, and a small road runs into it, but we were debarred from entering it by car. We did how-

Isopyrum thalictroides

ever drive into the north-west side. It was a bad road, but ran through beautiful scenery and there were many interesting flowers. In the woods we found *Asarum europaeum, Cardamine kitaibelii, Cephalanthera longifolia, Corydalis bulbosa* and *C. ochroleuca, Erythronium dens-canis* (just setting its seed in May), *Isopyrum thalictroides, Lathraea squamaria* and *Paris quadrifolia*. In more open and rocky places the leaves of *Iris sintenisii* and *Crocus vernus vernus* (*heuffelianus*) were seen.

The Titograd road runs between this National Park and another centred upon Durmitor (2522 m.). We did not visit this area, but Mr. and Mrs. Barrett (*Bulletin* Vol. 37, p. 142) travelled there from Nikšić (a rather uncomfortable bus-ride) and stayed at the hotel at **Zabliac**. It is clear from his account that it is a very attractive area scenically, and contains some interesting flowers, though unfortunately it was excessively grazed. The flowers included *Fritillaria messanensis gracilis, Armeria maritima alpina, Linum capitatum, Veronica prostrata, Viola calcarata zoysii* and *Potentilla clusiana*.

Another area of special interest is the Cakor Pass, lying on the boundary between Montenegro and southern Serbia. It is reached, albeit by a very circuitous route, from Titograd via Kolašin and Andrijevica. The main road from Titograd to Kolašin is magnificent, following the gorges of the River Moraca. Here was *Moltkia petraea* again, and among the lovely purple salvias that coloured the roadside banks was a fine white form. *Dictamnus albus* was also white here (despite its name the form with purplish-red flowers seems to be rather commoner), and the odd and attractive pomegranate (*Punica granatum*). There is a 'Motel' on the main road at **Kolasin**, conveniently placed but rather grubby, and from here a mountain road crosses the Trešnjevik Pass to Andrijevica. Judging by accounts we were given of the road it is probably better to take the longer route round by Ivangrad, which is another beautiful drive. The Cakor Pass lies between Murino and Pec. The road is steep and twisting, and rather rough in places, but adequate, and we found many beautiful flowers, some of which we could not identify. Under the roadside trees on the lower slopes were the yellow *Anemone ranunculoides* and snowdrops (*Galanthus nivalis*), and in the turf between the woods magnificent lady orchids (*Orchis purpurea*), two species of polygala (one of them with fine large blue-purple flowers was probably *P. major*), *Scilla bifolia*, *Primula veris columnae* and *P. elatior*. These two last are part of the alpine flora too, and here as in the Alps they were growing at the edge of the retreating snow on the 8th May. Also by the edge of the snow, and again recalling the Alps, were crocuses, but here they were *C. vernus vernus*. There were beautiful large violas, some yellow and some a good carmine-red. We also failed to identify these; there are more than a dozen species of alpine 'pansy' in southern Jugoslavia. But of all the flowers on the Cakor Pass the most brilliant was the spring gentian. There are few alpine plants more widespread in Europe than *Gentiana verna*. Centred on the Alps, it extends to Northern England and to the Arctic, to the Sierra Nevada in Southern Spain, and away through the Balkans to Greece and Turkey. But the eastern forms are special. We have already met subsp. *tergestina*, with its winged calyces, in the Karst country in northern Jugoslavia, and here it is again on the Cakor Pass with huge flowers (some were a measured 5 cm. across) with no loss in the deep brilliance of their colouring. Up on the pass itself it was cold and snowing but not so heavily as to prevent us from visiting the screes above. Here was a plant new to us in the wild, *Androsace hedraeantha*, like a very beautiful, slightly enlarged, rather broader-leaved *A. carnea* with rose-pink and white flowered plants in about equal numbers. It was growing among bilberry plants straggling through the turfy scree, and it seems that this limited area is either of acidic rock (it appeared shaly) or, if the underlying rock is limestone, it is either leached out or heavily overlain with acid soil. There were outcrops of what seemed to be hard limestone, and here was a fine-leaved edraianthus (*E. tenuifolius*) not yet in flower, characteristically a limestone plant. We also found by the roadside on the pass an especially beautiful and distinct blue-flowered lithodora (or one of the allied genera) which we could not identify. Mathew and Grey-Wilson recorded here *Corydalis ochroleuca* and *C. bulbosa marschalliana*, a cream-flowered form.

Driving eastward from the pass we enter Serbia, and yet again drive through fine limestone gorges to Pec, a town which is now both cleaner and duller than when Roger-Smith described it. Here we found a satisfactory hotel for a night's stay before driving southward to Prizren on the northern side of the Šar Planina, a mountain range that forms part of the border between Serbia and Macedonia.

MACEDONIA

The ancient kingdom of Macedonia comprised what is now the southernmost Socialist Republic in Jugoslavia, Northern Greece and I believe a bit of Bulgaria too, and modern Jugoslavian Macedonia has mountain frontiers with Albania, Greece and Bulgaria. The change-over from alpine to Balkan flowers, which we have been witnessing as we have travelled southward through Jugoslavia, is here almost complete. Macedonia is not only more southerly, it is more influenced by the warm Adriatic and Aegean seas, and plants from the lower levels are not reliably hardy in English gardens.

THE ŠAR PLANINA

This range of mountains, running north-eastward from Mt. Korab (2764 m.), which is on the Albanian frontier, to Mt. Ljuboten (2499 m.), forms part of the northern border of Macedonia. There is access to the hills from the small town of **Tetovo**. This is a popular tourist and winter sports area, and the one place where we did not manage to secure a room in the hotel. There is a cable railway from Tetovo up into the hills at Popova Šapka (1750 m.), a winter sports centre where there are mountain hotels.

An early account of a visit to these mountains is to be found in the *Bulletin* (Vol. 11, p. 30) where the Rev. H. P. Thompson told of his travels in Macedonia in June 1937. On the Popova Šapka (even then a ski resort) he found *Geranium cinereum subcaulescens*, that most startlingly coloured of all Balkan flowers, and *Crocus scardicus*, *Soldanella hungarica*, *Primula elatior intricata*, *Saxifraga marginata*, *Hutchinsia alpina brevicaulis*, *Sempervivum macedonicum* and *Edraianthus graminifolius*. On Ljuboten, Thompson found also *Thlaspi bellidifolium*, *Saxifraga sempervivum*, *Gagea peduncularis*, *Viola grisebachiana* and *Lilium carniolicum albanicum*. Roger-Smith also visited Ljuboten, reporting *Bruckenthalia spiculifolia* (an ericaceous plant, suggesting that in places there is acid soil over the limestone) and an attractive dianthus which may have been *D. scardicus*. More recently (*Bulletin* Vol. 39, p. 190) Mathew and Grey-Wilson found yellow and blue forms of *Iris pumila*, and *Scutellaria orientalis*. It is clearly a rich area.

Mt. Korab is now inaccessible to the plant seeker, and indeed so is the whole of mountainous Albania. This is unfortunate, for it appears to be a most interesting country for its flowers. Roger-Smith referred

187

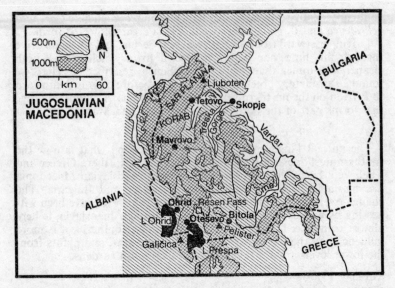

to rich alpine meadows on Mt. Korab, and special plants included *Androsace hedraeantha*, *Ranunculus wettsteinii* and the white-flowered *Edraianthus graminifolius niveus*. Dr. and Mrs. Giuseppi visited Albania, not without discomfort and perhaps some danger, and found among other rare plants *Wulfenia baldaccii* and *Convolvulus boissieri compactus* (*Bulletin* Vol. 3, p. 7).

From Tetovo a good road runs southward through Gostivar to **Mavrovo** on the lake (now enlarged as a reservoir) of that name. It is an attractive area and much of it is a National Park. We spent a few days in a 'Motel' by the lake, finding it adequate if a little unedifying. The lake itself is beautiful, and from its western end the Debar road runs through a gorge, the Volkovija Schlucht. Here were *Saxifraga sempervivum* and either a form of the variable *S. marginata* or the closely related *S. scardica*, *Alyssum saxatile*, *A. ovirense*, *Achillea ageratifolia* (widespread and variable in Southern Jugoslavia), and *Jovibarba heuffelii*, but the most colourful plant we saw in the gorge was an annual, *Malcolmia angulifolia* or *M. illyrica*. Mathew and Grey-Wilson reported also *Ramonda serbica* from this area. In meadows by the river, *Narcissus poeticus radiiflorus* was just coming into flower on the 9th May, and there were small colchicum leaves (*C. ? hungaricum*) and orange-yellow *Lathyrus laevigatus*. We found a small road branching off northward to the village of Nicpur, and took it, and it led us up into the hills. Here were many of the lovely flowers already recorded, masses of the widespread and variable *Chamaecytisus hirsutus*, lady orchids, leaves of a campanula which was probably *C. versicolor*, and, higher up among the turf and rocks, *Gentiana verna* (both 'winged' and 'unwinged') and the leaves of

188

Sternbergia colchiciflora, which has such squinny-petalled flowers that it sometimes does not bother to open them above ground at all. The road got progressively higher and worse, and it was here that we finally found ourselves at some sort of army outpost (probably on the slopes of Mt. Korab) and were politely but firmly escorted back to Mavrovo.

To the south of Mavrovo is a mountain (Bistra, 2102 m.), and a new road for winter sportsmen runs up on to its lower slopes. Here we found purple crocuses (probably *C. veluchensis*) flowering at the edge of the snow, *Saxifraga marginata, Daphne oleoides*, red *Geum coccineum, Iberis saxatilis, Pinguicula leptoceras* and leaves of a lily (probably *L. carniolicum albanicum*) and of other plants not yet in flower—*Gentiana cruciata, Geranium cinereum subcaulescens* and various crocuses. Two other wide-spread plants, both particularly beautiful in the Mavrovo area, were the blue *Ajuga genevensis* and the rose-flowered, delicate-leaved *Geranium tuberosum*.

Geranium tuberosum

OHRID, GALICICA AND PRESPA

From Mavrovo a fairly good fast road runs via Kicevo to **Ohrid** (Ochrid) on the lake of that name, which is shared with Albania. It lies in a warm valley, and this was reflected in the animals and birds we saw as well as the flowers. Large tortoises lumber around and on the roads they all too often suffer the fate of hedgehogs on the roads in England. Lizards abound, especially a stout 25 cm. brilliant emerald-green fellow with a blue throat. Nightingales, common throughout Jugoslavia, are even commoner here, and there are brilliant bee-eaters and roller birds. Two attractive yellow-flowered plants by the roadside as we drove to Ohrid were *Linaria peloponnesiaca* and *Scutellaria orientalis*. Ohrid, an ancient cultural centre, is a fascinating mixture of old and new, and even the most dedicated flower-seeker should take time off to visit the old town. An intriguing feature of one straight narrow street was to find several men by the roadside equipped to weigh and measure the passer-by. There are several hotels in the newer part of the town, but those which we saw looked very cosmopolitan and expensive, and we drove to **Gorica** on a headland by the lakeside a few miles south of Ohrid. Here there is a hotel complex, and one may secure accommodation at a moderate price to a moderate standard in a modern hotel, with only nightingales to disturb one's sleep.

The lakeside road continues southward through Peštani, crossing rocky headlands where the beautiful *Convolvulus althaeoides tenuissimus*, *Ajuga chamaepitys chia*, an attractive mullein (*Verbascum* ? *undulatum*) and the cheerful little sugar-pink annual *Crepis rubra* grow. There were orchids too by the roadside in May, including the odd little *Ophrys scolopax cornuta*, with a pair of large curved forward-pointing spikes on each flower. In early June *Limodorum abortivum* appears, and *Himantoglossum hircinum calcaratum*, a Balkan relative of the lizard orchid but a more delicate and beautiful plant whose flowers are predominantly rosy-pink. The road goes on to the southern end of the lake where on the Albanian frontier is the fine old monastery church of Sveti Naum, a great tourist attraction. It lies at the foot of Galicica, a mountain mainly in Albania. To the north of Galicica, in Jugoslavia, is an outlying peak called on one of our maps 'Goga' (1737 m.), a name which we have not found on other maps and which did not seem to be known locally, but Goga it is to us. A good road climbs steeply from Trpejca, just south of Peštani, to cross the col between Galicica and Goga. We have twice driven up to this col and climbed Goga, and a most rewarding area it is. By the roadside we found a plant quite new to us, *Erodium guicciardii*, with finely cut silvery leaves like those of *E. chrysanthum* and carmine flowers, a beautiful, hardy and excellent garden plant. The violas here were wonderful too. We called them *V. dacica* but with no great certainty. They were neat plants with large flowers which, on separate plants, were violet, clear strong yellow, white or cream. Up on the pass we found a very attractive anchusa with low spreading sprays of brilliant blue flowers. It has been named for us as *A. macedonica*, but it is a soundly perennial plant. A surprising find was the lovely *Vicia onobrychioides*, which we had last seen at Vinadio in North-West Italy. Among the rocks were two daphnes, not yet in flower. One was certainly *D. oleoides*, the other probably *D. alpina*. Above the pass, on Goga, at our first visit were many lovely flowers; *Centaurea pindicola*, *Colchicum* ? *hungaricum*, *Crocus chrysanthus* and *C. sieberi*, a very large-flowered ornithogalum (*O.* ? *montanum*), *Saxifraga marginata* (including some beautiful rosy-flowered forms), *S. scardica* and possibly *S. spruneri*, and *Sempervivum ciliosum*. On the occasion of our first visit, in early June 1970, the crocuses were flowering and the top of the mountain was under snow. Oddly, when we visited in mid-May in 1977 the ridge was clear of snow and the crocuses and saxifrages were at the end of their flowering. Elsewhere in Macedonia we had found the flowers less advanced in May than on our June visit, as we expected. We can only suppose that in 1970 there had been a late snow-fall on Goga which had held the flowers back; such are the freaks and mysteries of seeking flowers in the mountains!

In 1977 on Goga we found fritillaries in flower, little reddish-brown chaps with almost spherical bells only about two centimetres across. There were many other flowers. *Prunus prostrata* made a good show, *Euphorbia myrsinites*, *Asphodeline liburnica*, *Draba* ? *tomentosa*, the leaves of *Sternbergia colchiciflora*, *Dianthus gracilis armerioides* (with neat glaucous cushions and cherry-red yellow-backed flowers) and *Edraianthus tenuifolius*. Mathew and Grey-Wilson reported *Astragalus baldaccii*, *Arabis caucasica* and *Thymus cherlerioides*.

The road on the eastern side of the pass at first zigzags down among rocks where we found the attractive and unusual, yellow-flowered *Haplophyllum boissieranum*, a relative of the rues, plum-coloured *Lychnis viscaria atropurpurea*, and *Hypericum rumeliacum*. Lower, the road runs through woodland, where there were leaves of crocuses and of *Iris sintenisii*, before dropping down to Oteševo on Lake Prespa, another beautiful lake at a higher level than Ohrid, and shared between Jugoslavia, Albania and Greece.

At **Otesevo** there is a hotel complex by the lakeside. Storks and pretty white egrets feed by the lake, and at its northern end there is a vast marshy area which was rosy-purple with thousands of beautiful *Orchis laxiflora*. From here the road continues eastward over the Resen Pass to Bitola. This pass can also be reached from Ohrid via Kosel and Resen, and the round trip is a pleasant day's drive. The Resen Pass (1181 m.) is unspectacular but pleasant and interesting. It crosses a ridge of hills extending northward from Pelister (2532 m.) which separates Lake Prespa from the wide river valley in which lies Bitola. There is another pretty and distinct viola on the Resen Pass, dwarf forms of *Chamaecytisus hirsutus*, and we found the leaves of *Crocus pulchellus*. In June, *Scorzonera purpurea rosea* was in flower.

PELISTER AND BITOLA TO SKOPJE

Bitola is a town of some size, though in 1977 there was only one hotel, which was new, large, adequately comfortable and less expensive than it looked. The town, only some 16 km. from the Greek frontier, is in a wide and pleasant plain, with attractive hills to the east and impressive Pelister (2532 m.) to the west. At the edge of the town is Heraklea, an interesting Graeco-Roman site which is being steadily uncovered.

Pelister is clearly Roger-Smith's 'Peristeri', though he put it to the north of the town, and the spelling 'Peristeri' can lead to confusion with the mountain of that name near Metsovon in Greek Macedonia. It is a National Park, and a fine mountain. It is semi-circular, facing north, and there is a dead-end road leading up to some villages in the fold of the mountain. This road, to be avoided if one's objective is to drive as high as possible, is a left-hand turn off the 'main' road, which continues as a fine and interesting drive up the western shoulder. There is ski-ing here, and a little above the end of the road a small mountain hotel. There is a marked path to the summit—or rather a series of red rings. Indeed there is not always a clear path, but if the Gods of Pelister love you, you may be adopted at the hotel by a small shaggy dog who knows the way perfectly and in return for a share of your lunch will guide you and nibble your ankles if you go too slowly. Among the flowers by the path side are *Geranium cinereum subcaulescens*, the same attractive viola (possibly *V. orphanidis*) as on the Resen Pass, *Fritillaria pontica*, and higher up *Crocus veluchensis*, *Lilium carniolicum albanicum*, *Jovibarba heuffelii* and, in the shade of rocks among the screes near the summit, a mossy saxifrage, *S. pedemontana cymosa*. Two other plants mentioned by Roger-Smith as growing on Pelister were *Ranunculus crenatus* and *Dianthus myrtinervius*, while Trevan and Whitehead (*Bulletin* Vol. 42, p. 302) reported also the purple-flowered *Centaurea napulifera* and *Gentiana punctata*. This last is one of the infrequent links in Macedonia with the flora of the Central Alps. Pelister is a laborious mountain to climb in its upper reaches—a vast jumble of huge boulders—but the views across Southern Jugoslavia are magnificent.

From Bitola it is a fine drive to Skopje, the capital of Jugoslavian Macedonia, first crossing the fertile plain of Bitola to Prilep. From here there is a smaller, interesting-looking road going across the hills to Titov Veles, but we followed the main road over the Pletvar Pass (990 m.) because we wished to visit the classical site at Stobi. This pass is through knobbly jumbled mountains where Prilep marble is quarried, and here were some very lovely flowers, tending to be 'Mediterranean' in type—*Convolvulus cantabrica*, *Linum tenuifolium* and an exceedingly beautiful annual blue flax, a yellow centaurium, *Onosma* ? *echioides* and *Stachys iva*. Beyond the pass the road runs through limestone gorges, and here we saw what was perhaps the most striking plant of our visits to Macedonia —the huge-belled powder-blue *Campanula formanekiana*, spread tightly against the faces of a limestone crevice. How incomparably finer it seemed than the upright white-flowered forms that we see on the show bench! Giuseppi introduced this plant, around 1930 I believe, and there is an account of it in Vol. 1 of the *Bulletin* (p. 110).

The classical site at **Stobi,** some 30 km. south of Titov Veles on the *autoput*, is well worth visiting for its own sake. It was here that we first encountered *Haplophyllum boissieranum*, an attractive species and a complete puzzle to us at the time. There is a small but adequate hotel near by. At Titov Veles there is reported to be a roadside stone bank smothered with *Ramonda nathaliae*. We ourselves did not find it here; the roaring traffic demanded all our attention. From this town a road runs eastward to the Bulgarian frontier, and Thompson (*Bulletin* Vol. 11, p. 30) explored this area but found it florally dull. Solunska (ca. 2300 m.), to the west of Titov Veles and south of Skopje, was visited both by Thompson and by Giuseppi. It sounds an interesting area; they found *Ramonda nathaliae*, *Viola grise-*

192

A high alpine meadow,
Col du Lautaret, French Alps (p. 100)

Photo:
D. Holford

Pulsatilla alpina in seed,
with Jungfrau, Bernese Oberland

Photo: C. Baron

194

Androsace vandellii,
near Zermatt, Canton Valais (p. 38)

Photo: D. Holford

Gentiana clusii,
near Zermatt, Canton Valais

Photo: D. Holford

Primula hirsuta,
Bernina Pass, Engadine (p. 44)

Photo: R. Elliott

Gentiana punctata,
Flüela Pass, Engadine

Photo: G. D. Dawson

Crocus vernus,
Sella Pass, Dolomites (p. 60)

Photo: D. Holford

The Cimon della Pala,
Dolomites (p. 61)

Photo: G. D. Dawson

Anemone narcissiflora,
Gran Sasso, Abruzzi

Photo: D. Holford

198

University of Grenoble alpine garden,
Col du Lautaret (p. 100)

Photo: M. G. Hodgman

Saxifraga callosa,
Alpes Maritimes (p. 103)

199   *Photos: D. Holford*

Primula marginata,
Alpes Maritimes (p. 104)

Narcissus poeticus,
Eastern Pyrenees

Photo: *D. Holford*

200

Antirrhinum molle,
on limestone cliffs, E. Pyrenees (p. 116)

Photo: *M. G. Hodgman*

Gentiana pyrenaica,
Eastern Pyrenees (p. 118)

Photos: D. Holford

Ramonda myconi,
Western Pyrenees (p. 124)

Narcissus requienii,
Western Pyrenees (p. 126)

Photo: *D. Holford*

202

Narcissus pseudonarcissus ssp. *nobilis,*
Col du Pourtalet, Western Pyrenees

Photo: *M. G. Hodgman*

Crocus nevadensis,
Sierra Nevada (p. 150)

Photos: D. Holford

Ophrys lutea,
Andalusia (p. 152)

Leucanthemopsis alpina,
Hintertux, Austria

Photos: D. Holford

Doronicum grandiflorum,
Turracher Höhe, Austria

Helleborus niger and *Daphne mezereum*
near Berchtesgarten, Bavarian Alps

Photo: W. Schacht

Campanula formanekiana,
Jugoslavian Macedonia (p. 192)

Photos: L. J. Bacon

Potentilla nitida,
Julian Alps (p. 181)

Iris pumila var. *attica*,
Southern Greece (p. 223)

Photos: D. Holford

Anemone coronaria,
Southern Greece (p. 227)

Daphne arbuscula,
Muran Hills, Czechoslovakia

Photo: J. Starek

208

Dianthus callizonus,
Romania (p. 253)

Photo: W. Schacht

bachiana, Saxifraga scardica, S. spruneri, Delphinium fissum and *Tulipa boeotica.*

Skopje is now a city of modern buildings, largely rebuilt since it was destroyed by an earthquake in 1963. We found a pleasant 'Camping Hotel' on the Tetovo road close to the entrance to the Treska Gorge. This is famed for its flowers, though these have perhaps been reduced (or at any rate the scene has been changed) since the Treska was dammed to provide hydro-electric power for Skopje. One can drive to the mouth of the gorge, where there is a monastery with XIVth Century frescoes, and then there is a twisting little footpath along the northern wall of what is now a long narrow sinuous lake, with magnificent cliffs falling into it on either side. Photography unfortunately is forbidden. Here is *Ramonda nathaliae,* coming into flower in late May; on the south-east-facing stone some of it was shaded by scrub of box, lilac, bladder senna, etc., but some of the plants were in full sun. Other flowers in this fine gorge include *Saxifraga grisebachii, S. sempervivum* and *S. marginata, Dictamnus albus, Achillea ageratifolia,* a dianthus on the lines of *D. sylvestris, Sedum sartorianum* and *Matthiola fruticulosa.*

A visit to the Treska Gorge makes a fitting end (or start) to a holiday in this exciting country of Macedonia.

Jugoslavia in the *Bulletin*:

3, 7 Giuseppi, P. L.
    Macedonia
11, 30 Thompson, H. P.
    Macedonia
22, 349 Hodgkin, E. Slovenia
26, 9 Hodgkin, E. Slovenia
31, 238 Hecker, I. M. Slovenia
32, 129 Barrett, G. E. Kamnik
    Alps
34, 182 Barrett, G. E.
    Slovenia

37, 142 Barrett, G. E.
    Montenegro
39, 15 Grey-Wilson, C.
    Macedonia
39, 107 Mathew B. &
    190 Grey-Wilson, C.
        Jugoslavia
41, 209 Kelly, J. Triglav
42, 302 Trevan, D. J. &
        Whitehead, M. J.
        Macedonia

11

GREECE

Greece is in some ways the most varied and complex country to be considered in this book. It is largely mountainous, but is at the same time a huge peninsula projecting into the Eastern Mediterranean with a long and complicated coastline and a very large number of islands off its western, southern and eastern shores. The largest of these islands, Crete, though politically a part of Greece, is given separate treatment in this chapter. Many of the most easterly islands lie close to the Asiatic mainland of Turkey and, following *Flora Europaea*, I shall give these scant attention here. The northern frontiers of Greece are with Albania, Jugoslavia, and Bulgaria, and to the north-east with European Turkey.

In a country so large and varied there is inevitable diversity in the flowers and to some extent in the culture of the people, in the terrain and in the climate. The number of places in Greece that it would be delightful and interesting to visit 'had we but world enough and time' is legion. Here I must select, and in mainland Greece we will visit only Macedonia, Thessalian Olympus, Delphi and Parnassus, the Peloponnese, and then sample a small number of the many islands.

The quickest and easiest way to reach Greece is to fly to Athens, where cars can be hired, and there are 'Fly-drive' holidays. One can also fly to Thessaloniki (Salonica) and hire, and this provides the easiest access to Northern Greece from the Albanian to the Turkish border, and to the area of Mount Olympus. Taking one's own car to Greece involves a very long journey, either driving or train-ferrying the car to Northern Jugoslavia (p. 176) and then driving down through Jugoslavia to Greek Macedonia, or driving the length of Italy to Bari or Brindisi and ferrying it by sea to Igoumenitsa in Northern Greece or on to Patrai (Patras) in the Peloponnese.

There are now good fast main roads between the mainland towns. The mountain roads are very varied, and what has been said of Jugoslavian roads applies also to Greece. There are railways from Athens to the main towns of the Peloponnese, to Thessaloniki and thence on to Turkey, and to a few others, but most parts of mountainous Greece are better served by buses than by rail.

The classical sites of Greece are numerous and wonderful, and even a plant-seeker would be stupid to pass them by. Besides, because goats are generally excluded, the flowers on these sites are often rich and beautiful. Many of the furnishings and movable objects from the sites are now in museums, such as those in Athens and Olympia. We found it better when possible to visit the museums first—having seen the contents helped to bring the ruins to life—but it is well to check the opening times in advance. Much of the tourist industry is centred upon these sites, and in their vicinity are hotels, including *xenias* (Government hotels) and restaurants, where the food is likely to be more or less cosmopolitan. Apart from such areas, and particularly in the mountainous districts, hotels are infrequent and the food in the small inns may or may not appeal to the Western European palate. Dried spiced meats, fried veal and kebabs, with chip potatoes are widely available. Some of the hotels are of the 'bed and breakfast' type, and you must dine out. It seems to be in order to go into the kitchen and choose your food.

The language is of course Greek, and there is no other widely used second language. However, many Greeks have some German, French, Italian or English, and are very willing to use it, and generally someone can be found to translate. Road-signs, menus, etc., are mainly in the Greek alphabet, and it is very helpful to learn this alphabet (both the small and the capital letters) if only to be able to read the road signs.

The flowers are wonderful. In Northern Greece (Macedonia) they are similar to those in Jugoslavian Macedonia. In Southern Mainland Greece and on the islands the flora is predominantly Mediterranean. In addition however to both these elements, and particularly in the mountains and in the islands, there are more or less local plant populations. For example the flora of Tymphi and Smolikas in Macedonia, of Olympus in Thessaly, of Parnassus near Delphi, and of the Aroanian Mountains in the Peloponnese is in each case excitingly distinctive. Similarly many of the islands each have a few distinctive plants as well as a fair sample of the Greek flora. The range is tremendous, and there are said to be more than 6000 species native to Greece.

The time to visit is perhaps even more difficult to specify in Greece than in other countries. Spring starts in February on the southern coasts, in May or June in the northern mountains. We found early April a delightful time for our first sight of the main flush of spring flowers in the Peloponnese, but could not climb high on to Ziria because of the snow. The weather was warm, but not excessively hot. In early June in Macedonia it was indeed hot at the lower levels; hot and somewhat arid, partly because here, as throughout the Mediterranean area, the goats and sheep had cleared the herbage, but in the mountains, for instance on the Katara Pass, it was cooler, and many fine plants were in flower and yet others still only in bud. On Olympus in June the 'specials' of the high screes were still under snow and for these an August visit has been recommended. Greece in autumn too has its attractions, especially for those with an interest in crocus and colchicum, as Mr. and Mrs. Crook's account on p. 224 shows. In brief, there is no one right time

211

to see the flowers of Greece. You must go many times, to many places, and in many seasons. For the classical sites, a visit 'out of season', that is, early or late in the year (and early or late in the day) has much to commend it.

THE MAINLAND

MACEDONIA AND THE EPIRUS

This, the most north-westerly part of Greece, is botanically, and was in classical times politically, continuous with Jugoslavian Macedonia, and so is our most logical point of entry into Greece. We travelled south from Bitola in the second week of June and drove via Florina to **Kastoria**, a pleasant little town on a lake. There is a direct road from Florina to Kastoria, but a permit is (or then was) required to travel on it, for this is a 'sensitive' area near the Albanian frontier. The route through Aetos is longer, but a good road and pleasant. There is a *xenia* as well as other hotels in Kastoria. From here a road runs southward through mountainous country (the eastern foothills of the Pindus range) to Kalambaka, and here one turns westward on a fine new road across the Katara Pass to Joannina. There are attractive flowers by the roadsides, a pleasant hypericum (*H. apollinis*), *Orchis papilionacea*, *Potentilla ?inclinata*, *Cephalanthera rubra*, *Cistus incanus creticus*, *Convolvulus cantabrica*, *Dictamnus albus* and *Iris sintenisii* among others, but it was not until we reached the Katara Pass that we encountered the more rare and special plants of the Pindus Mountains. This is an exciting area, with marshy meadows on one side of the road and steep rocks on the other. In a long list of interesting plants there were a pretty white, very sweet-scented allium, the showy annual *Campanula ramosissima*, *Chamaecytisus hirsutus*, *Fritillaria pontica*, *Helleborus cyclophyllus*, *Jovibarba heuffelii*, *Narcissus poeticus radiiflorus*, *Saxifraga rotundifolia*, *Sempervivum ciliosum*, another sempervivum which was probably *S. marmoreum reginae-amaliae*, *Tulipa sylvestris* in fine flower (a surprise, this) and leaves of *Soldanella pindicola* (does this *ever* flower?), *Lilium chalcedonicum*, *Crocus chrysanthus* and a colchicum which was probably *C. lingulatum*. Another interesting plant which has been reported from this pass is *Daphne blagayana*.

The Katara Pass is the only road-crossing of the Pindus Mountains, a somewhat diffuse range that runs from north to south through Northern Greece. They reach their maximum height in Smolikas (2637 m.) near their northern end. Tymphi (2497 m.) lies a little to the south of Smolikas, and Peristeri (2295 m.) further to the south-east behind Joannina. The Katara Pass road, between the pass and Joannina, skirts the northern side of Peristeri, though separated from it by a deep river-valley. This is a beautiful and spectacular drive. Between the mountain and the road lies the little hillside village of **Metsovon**, where there are hotels—a good place to stay for exploring both the pass and the mountain. One of the pleasures of mountain holidays is to chance upon spectacular local events. We found Metsovon a seething mass of happy people, many of them in their national costume; a wedding had just taken place and there was dancing on the green to a four-man band of drum, tambourine, flute and bazouka. We were told they would keep it up for three days!

Joannina is a bigger, lower and hotter town, beautiful on its lake and well placed for a visit to the coast at Igoumenitsa or for exploring Tymphi and Smolikas. However, a permit from the military is required to climb these mountains (or was, in 1970) and although we at last secured one in Joannina, and drove northward to Konitsa, the officer in the barracks there would not accept the permit and so we were disappointed. Dr. Giuseppi visited Smolikas in 1935 (*Bulletin* Vol. 3, p. 7) and reported that it is a mountain of schists and serpentine—the Pindus generally is I believe limestone—with some interesting plants including *Campanula hawkinsiana, Viola magellensis, Dianthus haematocalyx pindicola* and *Pinguicula hirtiflora*. Goulimy visited Tymphi (also called Gamila) in 1955 (*Bulletin* Vol. 23, p. 238), describing it as a wild and unexplored area where wild goat, boar, cat and bear were still at large, and the flowers he mentioned included *Viola orphanidis, Alyssum corymbosum, Linum elegans, Allium flavum* and *Campanula hawkinsiana*. While we ourselves were disappointed, we nevertheless found the visit to Konitsa rewarding. The road was under reconstruction and was atrocious in parts, but probably is now good. It would be well to confirm in Joannina whether a permit is required to go to Konitsa. This little town lies near the mouth of a spectacular gorge, the Xaradra Bikou, on the River Aoos that separates Smolikas from Tymphi. Beside the small path running

along the gorge we found *Pterocephalus perennis bellidifolius, Ramonda serbica* and *Saxifraga marginata* var. *rocheliana*. We also found roads running up across the lower slopes of Tymphi to reach the upper end of the same gorge near Koukouliou, and in this very pleasant area there were attractive flowers—*Anemone coronaria, Aubrieta* ? *intermedia, Digitalis lanata, Fritillaria pontica, Hypericum apollinis* and the Madonna Lily, *Lilium candidum*. It seems that there is still dispute as to whether this last is a truly native plant of Greece. It is certainly thoroughly naturalised.

Ramonda serbica

A few miles to the south of Joannina is Dodoni, a magnificently sited and well-preserved Greek theatre on a hillside, where we found

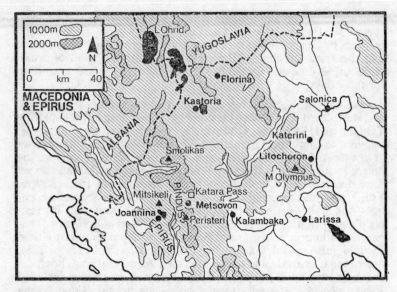

the leaves of *Campanula versicolor*, *Colchicum bivonae* and crocuses, muscari and ornithogalum.

To reach Peristeri from Joannina it is well to take the Katara road again and approach the mountain from its northern side: we attempted first to get at it from the south without much success. A small side road crosses the river to reach the tiny hamlet of Krapsi, and from this road there is a track up Peristeri. Among the delightful flowers that we found on this mountain were white *Astragalus spruneri*, one of the aubrietas, *Cerastium* ? *moesiacum*, *Daphne oleoides* and the aggressively brilliant-flowered *Geranium cinereum subcaulescens*. Up by the snow-patches were *Crocus veluchensis* and *Scilla bifolia*, and on the hot slopes below, *Putoria calabrica*, *Iberis sempervirens* and *Serapias lingua*.

OLYMPUS

Mount Olympus (2911 m.), the highest mountain in Greece, is a jumbled mass lying just inland from the Aegean sea in Thessalia. The nearest sizeable town, Katerini, lies on the main road which runs down Eastern Greece from the Jugoslavian frontier, where it is continuous with the autoput, to Athens. The quickest approach from England is from the airport at Thessaloniki. One can also approach it, as we did, from Joannina, crossing the Katara Pass and travelling via Trikala and Larissa. One advantage of the latter approach is that one passes close to, and should certainly visit, the remarkable rocks at Meteora; red volcanic outcrops sticking up fantastically from the valley of Pinios. In times past men have burrowed into them to create

214

impregnable monasteries, and they now contain museums of Byzantine art. On the rocks we found a pretty little pink allium, possibly *A. frigidum*, and *Romulea* ? *linaresii graeca*.

At Larissa one joins a toll-road that runs through the Vale of Tempe, a rocky gorge with fine views of conical Ossa ahead. Left to itself this would have been a beautiful place, but it has been extensively 'improved' with cement and garden roses.

Olympus can be tackled from several angles, but the usual and easiest approach is via **Litochoron**. The mountain block is like a great arm-chair with a little river, the Vrissula, emerging from it to the east through the Enipeus Gorge to run down to the sea. Litochoron lies at the mouth of the gorge, on a side-road running in from the coast. There are now probably several hotels, for winter sports are developing on the mountain. In 1970 we found a small modern hotel, but had to take all our meals, including breakfast, at one of the restaurants in the centre of the village.

A footpath, which is in fact a paved-over aqueduct, runs up the Enipeus Gorge for a short distance, providing an easy little walk among the rocks where aubrieta and *Saxifraga rotundifolia* grow. It ends at the stream, but we were told that by crossing the stream one can continue upwards into the heart of the mountain. However, there is nowadays a much easier approach, for a road has been built that climbs the northern 'arm' of Olympus to Stavros and then continues to the spring at Prioni, from which it is a relatively short, though steep, climb to Refuge 'A', one of four mountain huts on Olympus. In 1970 we were able to drive only as far as Refuge 'D' at Stavros, but even this saved an hour's climbing. Earlier plant-seekers had a much tougher job, and indeed before the war Dr. Giuseppi had a military escort because brigands were still at large on the mountain. We were not able to obtain a local map, as we arrived at a holiday week-end, and everything was shut, but the Greek Alpine Club (E.O.S.) had set up a board in the square in Litochoron on which the main footpaths were shown.

Even the drive to Stavros produced some lovely flowers. Many of them were old friends, such as *Cephalanthera rubra*, *Cistus incanus creticus*, *Limodorum abortivum* and *Platanthera bifolia*, but there were also some new to us, such as *Linum thracicum turcicum*, *Silene radicosa* and *Anthemis tinctoria*. At Prioni one is among the exciting flowers of Olympus. The whole mountain is now a protected area where it is forbidden to pick or collect plants. *Jankaea heldreichii*, that exceptionally charming Olympian endemic, is here. Outlying colonies have been reported as low down as the Enipeus Gorge, and also it occurs above Refuge 'A', so its altitudinal range is very considerable, and so therefore is the range of season in which it can be seen in flower. On June 15th it was in flower at Prioni but was snow-covered above the refuge. I found it in sunshine at 8 a.m. when I was having my second breakfast, but it was on north-facing rocks and

215

probably would receive no sun for the rest of the day. All the other plants I saw were in shade.

The climb from the valley to Refuge 'A' is steep and hot, even in June in the early morning, but beautiful and florally exciting. Among the many flowers to be seen were an alyssum (probably *A. corymbosum*), *Fritillaria graeca* and *F. messanensis*, *Iberis sempervirens*, *Potentilla deorum*, *Viola gracilis* (the true plant, very much more aristocratic than *V. gracilis* of gardens), *Silene multicaulis*, and *Geranium macrorrhizum*, with one of those brilliant green blue-throated lizards peering out from it.

At Refuge 'A' the warden spoke English and knew and enjoyed his flowers. It was interesting that the special show-piece in his eyes was not *Jankaea*, nor *Viola delphinantha*, which I was too early to see, but *Gentiana verna pontica*, brilliant and beautiful as the spring gentian nearly always is, and in Greece a rare plant. Most people visiting Olympus to see the flowers spend a night at the refuge. I had only four hours there, but it was long enough because in mid-June the snow was still down almost to the refuge, so there was no question of seeking the higher plants. But round the hut the rocks were clear of snow and there were delightful flowers. *Campanula oreadum*, with large shapely bells on neat small tight-foliaged plants was beautiful, and *Edraianthus graminifolius* was still in leaf in the rock-crevices where *Saxifraga marginata rocheliana*, *S. scardica*, *S. sempervivum* and *S. spruneri*, and a sempervivum which I took to be *S. marmoreum reginae-amaliae* grew.

Others who have travelled to Olympus later in the year have reported many other beautiful plants from the higher rocks, and there

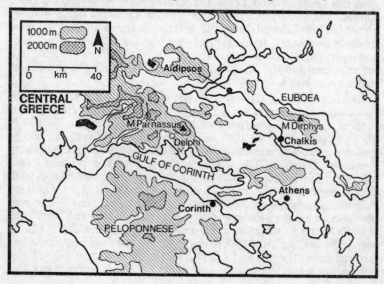

is a full and nicely illustrated account of these by Grey-Wilson in the *Bulletin*, Vol. 37, p. 255.

Litochoron is not the only point of entry to the high peaks of Olympus. Giuseppi entered, I think from the west, near the present Refuge 'B' (*Bulletin* Vol. 3, p. 7) finding much the same flowers, and reporting also *Trachelium jacquinii rumelianum*, *Viola delphinantha* and *Omphalodes luciliae*.

Small and sometimes bad, but negotiable, roads encompass the entire bloc of Olympus. On the south side one can drive high into the hills by a road that runs away from the coast through Leptokaria and Karya, a lovely if rather exciting drive, because of the state of the road. We saw white pyramidal orchids, white primroses and a potentilla of the *P. recta* group. On the north side a road runs from Katerini to St. Dimitrios. It is separated from the mountain by a river, but this can be crossed by a small road that climbs up to the Petras Monastery. This also is a poor road, and it deteriorated into a dirt and stone track, but it was a pleasant place, and we found leaves of *Colchicum cupanii* and *Crocus flavus*, and also found one of the loveliest dianthuses we have ever seen. It 'keyed out' in *Flora Europaea* more or less as *D. deltoides*, but was far more beautiful than any we have seen in gardens under that name.

These roads that encircle Olympus are in places very attractive, for one is looking into the mountain mass, but truth to tell we did not find it a very beautiful mountain. It is too much of a jumbled hotch-potch of knobs from which no one peak stands clear. The explanation is, I understand, simple. Each god had his or her own peak to sit on, and the jealousies of the gods, or perhaps it was Grecian democracy, permitted only minor differences of status between them.

Delphi and Parnassus*

Every visitor to Greece should go to **Delphi**. Its setting is quite superb, below the great vertical cliffs of Mt. Parnassus and looking south to the Gulf of Itea, over the enormous olive-grove which carpets the floor of the Gorge of Pleistos far below. The classical remains, rather charmingly referred to by a certain Guide as "the Ruinations", are surely the most beautiful and possibly the most interesting in all Greece. That they are naturally one of the main tourist attractions provides its own problems, but there are compensations. It means that access is easy and accommodation of all categories is good. Within the site, which is fenced against sheep and goats and non-paying visitors, the wealth of wild life, particularly plants, is really spectacular, especially in the spring and autumn. In an average year the first half of April and of October would be the best times to see the most flowers.

So great is the wealth of plants to be found here that mention can be made of only a very few. First to catch the eye by the roadside will be *Verbascum undulatum* with its woolly grey wavy rosettes. Next,

* Contributed by Mr. I. B. Barton

adorning the walls of "the Ruinations" will be the purple star-fishes of *Campanula rupestris* and yellow clumps of *Alkanna graeca* and the golden drop, *Onosma frutescens*. The dainty pinkish spikes of *Asphodelus fistulosus* emerge from between the stones, and the brassy yellow *Asphodeline lutea* is quite common, especially higher up. Bulbs, in their widest sense, are everywhere, but particularly orchids, which in form and variety it would be hard to match. There is also a brilliant Prussian-blue grape-hyacinth, *Bellevalia dubia*, to be found all through the site. *Muscari comosum* is very common, and in the autumn *Sternbergia lutea* and *S. colchiciflora* brighten the scene, especially below the cliffs above the Stadium. Here too are massive clumps of *Euphorbia characias wulfenii* and great spiny cushions of *E. acanthothamnos*. Possibly the most charming plant to be found in Delphi, however, is the delicately lovely *Daphne jasminea* in a particularly good dwarf form. One such plant, perched on top of a boulder, was some 12–14 inches across in 1962, and only a little larger, but still thriving, in 1976.

Outside the site, on the lower slopes of Mt. Parnassus, are many more interesting and beautiful plants, including the brilliant scarlet *Tulipa boeotica* in the stiff red clay of the cultivated area. *Iris pumila attica*, further up, varies from white with brownish-green falls through shades of yellow to deep purple, but the white and pale yellow forms only are sweet scented. *Fritillaria graeca* is another nice plant to be found here above the site.

Near Delphi is the picturesque village of Arachova, whence a good road climbs up Mt. Parnassus, along a high plateau and finally up through thick forests of fir to a ski-lift which starts above the tree-line. This provides easy access to high alpine plants of great interest and variety. Drifts of *Crocus* species, especially *CC. veluchensis*, *cancellatus* and white *cartwrightianus*, occur here, and some particularly fine campanulas of the *C. rupestris* persuasion as well as other species grow on the rocks, and spiny tufts of *Anthyllis hermanniae* on the more open ground. Near the summit are enormous cushions like 'vegetable sheep' which I have not identified, and amongst them a tight, rather prickly dwarf dianthus, with numerous plants of *Sternbergia colchiciflora*.

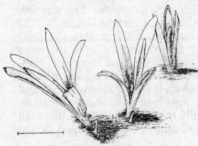

Sternbergia colchiciflora

On the road to Athens, an excursion to the marvellous Byzantine monastery of Ossios Lukas is well worthwhile. Here, in an almond orchard, are not only many *Asphodelus aestivus* (*microcarpus*), but also great numbers of orchids, especially forms of *Ophrys sphegodes* which in some years make quite a purple haze, and the giant orchid, *Barlaea robertiana*, and many others.

Before finishing this very cursory introduction to the plants one can see round Delphi, perhaps one should mention that it is a very exciting place for the variety of its birds and butterflies. Almost always there are griffon vultures, so often mistaken for eagles, gliding gracefully along the cliffs, red-rumped swallows by the Castalian Spring, and many more.

The Peloponnese

The Peloponnese is the southernmost part of Mainland Greece, almost separated from the rest by the Gulf of Corinth and connected only by the narrow Isthmus through which is cut the Corinth Canal. A new main road traverses the Isthmus, connecting Athens with Corinth, and this is the only approach to the Peloponnese by land. There is however a car ferry between Rion and Antirion at the narrowest point of the Gulf of Corinth, and there are also car ferries from Italy to Patras (Patrai).

The Peloponnese contains several of the best-preserved and most beautiful of the Grecian sites, and also a number of mountain ranges, of which the two highest and most distinctive are the Aroanian Mountains in the north and the Taygetos in the south. Each of these has endemic plants of special interest, and the lowland areas have an especially rich and beautiful spring flora of Mediterranean type.

We travelled from Athens to Corinth on 7th April, and spent a week making a circuit of the peninsula. The new toll-road to Corinth is fast, but the old road, which is still maintained, though slower is much more beautiful and interesting. Driving out of Athens can be a bit of a strain, especially if you have just taken over a hired car, and a

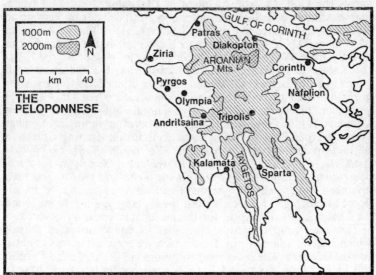

stop at the Byzantine monastery at Daphne, where there is a good restaurant, can be recommended. Alongside the old road, running between limestone rocks, there are plenty of flowers. *Asphodelus fistulosus*, dwarf with pink flowers and the prettiest of a race of plants generally most effective from a distance, grows by the roadside with the handsome annual grass *Briza maxima, Convolvulus althaeoides tenuissimus*, and white *Gagea* (*Lloydia*) *graeca*. We have not found *G. graeca* to be reliably hardy in our Hampshire garden, but it comes through some winters, sets good seed regularly, and is a good alpine house plant. In general the lowland plants of the Peloponnese have to be suspected of frost-tenderness, but there are some surprising exceptions, and of course plants such as *Anemone blanda* which flourish in the lowlands but also climb into the hills are more likely to be hardy. Also by the roadside on the way to Corinth are various orchids, such as *O. papilionacea* (a smaller-flowered but deeper-coloured form than we have met in Spain), *Ophrys speculum* and *O. ferrum-equinum*. It is also one of the sites of the rare Greek endemic *Daphne jasminea*. *Cyclamen graecum* and *C. hederifolium* (leaves only of course in April) are in the rocks, as is *Campanula 'rupestris'*, or one of its group: *Flora Europaea* does not seem to admit the true species as growing in the Peloponnese. By the Corinth Canal there were masses of a pretty hypecoum, either *H. procumbens* or *H. imberbe*. Altogether this road, taken slowly, is a fine introduction to the flowers of the Peloponnese.

But if you continue along the coast road towards Patras it is a different story; a flat featureless shore scattered with little shacks and bungalows, with a redeeming view of snow-covered Parnassus across the Gulf. We spent a night at **Diakopton**, in a hotel which may charitably be called adequate, hoping to drive from here up to Kalavryta and thence to explore Chelmos (2341 m.) in the Aroanian Mountains. There is a road up to Kalavryta, but it does not run directly from Diakopton: the latter is on the new coast road, but the Kalavryta road branches southward from the old coast road which runs further inland. There is also a railway following the river gorge and said to be a very spectacular ride. When Dr. Giuseppi went there before the war 'the only mountain hut in Greece' was on Chelmos. It is the source of the River Styx (of mythological fame as an underground travel facility) and contains an exciting collection of local plants—*Asperula boissieri, Globularia stygia, Campanula spatulata, C. aizoon, Trachelium asperuloides, Saxifraga taygetea, Macrotomia densiflora, Aquilegia ottonis, Fritillaria graeca, Teucrium aroanium* and (recalling Olympus) *Gentiana verna pontica*. A magnificent assemblage of 'specials': but these plants are not to be found on Chelmos in early April, for the mountains are snow-covered.

The coast road improves somewhat as one approaches Patras, which is quite a large town, from which we travelled across country to visit Olympia. The coast road continues via Lechaina and Pyrgos: this looks a long way round, but it is a much safer bet if you have to be at Olympia by a specified hour. However, our cross-country route via Boykovina was a pleasant if at times frustrating experience. The road was atrocious in places, and we had no food and found never a shop or restaurant, and there was a remarkable dearth of signposts and village name-signs. But we traversed a beautiful range of hills around Chiona and drove among brilliant flowers— *Anemone pavonina, A. fulgens* and *A. blanda, Aethionema saxatile, Alkanna orientalis, Aristolochia rotunda, Globularia alypum* and orchids including the monkey orchid (*O. simia*) and *Ophrys sphegodes mammosa*. Especially beautiful was the Peloponnese form of *Iris unguicularis*. This is probably a form of subspecies *cretensis*, but is intermediate between the tall large-flowered African form which we grow in our gardens as *unguicularis* and the exceedingly fine-leaved and small-flowered dwarf form of *cretensis* in Crete. The Peloponnese form has the best of both. There were also crocus leaves: crocuses abound in the Peloponnese, and are very beautiful, the range including *CC. boryi, crewei, goulimyi, niveus, flavus, sieberi,* and *olivieri*.

At **Olympia,** a tourist centre, there is a *xenia* as well as other hotels. There is also a museum. We found it closed when we tried to visit on a Monday and our guide-book had not told us this— so check! The Olympic stadium and temples are wonderful, and we found them set in a riot of flowers. Goats are excluded and so early in the season the flowers were relatively untrodden by man. Especially lovely were the Judas trees, *Cercis siliquastrum*.

Another beautiful building, set wildly out in the hills, is the Temple of Apollo at Vassai. To reach this from Olympia you must drive down to Pyrgos, and then turn back eastward at first along the coast and thence to Andritsaina. The roadsides were rosy with *Silene colorata* and a pretty geranium rather like an improved *G. pyrenaicum*. Also there was the beautiful *Onosma taurica* and a magnificent large white astragalus, *A. lusitanicus orientalis*, as well as *Anemone hortensis, Cyclamen graecum* and other plants we had met before.

It is a lovely drive from Olympia to Tripolis, which is a main communications centre in the Peloponnese. The road winds delightfully among the hills: mostly these were close-cropped by the goats and sheep in April. All the same we found many flowers, and one could hardly sit down without finding the leaves of crocuses and other bulbous plants. From Tripolis we travelled down through similar country to Sparta. The whole was an easy day's delightful travel. We found many of the plants already mentioned, and dianthus, gageas, *Galanthus nivalis* in seed, and a hairy-leaved ornithogalum. At **Sparta,** there are hotels including a *xenia*, and the Taygetos Mountains, snow-topped in April, form a wonderful back-cloth. The show-piece for most visitors is the ruined Byzantine town of Mistras, with its eight surviving churches, chapels and monasteries. It is set steeply upon a hillside, and is best seen from above. As at Olympia, the exclusion of goats means that there are beautiful flowers among the ruins. *Anemone fulgens* glows hot in the grass between the old walls, and especially impressive is the fine large spurge which is probably *Euphorbia characias wulfenii*. There are bold masses of phlomis, and mats of deep blue pimpernel.

From Mistras one looks straight across upon the main ridge of the Taygetos Mountains, and this ridge is cleft by a deep gorge—the Porori Gorge. I spent an hour or two there, and never elsewhere have I seen such a wealth of bright flowers. Mostly they were the anemones, campanulas, and so on, that we had already met, but among new flowers were *Malcolmia maritima*, *Hypericum empetrifolium*, a charming white, brown and purple toadflax in a crevice (it was probably a cymbalaria or a kickxia), the leaves and seed of *Galanthus nivalis reginae-olgae*, and—the *pièce de résistance*—the lovely 'Pelops' form of *Cyclamen repandum*, growing both in light woodland by the stream at the bottom of the gorge and also higher up among the rocks. The Greek snowdrops are interesting in that plants from different localities seem to have very different flowering times, the extreme form is *G. reginae-olgae* which blooms in the autumn before its leaves appear. It was the sheer volume and brilliance of the flowers (particularly the anemones) that took one's breath away in the Porori Gorge. Clearly it had not been grazed, but as I went on up the valley I met a vast flock of goats coming down, and on my return I found the whole place stripped bare. How beautiful Greece (and indeed I suppose the whole Mediterranean area) would be if it were not so heavily grazed!

In April the snow was still fairly low on the Taygetos hills. Others have been there later, and reported fine flowers, including *Acantholimon androsaceum*, *Campanula papillosa*, white primroses, *Crocus sieberi*, *Colchicum boissieri*, *Tulipa boeotica*, *T. goulimyi*, *Verbascum acaule* and *Mandragora autumnalis*.

Another rich and beautiful area is the easternmost of the main 'tongues' of the Peloponnese, surrounded by the Saronic Islands. A convenient centre for this area is **Nafplion (Nauplia)**, beautifully set on a little headland at the head of the Argolikos Bay. It is a popular tourist centre, and there are hotels. Small roads over the hills lead to coastal villages such as Galatas (opposite the island of Poros) and the area is full of flowers. Among others new to us in the Peloponnese were *Alyssum saxatile orientale*, *Campanula spatulata*, *Euphorbia acanthothamnos*, *Orchis quadripunctata*, *Ajuga chamaepitys chia*, *Alkanna orientalis* and *Linaria triphylla*.

A showpiece of the area is the ancient theatre of Epidauros, with a stadium and the medical treatment centre of Asclepias and a museum alongside it. We arrived here in the late afternoon just as all the coaches were leaving—an excellent piece of timing. Among the ruins we saw a white *Serapias vomeracea*, white *Muscari comosum*, *Barlaea robertiana*, and *Campanula drabifolia*. A sad discovery was that weed-killer had been applied to the turf on the banks of the stadium, and rare and lovely plants were dead or dying.

Epidauros is but one of several classical sites in this area. Of the old fortress at Tiryns, some of it dating from the XVIIth Century B.C., one can but write in wonder at its age; but at Mycenae, in its fine setting among the hills, there is great variety and beauty too, enhanced by *Campanula rupestris* and *Onosma taurica* draping the man-made structures as well as the wild rock around them. We found *Ophrys ferrum-equinum* here, *O. lutea* and *O. speculum*, and the attractive, spiked *Ornithogalum narbonense*.

Driving back from Nafplion to Corinth one passes close to Nemea, where Hercules strangled a lion, Zeus had a temple, and excellent wines are made. From here you can travel westward through the hills to Kaliani, beside its dried-up lake, and from the little village of Bousi a path leads up towards Mt. Ziria (syn. Cyllene or Killini) (2376 m.) the highest mountain in the Peloponnese; here we are once again in the Aroanian Mountains. This is perhaps not the best approach to Ziria: I believe it can also be reached from the north coast via Trikala. In any case, in April there was no question of getting very high up it, because of the snow. Even so, it was well worth the steep hot scramble. Pale yellow *Iris pumila attica* grew in hot, south-facing crevices, its rhizomes exposed. *Hermodactylus tuberosus* reached a fair altitude, and *Anemone blanda* accompanied me right up to the snow's edge. Other plants of the hot rocks were *Sternbergia colchiciflora* (in leaf), *Thymelaea tartonraira*, a handsome broomrape (*Orobanche crenata*, I think), *Orchis quadripunctata*, *Iris unguicularis cretensis*, and pink *Crepis rubra*. Up by the snow there were a few late flowers of *Crocus flavus* (the only crocus we found in the Peloponnese flowering in April), and an odd little variant on the lesser celandine, *Ranunculus ficarioides*, with scalloped leaves. Down near the dried-up lake there was a field of beautiful *Ornithogalum nutans*, a rare introduced plant in England.

GREECE IN AUTUMN*

There can be few places in the northern hemisphere so rewarding for the flower-lover in autumn as Greece. A number of Mediterranean plants, particularly bulbs, are summer-dormant and many flower in the autumn ahead of their leaves, which follow soon after or in the next year. Chief among these are crocus and colchicum, of which Greece has an unrivalled selection. The weather can be expected to be fairly good in October, but becomes wetter and colder in November. This is a good season for the classical sites: lack of haze helps photography, and there is not the pressure of tourists. Most of the plants are to be found at lower levels, but some of the

* Contributed by Mr. and Mrs. H. L. Crook

best prefer the hills, so that places like Mt. Parnes, Delphi and the Katara Pass are all worth visiting, in addition to the Peloponnese, where it can be expected to be warmer and drier than in the north.

In early October appear *Crocus hadriaticus*, *C. cancellatus*, *Cyclamen hederifolium* and *Biarum tenuifolium*. All are widely distributed and common. *Crocus hadriaticus* is scattered around Joannina, abundant above Delphi and by the thousand between Tripolis and Sparta, where there are some blue-tinted forms. *C. cancellatus* always grows scattered and continues over a long period into November. It too is abundant above Delphi in both white and blue forms. On Mt. Parnes are the earliest forms of *C. laevigatus*, mostly white or lightly marked: it flowers much later in Euboea and the south-east Peloponnese. The following crocuses are found in the Peloponnese: *C. boryi* comes shortly after *C. hadriaticus*, towards the end of October *C. crewei* comes up where *C. hadriaticus* was, and *C. laevigatus* follows and overlaps *C. boryi*. One of the best shows is given by the crocuses of the Mani Peninsula in early November. Both *C. goulimyi* and *C. niveus* cover large areas of ground locally and are often accompanied by scattered plants of *C. boryi*.

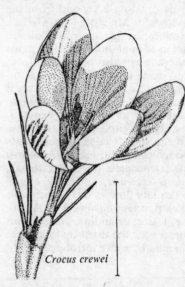

Crocus crewei

Colchicums are widespread but are always localised. The best is *C. bivonae* (*sibthorpii*), with large tesselated flowers. There are many others with smaller flowers looking rather alike but of great interest to the connoisseur.

Cyclamen graecum makes an unrivalled show in October on Mt. Parnes, in a wide variety of forms of flower and leaf. It is found in many places but is not generally common. *Scilla autumnalis* is ubiquitous and abundant usually in a form taller and pinker than our native plant. There are also albinos. *Narcissus serotinus* is a beautiful scented plant of the coast and lowlands, sometimes making large colonies in semi-cultivated ground in the south. In damp places in the Taygetos mountains one may come across the rare autumn snowdrop, *Galanthus nivalis reginae-olgae*. However, the real glory of Greece in the autumn is the profusion of *Sternbergia lutea*. It is widespread over the whole of Greece, but is seen at its best in the Peloponnese (between Tripolis and Sparta, or between Kalavryta and Vytina) where the lovely yellow crocus-like flowers light up south-facing hillsides. The tiny *S. colchiciflora* is less common, on hills and mountains.

There are also non-bulbous autumn-flowering plants. *Erica manipuliflora* (*verticillata*) is a showy small shrub; *Dittrichia* (*Inula*) *viscosa* is a roadside weed, lining long stretches of the verges with its yellow flowers; the autumnal lady's tresses (*Spiranthes spiralis*) is an uncommon orchid. *Erodium chrysanthum, Pterocephalus perennis* (*parnassi*) and *Convolvulus cantabrica* are still in flower above Delphi in October, as is also at lower levels the tender *Daphne gnidium*. There are many plants in berry or in fruit, and autumn colour is provided by poplars and other deciduous trees, notably the rhus, (*Cotinus coggygria*). But the most abiding memory is of the road climbing above Colos, with the rocky slopes covered with a mixture of sternbergia and *Cyclamen graecum*.

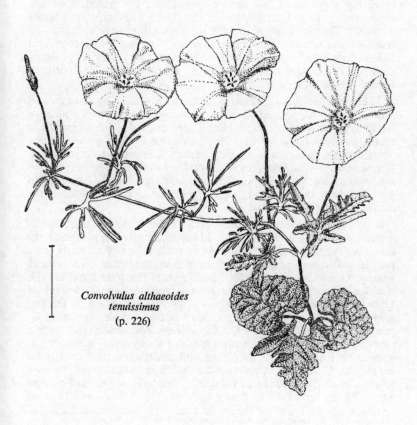

*Convolvulus althaeoides
tenuissimus*
(p. 226)

Of the large number of Greek islands only a small 'sample' can be considered here. As would be expected, their flora tends to be similar to that of those parts of the mainland nearest to which they lie. The islands chosen here—Corfu in the Adriatic, the Saronic group off the Peloponnese, Euboea off the Greek mainland in the Aegean, and Lesbos and Rhodes off mainland Turkey—form a series in which the affinities of the flowers progress from those of Greek Macedonia towards the Eastern Mediterranean with its Asiatic influence.

CORFU (KERKYRA)*

This is an exquisitely beautiful island, with long associations with Britain, and English is spoken almost universally. Access is easy, accommodation varied and good (but avoid the Greek Easter), and there is an extensive bus service throughout the island. Cars are expensive to hire, but mopeds can be hired and taxis are readily available. Rainfall is high, making the vegetation more lush than on some of the islands. Corfu lies close to the coast of Greece (and indeed 'overlaps' Albania) with a frequent ferry service to Igoumenitsa. From here there is access to Joannina and the Northern Pindus mountains.

There is a maquis of Mediterranean plants, such as cistuses and *Phlomis fruticosa*, among which grow many of the flowers which we have encountered on the mainland, for example, *Iris unguicularis cretensis*, *Convolvulus althaeoides tenuissimus*, *Verbascum undulatum*, *Acanthus spinosus*, *Lamium garganicum*, *Campanula ramosissima*, *Gynandriris sisyrinchium*, *Hermodactylus tuberosus*, *Anemone pavonina* and *Allium roseum*. Two fritillaries are reported, *FF. graeca* and *graeca* subsp. *thessala*, and other plants of interest include *Arum italicum*, and *Crepis incana*.

It is however particularly for its orchids that Corfu has acquired its reputation among flower-seekers. Many kinds grow in profusion. In the lower marshy areas *Orchis laxiflora* makes the wettest parts quite purple, and there are several species of *Serapias* in the drier ground nearby. One may also find the local form of the pyramidal orchid, *Anacamptis pyramidalis brachystachys*. Amongst the prickly scrub of *Quercus coccifera* are many species of ophrys, including *O. ferrumequinum* and *O. scolopax cornuta*, and also of orchis, including *O. quadripunctata* and *O. simia*. *Limodorum abortivum*, the purple saprophytic orchid which can be (but isn't always) very attractive, is also to be found. There are other bulbous plants, such as *Crocus boryi* and *C. olivieri*, *Cyclamen hederifolium* (usually the scented form), and in the lower areas sometimes can be found the tall conical dark blue spikes of *Scilla hyacinthoides*. One of the specialities of

* Contributed by Mr. I. B. Barton with additional information from Mr. J. D. Aldridge, Miss M. Fishwick, Mr. C. W. Henderson, Mr. F. E. Heppenstall and Mr. W. K. Weston

Corfu is the form *corcyrensis* of *Galanthus nivalis reginae-olgae*, the autumn-flowering snowdrop, particularly on the higher ground, though it is difficult to discern its leaves in the spring.

THE SARONIC ISLANDS*

This group of islands, of which the largest are Aegina, Poros, Hydra and Spetsai, lie to the south of Athens on the eastern side of the Peloponnese. They are served by the rather marvellous Greek ferries. From Athens the port of Piraeus is easily reached by train, bus or taxi, and here one picks up the ferry for Spetsai, calling at Aegina, Poros and Hydra. One can stay on any of these islands, all of which have good hotels and tavernas. Transport on the islands varies from car-hire (or taxi, bus, horse-drawn vehicle, bicycle-hire or scooter-hire) on Aegina to mule or donkey on Hydra. On all there is good walking and fine scenery, and there are ancient sites on Poros and Aegina.

Flowers are everywhere in profusion in the spring (March and April) and in October. They are essentially the same as those of the lower levels of the Peloponnese mainland, including such species as *Gladiolus illyricus*, *Cyclamen graecum*, *Gynandriris sisyrinchium*, *Serapias cordigera*, and *Silene colorata*. The flowering times are a little earlier on the islands than on the mainland.

In the grounds of the museum at Aegina is an altar slab with *Anthemis chia* engraved on it and the same plant growing round it—an example of 'stone botany'—another slant on flowers?

EUBOEA†

This is the narrow island, some 160 km. long, lying off the eastern coast of mainland Greece, separated by only a very narrow channel opposite the main town of **Chalkis**. Being so large, it contains all types of terrain, including some quite high mountains. The highest of these is Mt. Dirphys (1734 m.), some 25 km. east of Chalkis. It contains many good plants, including, it is said, *Daphne jasminea*, though this does not seem to have been found there in recent years. A road crosses the shoulder of the mountain, through dense chestnut woods, making it relatively easy to reach the open ridge below the gaunt summit. Amongst the chestnuts are plenty of bulbs, notably the dainty green and white *Ornithogalum nutans* and a good form of *Crocus sieberi atticus*. There are some quite good species of *Hypericum* here too, including *H. barbatum*, and quantities of *Erica arborea*, which provides one of the main sources of honey for enormous numbers of bee-hives.

On the high ridge of Mt. Dirphys is a colourful alpine meadow, with quantities of *Anemone coronaria* and various species of crocus, especially *C. cancellatus*, the corms of which are eaten by the local shepherds. A grove of the Greek fir *Abies cephalonica*, some of them

* Contributed by Mr. F. W. Buglass
† Contributed by Mr I. B. Barton

plastered with mistletoe, shelters a number of interesting plants, including *Daphne oleoides*, the rather taller *D. gnidium* (or possibly *D. gnidioides*), small drifts of *Doronicum orientale*, and, rather surprisingly at this height, *Anchusa azurea*. On exposed rocks here-abouts grows a very attractive campanula of the *C. rupestris* persuasion but with soft grey very velvety leaves. Near the summit, amongst large sharp stones, grows *Saxifraga scardica*, whilst a little lower is a rather dull form of *Geranium cinereum subcaulescens*. On the borders of the tree-cover is *Lilium chalcedonicum* (perhaps the form *heldreichii*), and in a remote area of the eastern slopes is a lovely white paeony, whose identity remains to be established.

Saxifraga scardica

The south of the island is less high, but is where one of the uncommon species of fritillary occurs—*Fritillaria ehrhartii*.

Recent road-building has opened up the attractive northern part of the island, and the small spa at **Aidipsos** has quite reasonable accommodation, while two good car-ferries provide an easy and pleasant way of reaching the mainland, especially Macedonia.

The two remaining islands to be considered are examples of the large group more or less adjacent to the Turkish coast. Politically they are Greek, but geographically they are linked with Asia and this is reflected to some extent in their flora. They are excluded from *Flora Europaea*.

LESBOS*

Lesbos is not so firmly on the tourist map, but there are good hotels at the main town of **Mytilene**, as well as at **Mithymna** in the north, **Sigrion** in the west and, perhaps most picturesque of all, **Plomarion** in the south near the highest point, Mt. Olympus (967 m.). Access is from Athens by sea or by air to Mytilene.

Whilst Samos is noted for its vineyards and wine, Lesbos claims ten million olive trees and the best olives, as well as the best ouzo, in the world. Below and between the olive trees is a dense cover of colourful shrubs; especially pungent-smelling labiates, several species of *Cistus*, and also various leguminous plants ranging from dwarf cushions of a species of *Genista*, bright with very small flowers in May, to dense thickets of *Spartium junceum*. *Nerium oleander* has established itself by the banks of streams, and in one or two similar places *Rhododendron luteum* (*Azalea pontica*) is to be found in one of its few European stations.

* Contributed by Mr. I. B. Barton

Bulbs are numerous, particularly orchids in great variety. One of the best is *Orchis laxiflora palustris*, a rather superior subspecies and found like the type plant in boggy places. Even more striking is *Comperia comperiana*, found high on Mt. Olympus. It has a most extraordinary lip with long trailing filaments, and is one of the plants more closely associated with Asia. Commonly seen by the road verges on Mt. Olympus is the rather straggly *Campanula* ? *betonicifolia*, and under the chestnuts are the dwarf *Tulipa orphanidea* (*hageri*), a paeony (probably a form of *P. mascula*) and a delightful fritillary, *F. pontica stipitata*. At the tree-line and above grows *Crocus nubigenus*, a really lovely January-flowering species related to *C. crewei*. The top of Mt. Olympus is devoid of trees, and consists of a steep rock outcrop, complete with military outpost, so that one may not visit the top! It was possible to find a densely caespitose Campanulad, possibly an asyneuma, with dark purple starry flowers, before being turned back.

Down on the plains, around one or other of the great inland gulfs that are a feature of the island, are quite spectacular stands of the white and yellow *Iris ochroleuca* (*orientalis*) *monnieri*— a splendid plant.

Comperia comperiana

Lesbos is not only an exciting place for plants and scenically so beautiful; it is also one of the most marvellous places for the bird-watcher, being on the migratory route up the west coast of Turkey. All-in-all it is a fascinating island, friendly, beautiful, rewarding, and incidentally car-hire is only about half the price of the very high rate on the mainland.

RHODES*

Rhodes is a Greek island about 80 km. long by 30 km. wide, wooded

* Contributed by Mr. and Mrs. H. L. Crook

and hilly, rising to 1215 m. on the treeless, rather bare Mt. Ataviros. It lies in the Eastern Mediterranean close to South-West Turkey and in consequence has a rather warmer climate in winter and spring than Crete. The flora is largely Mediterranean with a number of plants from Asia Minor and a few endemics.

Access is good by air, directly or via Athens. The main roads are good and the minor roads adequate. There are abundant facilities for the hire of cars and other vehicles. The best time to see the flowers is mid-April, and as this is out of season hire-charges are considerably less than those quoted by travel agents in England. The main town is **Rhodes** (Rodos) with ample hotels of all categories, and it is the best centre from which to explore the island. There are coach-trips to various places of interest to tourists, all of which have also some botanical interest.

Mt. Profitis Elias (798 m.) is well wooded and carries two of the more notable endemics. The floor of the sparse pine woods is carpeted with *Cyclamen repandum rhodense*, differing from more western forms in having pure white flowers with a deep pink nose. With it grows the white-flowered *Paeonia rhodia*, and these two endemics are accompanied by *Iris unguicularis cretensis*. Other plants on this mountain

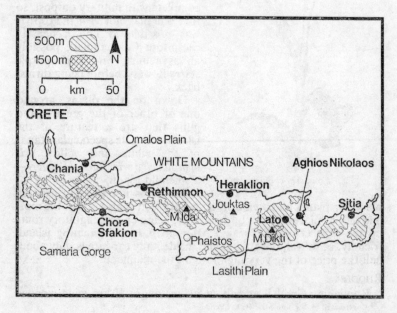

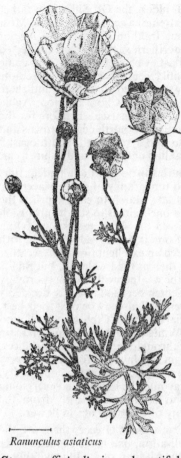

Ranunculus asiaticus

include *Rosularia serrata, Anemone blanda, Dracunculus vulgaris, Ophrys lutea murbeckii (minor), O. scolopax heldreichii, O. reinholdii, Orchis anatolica, O. provincialis* and *Neotinea intacta.*

Rhodes is noted for its orchids. In addition to those just mentioned, one can see, in the course of a fortnight's holiday, *Ophrys carmelii (attica), O. fusca iricolor, O. fusca omegaifera, O. sphegodes mammosa, O. ferrum-equinum, O. fuciflora candica, Serapias parviflora laxiflora,* and *Ophrys speculum regis-fernandii* which has a long thin labellum and is confined to Rhodes and South-West Turkey.

Cyclamen repandum rhodense is widespread at all levels, and on Mt. Philerimos (267 m.) it is in company with *C. persicum.* Here near the monastery is a striking giant fennel, *Ferula chiliantha.* Scattered over the island in light shade is an endemic fritillary, *F. rhodia,* with a small yellow bell. At Lindos can be seen *Ranunculus asiaticus* in its brilliant scarlet form and, on the castle walls, *Campanula anchusiflora. Arum dioscoridis* is a striking Asiatic with a red spathe and black markings, and *Styrax officinalis* is a beautiful, white-flowered shrub.

CRETE

Crete combines much of the beauty and interest of Greece with some distinctive features of its own. It is the southernmost land-mass of significant size in Europe—a long narrow island running from east to west, some 290 km. long and as little as 15 km. across at one place. And in this narrow strip there are high mountains; indeed the whole island is really a long narrow range of limestone mountains, with tiny coastal strips mainly on the north side. Though the hills are practically continuous through the length of the island, they rise here and there to greater heights, so that three main blocks can be identified—the White Mountains (Lefka Ori) near the western end, the Oros Idi containing Mt. Ida (2456 m.) near the centre, and the Oros Dikti

231

nearer to the eastern end. A fourth block, the Ori Sitias, are rather lower (reaching 1476 m.) near the extreme eastern end of Crete. Most of the towns—Chania, Rethimnon, Iraklion (Heraklion), Aghios Nikolaos and Sitia—lie along the northern shore and are connected by a good road. The southern coast, where the mountains come down more steeply to the sea, has until recently been relatively remote and inaccessible, but there are now improved roads here and there over the mountains leading to small towns (Chora Sfakion, Aghia Galini and Ierapetra) on the south coast. It is usual therefore for the visitor to Crete to stay in one or more of the north coastal towns and make excursions into the mountains and across to the south coast.* The usual approach is by air to Heraklion or Chania, and to hire a car.

As with most mountainous countries there is no one perfect time to visit, and indeed the latitude and topography of Crete exacerbate the problem. It is usually said that late March to early April is the ideal time, and doubtless this is so if one's aim is to see the profusion of delightful low-level flowers between the shore and, say, 1000 m. For a first visit, and particularly if one is not already familiar with the Mediterranean flora, this is indeed an excellent time. The weather is likely to be reasonably warm by then at the low levels, but rain is to be expected. By the end of April the weather will be drier (normally no rain falls in Crete from May to September) and it will be decidedly warm at low levels, where the flowers will already be past their best. On the other hand many of the special flowers of Crete are to be found in the mountains, especially the White Mountains, which remain under snow well into May. We, through force of circumstances, visited Crete during the first fortnight in May, and found this a very satisfactory time. The coastal belt was already becoming hot and dry, but one had to drive only a little way into the hills to find everything cool and fresh, and the snow had cleared sufficiently from the mountains to enable us to find many of the endemics in flower.

Our subject is flowers, but in Crete, as in Greece, there are the magnificent ruins of an earlier civilisation, one indeed much earlier than that of classical Greece, and the Minoan sites will inevitably to some extent influence the visitor's travels in Crete, if only because they have in part determined the roads and tourist facilities generally.

If you arrive at **Heraklion**, as we did, in the middle of the night, you will want to spend your first day quietly. Probably you will be in one of the new hotels that are set along the shore near the city, and if you wander on the beach you will find purple patches of matthiola, and an interesting collection of mostly annual plants—*Silene colorata*, viper's bugloss and anchusa, the leaves of *Pancratium maritimum*, and clusters of the orange egg-like berries of the mandrake, *Mandragora autumnalis*. But the hills call, and a few miles inland from Heraklion is Jouktas (811 m.), a northern outlier of the main Cretan range. For a first day's visit it has all the advantages. First, your road will take

* A south coastal road is now being built

you past Knossos, the most famed of the Minoan palaces. It is much reconstructed, which may or may not be to your taste, but you will have plenty of opportunity to see 'wild' ruins elsewhere. At Archanes there is a pleasant restaurant. On May Day it was crowded with cheerful people all garlanded with flowers—their hair and clothing, their bicycles, motor-bikes, and donkeys. All carried bunches, mainly of *Chrysanthemum coronarium* and its variety *discolor*, which clothed the roadside banks as well. A mixture of phrase-book Greek, German and gesture procured us omelettes, salads and beer, but we soon discovered that the wine is far better value for money than the beer in Crete.

From Archanes a little road runs between vineyards and then zigzags up the hillside of Jouktas to some sort of radio station; so, barely stretching your legs, you can find beautiful flowers including some of the Cretan endemics, of which there are said to be about 130. Among the garigue vegetation there are orchids and ophrys, including *Ophrys cretica*, softly blue-violet *Gynandriris sisyrinchium* in as fine a form as you will find anywhere, *Daphne sericea*, *Gladiolus italicus*, *Muscari comosum*, *Mandragora autumnalis* again, and, tucked under the bushes, a rather wistful, white-flowered *Cyclamen creticum*. It is a pretty flower, but decidedly a poor relation of *C. repandum* of which it was at one time thought to be a form. From the crest of Jouktas you can look *down* upon the nesting eagles. Here among the rocks is *Alyssoides cretica*, a smaller, neater silver-leaved version of *A. utriculata* of the Alps and another lovely silver-leaved plant, a helichrysum with pinky-gold flowers, probably *H. orientale*. Small compact starry-flowered *Hypericum empetrifolium* is here, and we found too the tiny grass-like leaves of *Iris unguicularis cretensis*, but its flowers were over. Mt. Jouktas is a location for the rare *Biarum davisii*. We did not find this—it would, I think, have been below ground—but we did find another biarum, probably *B. tenuifolium*. One of the showiest plants in the rock-crevices was a beautiful campanula with large tubular purple bells: we called it *C. tubulosa*, but the Cretan campanulas are confusing. We saw quite a lot during our stay, and tended to call them all *tubulosa*—but they certainly were not all the same!

The eastern end of Crete is hotter and lower than the west, so there is much to be said for going there first. We stayed two nights in **Sitia**, and spent a very pleasant day driving along the coast road to get there. The road takes one past the Minoan site at Malia to the pleasant but now over-popular little town of Aghios Nikolaos, on the site of an old port for the ancient city of Lato, set up in the hills a few miles to the west. For those with a car seeking peace and quiet the fishing village of **Elounda** a few miles to the north may appeal more as a place to stay.

A small road (a bus route) runs up to Kritsa, and from here a rough but negotiable road leads to Lato. It is a wonderful place to be, with the ruins of a IIIrd Century B.C. town straddling a high col, the man-made stones fading imperceptibly into the wild rock of the mountains on either side. There are carob trees among the ruins, and in the shady depths of the sunken rooms we saw the statuesque but stinking *Dracunculus vulgaris*. *Ranunculus asiaticus* here was bright yellow, and there were pyramidal orchids, ophrys past flowering, *Ornithogalum narbonense*, rue (*Ruta ?chalepensis*), *Allium subhirsutum*, a campanula rather like *C. patula*, *Hermodactylus tuberosus* and, hanging from the rocks, the lovely rose-flowered *Ebenus cretica*, like a robust giant sainfoin. An unusual plant growing here in fissures is *Ptilostemon chamaepuce*, a Composite looking more like a pale green dwarf pine but with deep pink centaurea-like flowers.

The drive from Aghios Nikolaos to Sitia is magnificent, mainly following the coast and its numerous bays and inlets, but at times crossing steeply over headlands and with many hairpin bends. At Sitia there are hotels, and it is a convenient base from which to explore the extreme eastern end of the island. We drove over the hills via Episkopi and Sitanos to Zakros, on tiny roads twisting among craggy limestone hills overlain with terra rossa. Already at the beginning of May the area was dry and full of 'spinies' such as *Sarcopoterium* (*Poterium*) *spinosum* and *Euphorbia acanthothamnos*. Peter Davis, in two most informative and entertaining articles (*Bulletin* Vol. 5, p. 385 and Vol. 7, p. 25) has a good deal to say about Cretan pricklies, mentioning among others *Berberis cretica*, *Satureja spinosa* and *Cichorium spinosum*. He visited this area in late May, when everything was very hot and dry, though cold at night, in the mountains. We found a few flowers still on *Anemone hortensis heldreichii* and *A. pavonina*. The former has, in the garden, a remarkably long flowering period, from early December till late April. It is a very distinctive form of the species, with small white flowers and blue stamens. We found too a neat white form of *Ranunculus asiaticus*, another lovely campanula (*C.? pelviformis*), a remarkably small form of *Gynandriris sisyrinchium* a few cm. high with 2 cm. flowers, *Gagea* (*Lloydia*) *graeca*, *Daphne sericea*, *Cyclamen creticum*, *Lythrum junceum* and charming *Trifolium uniflorum* (tap-rooted and I think tender), both rose and white. Another interesting find was a small yellow 'muscari', or one of the near relations of that genus, and Peter Davis adds to the plant-list here *Ranunculus cupreus*, *Fritillaria messanensis*, *Polygala venulosa* and *Asperula incana*.

Zakros is on the coast—a steep exciting descent through wild country and past two dramatic gorges. It is a beautiful place, with a recently discovered Minoan settlement. We saw a golden oriole, rollers, and dark blue backed egret-like birds. The site is partly under water, which has the effect of producing a very attractive water garden, with snow white egrets and little turtles.

From Zakros one can return to Sitia by faster roads through Palekastron and if time allows visit the Sideros Peninsula, the north-east tip of Crete. It is here, at Vai, that there remains the only natural palm-grove in Europe, of a Cretan form of *Phoenix theophrasti*. The palms are abundant, but likely to be outnumbered by the visitors to what might have been a very attractive beach.

Returning westward again, between Aghios Nikolaos and Heraklion there are roads leading up to the Lasithi Plain, a remarkable upland level area lying to the north of the Oros Dikti. There are several such upland plains in Crete, but the Lasithi Plain is unusual in being heavily populated by Cretan standards as well as intensively cultivated. It is also famous for its windmills—hundreds of them—which draw water from deep wells fed from the limestone mountains to the south. They were just having their sails attached for summer use when we arrived, but there were ominous sounds of electric pumps, and it seems sadly probable that the windmills are on their way out. This remarkable area has not only the great mountains behind it but also a rim of lesser hills on its northern edge. Where the road breaches the rim there is an eye-catching line of the remains of stone windmills, looking like forts, on either side of the col. By the roadside here was rosy pink *Crepis rubra*, and also some clear white forms of it, yellow annual *Linum trigynum*, *Ophrys lutea*, *O. fusca*, *O. omegaifera*, and *O. tenthredinifera*, as well as *Orchis coriophora*, *O. papilionacea*, *O. anatolica* and yellow *O. provincialis pauciflora*. *Cyclamen creticum*, hiding under spiny shrubs from the goats, was sometimes pale pink here. We found *Trifolium uniflorum* again, and also a few late flowers on *Iris unguicularis cretensis*—small, pale blue and yellowish, wholly different from the lovely Peloponnese form. At the southern edge of the plain is the Dikteon Antron, the alleged birthplace of Zeus, where you can burrow into the hill and see stalactites, but those who prefer instead to climb up the outside of the hill will find the iris and orchids that I have mentioned, and dittany (*Origanum dictamnus*) also grows here.

A road drops very steeply indeed from the Lasithi Plain via Mochos to Stalis. It may be better now, but in 1971 it was one of the worst roads we had ever been on—which is saying a great deal.

From Heraklion a road crosses the centre of the island over the hills to Timbaki, and in this area are three of the finest sites in Crete; Phaistos, Aghia Triada and Gortys. It is a magnificent drive, and an even finer one leads back from Timbaki via Spili to Rethimnon. On this journey we found *Linum caespitosum*, *Ornithogalum narbonense*, *Tulipa saxatilis*, *Gladiolus italicus* and *Orchis laxiflora* among other plants. Phaistos is famous for its orchids, largely because the guide, and even more so his father before him, has been specially interested in them. The Tourist Pavilion at **Phaistos** is an excellent place to spend a night, but as it has only five rooms it is well to 'phone ahead and book one.

The highest mountain in Crete, Mt. Ida, lies in the triangle between Heraklion, Rethimnon and Timbaki, appears to be remarkably inaccessible, and is by most accounts rather hot, dry and dull.

We visited the Ideon Antron, the cave on the eastern flank of the mountain, from Anogia, on an exceedingly bad road that winds through over-grazed and rather arid country. We found the beautiful cream-flowered *Arum creticum*, the leaves of *Colchicum pusillum* and of a crocus (probably *C. sieberi*) and of *Cyclamen graecum*, and *Putoria calabrica*. On the top of the mountain, if you can get there, there grow a few special plants (see *Bulletin* Vol. 5, p. 385).

Far more exciting, and at least in one place more accessible, are the White Mountains, near the western end of the island. A good centre for this area is **Chania** (Khania), the former capital of Crete, where there is a *xenia* and other hotels. It has a fine harbour, where you can sit and contemplate the octopuses strung out to dry in the sun. Chania lies at the neck of the Akrotiri Peninsula, famed for its display of early spring flowers, but now I believe rather heavily built-up in parts. Among the flowers which have been reported from this peninsula are *Campanula saxatilis*, *Verbascum arcturus*, *Dianthus arboreus*, *Tulipa cretica*, *Cytinus hypocistis* and *C. ruber*.

There is a fine drive across the island from Chania to Chora Sfakion on the south coast, and on the cliffs by the roadside we found an asperula (probably *A. idaea*), *Linum caespitosum*, *Muscari ?weissii*, *Petromarula pinnata* hanging effectively from the cliffs, and beautiful rose-pink forms of *Ranunculus asiaticus*. In addition to the white, pink and yellow forms of this latter plant which we found in Crete the bright red form is said also to grow here. This is the common form on Rhodes and Ogilvie-Grant (*Bulletin* Vol. 29—Conference Report—p. 60) has drawn attention to the affinities between the flowers of Crete, Rhodes and Karpathos.

A fine road runs southward from Chania to reach the Omalos Plain, another of the great Cretan high-level plains, lying to the north side of the White Mountains. The road as it leaves Chania runs at first through orange groves, and then climbs between hills where among the many flowers we found were *Cyclamen creticum*, *Anemone hortensis heldreichii*, *Arum creticum*, *Colchicum pusillum* (leaves), *Daphne oleoides*, *D. sericea*, *Orchis coriophora fragrans*, *O. papilionacea*, *O. quadripunctata* and one of the loveliest of all Cretan plants, the white-flowered, fine-leaved *Paeonia clusii*. The Omalos Plain is a well-known site for *Tulipa bakeri* (closely allied to, and perhaps a form of, *T. saxatilis*) which grows abundantly in the banks between the cultivated strips. At the southern end of the plain is a Tourist Pavilion, and from here a path leads up to the west into an outlying block of the White Mountains. It is a most exciting place to be—wild and rugged, with immense screes, still plenty of snow (in early May), and wide views across the island to the Mediterranean both to the north and to the south. Among the many special flowers here beside the path and at the edges of the snow are *Anchusa cespitosa* with its brilliant blue flowers, *Corydalis rutifolia uniflora*, *Verbascum spinosum*, *Euphorbia acanthothamnos*,

Prunus prostrata, Lithodora hispidula, Trifolium uniflorum, Acantholimon androsaceum, little chionodoxas varying from pale blue to near-white (probably both *C. cretica* and *C. nana*) and, loveliest of all, *Crocus sieberi* in its form *heterochromus,* shapely and colourful at the edges of the snow.

Below the Tourist Pavilion there is a small saddle where *Onosma erecta,* with delicate yellow flowers and silver leaves, grows and from here a path drops far and steeply towards the head of the Samaria Gorge. This gorge is by all accounts the show-piece of Crete, at least so far as its natural features are concerned. It is not easily accessible and not at all by car, for you must first descend the Xyloskalon, the wooden steps which commence the long drop down to the head of the gorge, and after an hour or more you will come to the deserted village of Samaria. This, alas, is as far as I have reached, but it is only the beginning of the real gorge, which continues for some five miles to reach the sea at Aghia Roumeli on the southern side of the island. From here you must either return the same way or take a boat to Chora Sfakion. The gorge can be visited by a regular long day trip by coach from Chania, or by bus to the top of the gorge and back from Chora Sfakion, necessitating either a very early start or a night at one of the small tavernas at Aghia Rumeli, as the last of the regular buses usually leaves at about four o'clock. It should be mentioned that the gorge is a Nature Reserve, and also that it is likely to be impassable until well into May.

While from its very nature the gorge is not abundantly flowered, there are plants of interest. White-flowered *Symphyandra cretica* is in the walls, and Dr. J. G. Elliott tells me that he found *Paeonia clusii* more abundant in the gorge than elsewhere, plenty of *Cyclamen creticum* on the way down, some remarkable stands of *Dracunculus vulgaris,* and quite a lot of *Ophrys fuciflora* and *Serapias vomeracea* just below Samaria.

Greece in the *Bulletin*:

Crete in the *Bulletin*:

5, 385 Davis, P. H.	**40,** 301 Raven, J.
7, 25 Davis, P. H.	**44,** 233 Ferns, F. E. B.
40, 188 Raven, J.	

Other reading:

Huxley, A. J., *Flowers in Greece*. The Royal Horticultural Society.

Huxley, A. J. & Taylor, A. W., *Flowers of Greece*. Chatto & Windus

12
BULGARIA*

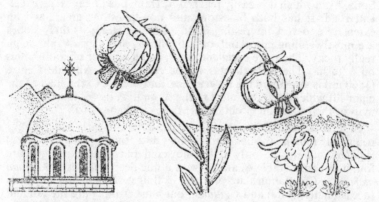

Situated in the extreme south-east of Europe, beside the Black Sea, Bulgaria is a country of considerable beauty. Nearly two-thirds of the country is mountainous, the main ranges being the Balkan, Rhodope, Rila and Pirin Mountains.

Sofia can be reached by air from London in about 3 hours. Cars may be hired there, and car travel is unrestricted. A leaflet, in English, *By Car Through Bulgaria*, which also includes a 1:800,000 road-map, may be obtained from the Bulgarian National Tourist Office. Main roads are usually good, but minor roads may be very rough. Rail travel is possible between main towns, but trains are very crowded and seats should be reserved in advance. There are buses from Sofia to the main holiday resorts. 'Balkantourist' also provides a long-distance taxi service for individual visitors at very reasonable rates.

Language can be a problem. Staff at hotels in remote areas are unlikely to speak any English, but German is widely spoken. Changing money may also be difficult, and if possible should be done in Sofia.

The weather generally seems to be rather more settled than in Romania, but it can be very hot during the summer months, with severe thunderstorms.

Mountain walking is popular, and the visiting walker is welcomed and there are no restrictions regarding access to the mountains except in certain frontier regions. Mountain huts are plentiful, though usually crowded. Accommodation and provisioning are very basic.

The flowers are good. There are elements of the 'basic' alpine flora, but generally the similarities are with the Balkan flora that we have met in Jugoslavia and because of the isolation of the Bulgarian mountain ranges there are many unusual and little-known species to be found there.

* Contributed by Mr. G E. Barrett

Vitosha (2290 m.) is an isolated mountain some ten miles south of Sofia, from which it is easily reached by tram, bus or car on an excellent road. It has both limestone and non-limestone areas, and an extensive and very interesting flora. Although steep, its turfy slopes are mostly rolling moorland, only the final peak, Cerni Vrah, being really rocky. There are excellent paths, and a number of good hotels on Vitosha. The Shtastlivetsa in the **Aleko** High Altitude Centre (1860 m.) is already in the flower zone, and is close to the start of the chair-lift which reaches almost to the summit. A useful tourist guide-map of the mountain is obtainable from 'Balkantourist'.

In several areas of the mountain in late June and early July the very beautiful *Lilium carniolicum jankae* and the equally beautiful *Aquilegia aurea*, the only yellow-flowered European aquilegia, are found in considerable quantity, with a fine deep red form of *Lilium martagon*. Campanulas are plentiful in Bulgaria, including *C. patula* (occasionally white) and *C. alpina*, but most striking are the tall and very beautiful pale blue flowered *C. moesiaca* and a little-known white-flowered campanula which has been named *C. stefanoffi*, although this name is not to be found in *Flora Europaea*. On the way up to the summit there is *Gentiana punctata*, also found in the Alps. Less familiar are the showy *Geum coccineum*, with bright red flowers, and *Dianthus microlepis*, a really minute 'pink', quite prostrate, with tiny flowers from deep pink through to pure white. The summit is very rocky, but there is no difficulty, and the meteorological station there will even provide the thirsty visitor with tea. On the northern side of the summit white *Ranunculus crenatus* is among the rocks, and other plants are *Dactylorhiza cordigera*, *Nigritella nigra*, *Senecio doronicum*, *Saxifraga rotundifolia*, *Pedicularis verticillata*, *Genista tinctoria*, *Acinos* (*Calamintha*) *alpinus*, *Geum montanum*, *Ranunculus aconitifolius* and *Jovibarba heuffelii*—an interesting mixture of 'Alpine' and 'Balkan'. Early spring or autumn might well disclose other interesting plants, particularly bulbs.

THE RILA MOUNTAINS

These mountains, some 55 km. to the south of Sofia, are very extensive, very rocky and very high. There are more than a hundred peaks over 2000 m. The highest, Mt. Moussalla (2925 m.), is also the highest mountain in the whole of the Balkan Peninsula. Many interesting flowers are to be found here, often species little known in Western Europe, such as *Primula deorum* which appears to grow only in these particular mountains, and there is great scope for further exploration.

The most convenient centre is **Borovets**, a small town and holiday resort only 65 km. by good roads from Sofia and at an altitude of 1300 m. It has two first-class hotels well used to catering for foreign visitors since Borovets is often included in Tours of Bulgaria although few British tourists seem to penetrate far into the mountains. There is also a chair-lift, which is inexpensive and very popular but of limited usefulness.

The outstanding expedition is the ascent of Mt. Moussalla itself, which has the advantage of including all the best of the flowers to be found in the area. It is a very long hard day, but there is no real difficulty. To reach the summit takes about five hours from Borovets: the first mile or more is along a good road and transport might be arranged for this section. In the lower part of the walk *Coronilla varia*, *Geum coccineum*, *Moneses uniflora*, *Geranium sanguineum*, *G. macrorrhizum*, *Pulmonaria rubra*, *Symphytum tuberosum* and *Campanula moesiaca* are to be found. On more open ground a little higher up the interesting *Bruckenthalia spiculifolia* becomes the dominant plant. After about 3 hours' walking, much of it over very rough paths, at a height of about 2100 m. more alpine plants begin to appear—*Dianthus microlepis*, *Campanula alpina* in various forms, *Viola biflora*, *Armeria maritima alpina*, *Senecio abrotanifolius* and *Gentiana punctata*. However it is not until after the large Moussalla Hut (2389 m.) has been reached that the greatest treasures are to be found. *Gentiana pyrenaica*, absent from the Alps, reappears here in great numbers. There is an especially good compact form of *Senecio doronicum*, *Jasione laevis orbiculata*, a dwarf centaurea with blue or occasionally white flowers, *Soldanella pusilla*, *Myosotis alpestris*, the lovely *Saxifraga pedemontana cymosa*, and again the beautiful silky white cups of *Ranunculus crenatus*. One of the most curious plants to be found here is the Balkan *Geum bulgaricum*. It is often large but it is a true alpine and is not found below about 2500 m. By a small lake grows the very rare reddish-purple *Primula deorum*, always in very damp areas, often in running water, usually in company with masses of the curious little *Plantago gentianoides*. Flowers of *Crocus veluchensis* often linger on here well into July.

Near the summit of Mt. Moussalla grows the uncommon *Gentiana frigida*. So also does *Geum reptans*. Surely fame if not fortune awaits the plant hunter who rediscovers the very rare hybrid of this plant with *Geum bulgaricum*, which may still grow there (*Bulletin* Vol. 4, p. 11).

Other very interesting walks in the area are to the former Royal Lodge at Saragjol, where traces of Wilhelm Schacht's rock gardens may still be seen, and via Mt. Deno to the Moussalla Hut again. For both these walks the chair-lift may be used. The flowers to be seen are similar to those described above, except that near Saragjol there is a fine form of *Gentiana lutea*, a scarce and strongly protected plant in Bulgaria. Also found here are *Nigritella nigra*, *Linum capitatum* and *Ranunculus platanifolius*. An interesting variation is to return from the Moussalla Hut via the Jastrabec Hut (2400 m.), where *Gentiana pyrenaica* and *Dianthus microlepis* are in great numbers; and *Dianthus carthusianorum*, *Jovibarba heuffelii*, *Swertia perennis* and *Asarum europaeum* are also to be found on this walk.

Another excellent centre in the Rila Mountains is **Malyovitsa**, some 36 km. to the west of Borovets, where there is an isolated hotel at a height of 1750 m. It is reached by a good road via Samakov and Govedarci and buses are available from Sofia. The hotel is splendidly situated with a fine view up the valley to the great peak of Mt. Malyovitsa itself (2739 m.). Unfortunately it may be difficult to book accommodation here as it is not a 'Balkantourist' hotel but is under the auspices of the Pirin Tourist Bureau. From the hotel there is an easy walk of about three-quarters of an hour to the Nalyovitsa Hut, but apart from this most of the walks are fairly hard, and the going rough, as Malyovitsa is primarily a mountaineering centre. Most of the flowers recorded for Borovets were also seen here, including *Primula deorum*, and, besides these, *Aquilegia aurea*, the very interesting *Polygala major* in red, white and blue forms, *Daphne mezereum*, *Primula farinosa exigua* and large quantities of *Primula minima*.

The 'Balkantourist' hotel adjacent to the Rila Monastery should also provide a suitable point from which to explore the neighbouring countryside. It is reached, again on good roads, from Stanke Dimitrov and Kocerinovo.

The Rhodope Mountains

These mountains, where Orpheus is said to have charmed the beasts with his lyre, form the frontier with Greece and may best be reached from Plovdiv in central Bulgaria, travelling south via Asenovgrad. Here by the picturesque Bachkovo Monastery there seems to be no sign now of the multitudes of plants of *Haberlea rhodopensis* which were said by earlier visitors (1951 *Conference Report*, p. 64) to be found on the cliffs nearby. The roads on this route, used by local buses, are very good.

Accommodation is easy to obtain in the large complex of excellent hotels at the popular tourist resort of **Pamporovo** (1600 m.), some 80 km. from Plovdiv. There are also one or two mountain huts in the Rhodope, but these are not easily accessible, and accommodation and service are unlikely to be very luxurious. Unfortunately Pamporovo is rather crowded, and the flowers in the immediate neighbourhood are not especially good, although *Dactylorhiza sambucina* in both its colour-forms is to be found even amongst the hotels. A little further afield are *Ornithogalum orthophyllum*, *Euphorbia epithymoides* and the interesting *Linum flavum* which is quite plentiful throughout the area. A two-stage chair-lift via the Studenets Chalet gives easy access to the summit of Mt. Snezhanka (1858 m.), the highest peak in the immediate neighbourhood of Pamporovo, where *Crocus veluchensis*, *Hypericum olympicum* with fine large flowers, and in the direction of the Smolyan Lakes *Euphorbia myrsinites* and *Jovibarba heuffelii* are to be found.

The very beautiful 'Rhodope Iris', a form of *Iris reichenbachii*, is to be found in considerable quantity in the gullies on the rocky summit of Mt. Mourgavets (1850 m.), an easy and interesting excursion from

Pamporovo. It is about 25 cm. tall, very free-flowering, and has bright yellow flowers. It is fairly widespread throughout the Rhodope Mountains. Generally speaking however the flowers here are not particularly good, and the mountains are little more than rolling hills, well-wooded almost to their summits with only very occasional rocky outcrops.

The highest mountain in the Rhodope is Goljam Perelik (2191 m.), a little to the west of the town of Smoljan and therefore at some distance from Pamporovo, but although it holds out considerable promise and there are good roads to the foot of the mountain, the western visitor may well be prohibited from climbing it owing to its proximity to the Greek frontier.

Another high peak, Goljam Persenk (2091 m.), may be reached by the side road leading to Zabardo from the Pamporovo-Asenovgrad road, which is quite appalling. This is unfortunate, firstly because it leads to the 'Stone Bridges', immense and quite fantastic natural arches of stone, and secondly because it is along such roads that the really interesting flowers are to be found. *Haberlea rhodopensis* appears in great numbers on the roadside cliffs, often accompanied by the somewhat strange but very desirable *Saxifraga stribrnyi* and occasionally *S. grisebachii*. Other flowers by the roadside or on the rocks include *Geum coccineum*, *Linum hirsutum*, *Iris reichenbachii*, *Globularia meridionalis*, *Astragalus angustifolius*, *Cortusa matthioli*, *Adiantum capillus-veneris* (the maidenhair fern), *Chamaecytisus hirsutus*, *C. supinus*, *Cytisus procumbens* and *Genista albida*.

Similarly rewarding, though in its later stages at least as rough a ride, is an expedition to the 'Devil's Throat', a very large swallow-hole and cave in limestone country near Trigrad on the River Kricim, some distance to the west of Smoljan. The approach roads are lined with colourful banks of flowers, including onosmas and many very showy leguminous plants. On the limestone cliffs above the river and near the cave itself the many thousands of plants of *Haberlea rhodopensis* are a really wonderful sight. On dry cliffs near the cave

Saxifraga stribrnyi

are the silvery rosettes of *Saxifraga sempervivum* and a magnificent purple edraianthus (*E. ? serbicus*).

Since elevations are relatively low, snow is not normally a problem here, and June is an excellent time to visit the area, especially for the haberlea. By then it is of course already quite hot.

The lack of good maps is even more apparent here, making the planning of routes extremely difficult, not only for walking but also even for visiting the 'recommended' beauty-spots. This, and the bad state of the roads, are particularly unfortunate as there is so much to be seen and so many areas still to be explored.

THE PIRIN MOUNTAINS

The Pirin range, in the extreme south-west corner of the country, are the wildest and most beautiful mountains in Bulgaria, and in their plants the most interesting. With eleven peaks over 2800 m., they are almost as high as the Rila range. The highest peak is Mt. Vihren (2915 m.). There is an exceptional abundance of lakes in these mountains many of which are very beautiful and add greatly to the landscape.

To reach the general area is relatively easy as there is a direct route almost due south from Sofia on good roads via Blagoevgrad to Simitli, but the final approach roads to the mountains are very rough.

There are several small towns such as Melnik, Sandanski, Bansko and Gotse Delchev which have suitable accommodation for tourists, but all are rather far from the mountains. The most convenient is

244

Bansko (935 m.), reached by a good road from Simitli via the Predel Pass and Razlog. There is an excellent new hotel here, but it is still some 16 km. from the foot of the mountains where the Banderitsa Hut (1770 m.) and the slightly higher Vihren Hut (1950 m.) are situated. A road connects Bansko with these huts, but its surface is bad, although a few cars and even small buses manage to make the trip successfully. One can stay at one or other of the huts. The Vihren Hut should be able to provide food as well as accommodation, but experience suggests that this is seldom available, and having to carry a sufficient supply of food and drink presents obvious problems. There are many other mountain huts scattered about the Pirin range, but their provisioning and accommodation are not of as high a standard as in similar huts in the Alps.

There are many fine walks in these mountains, but the most exciting and satisfying is to the summit of Mt. Vihren itself, reached by a fairly well defined path in about three hours from the Vihren Hut. The final peak, a vast dome of limestone rock, is very steep but not really difficult. On the saddle at the base of this peak at a height of about 2500 m. *Saxifraga ferdinandi-coburgi* is to be found covering the boulders in enormous quantities, and in a small level scree nearby the very rare and difficult *Leontopodium alpinum nivale*, a tiny and almost stemless form of edelweiss. Just below the summit there is a very beautiful dwarf form of the yellow alpine poppy, *Papaver pyrenaicum degenii*, probably endemic to these mountains. *Saxifraga pedemontana cymosa* grows here in unusually dry and exposed conditions, and other interesting plants are *Alyssum cuneifolium*, *Saxifraga spruneri*, and probably *Viola grisebachiana* on the west side of the peak. On the lower slopes of the mountain *Gentiana pyrenaica* flowers freely in the short turf, and in September these slopes are covered with thousands of flowers of another 'gentian', the minute annual *Gentianella bulgarica* with white or very pale blue flowers.

In the magnificent forests below the Vihren Hut are many fine trees of *Pinus leucodermis*. One giant, much revered, is said to be 1230 years old.

From the summit of Vihren may be viewed at close quarters the bizarre and quite extraordinary stark limestone ridge formed by the great peaks of Koutelo (2908 m.) and Banski Soukhodol (2884 m.), where the real treasures of the Pirin Mountains should be found; the almost legendary form '*crassense*' of the edelweiss, as much a giant as its near neighbour on Vihren is a dwarf, the rare and beautiful violet-flowered *Viola grisebachiana* and the equally beautiful yellow *V. rhodopeia*, *Saxifraga federici-augustii* (little-known from the wild), pink *Potentilla apennina stoianovii*, and the dwarf silvery-leaved *Centaurea triumfetti achterovii*. It cannot be guaranteed that all the plants listed here are still to be found on these peaks; there is considerable scope for some fascinating and indeed valuable exploration.

The original route, now only a track, to the Banderitsa and Vihren Huts makes quite an attractive walk, and a number of interesting flowers may be found along its length, including the decorative 'thistle' *Ptilostemon afer* in a dry stony area, *Allium victorialis*, *Scutellaria alpina*, *Soldanella hungarica*, the beautiful *Aquilegia aurea* and, nearer to the huts, *Draba lasiocarpa*, *Saxifraga luteoviridis* covering the rocks with its flat rosettes and *S. ferdinandi-coburgi* in large hummocks. A dianthus with small but vivid red flowers, a dwarf epilobium and a most interesting broom with fine silvery foliage and several other plants found here require further investigation.

From the Banderitsa Hut an interesting marked path leads up to the limestone ridge between Vihren and Koutelo, and here grow *Polygala major*, *Iris sintenisii*, *Daphne kosaninii*, *Saxifraga sempervivum*, *S. ferdinandi-coburgi* and *S. luteoviridis* in great numbers. The whole area is extremely picturesque and there are many splendid walks. That to the Demyanitsa Hut is particularly good, and although very long is not really difficult. It passes through the very heart of the range, crosses a 2580 m. pass, and runs beside a number of the very beautiful lakes that are such a pleasant feature of these mountains. Many flowers typical of the region are to be found on this walk—*Gentiana pyrenaica*, *Plantago gentianoides*, *Ranunculus montanus*, *Armeria maritima alpina*, *Soldanella pusilla*, *Jasione laevis orbiculata*, *Primula farinosa exigua*, *P. minima* in great quantity, *Senecio doronicum*, *Linum capitatum*, *Veronica "kellereri"* (? a dwarf form of *V. saturejoides*—very dwarf, with deep blue flowers), *Dianthus microlepis* here in a particularly large-flowered deep-coloured form, *Saxifraga pedemontana cymosa* and *Pinguicula leptoceras*.

In June when there is still much snow on the mountains vast numbers of *Crocus veluchensis*, its flowers variable but often of a striking rich imperial purple, cover the slopes.

The eastern part of the range is also somewhat difficult of access, although the Gotse Delchev Hut (1600 m.) can be reached by a very rough road from the village of Dobrinichte. Beyond the hut an even rougher timber-track leads high up into the mountains and gives access to the ridges and valleys descending from the Bezbog Peak (2645 m.). Here in river gullies is a soldanella which appears to conform in every way with that described by Professor Schwarz under the name of *Soldanella cyanaster* (*Bulletin* Vol. 43, p. 45).

An interesting excursion to the South Pirin Mountains was made by a Czechoslovakian Member of the Society, Mr. Zdenek Zvolanek. His approach was via Bansko and Dobrinichte and thence by taxi to the town of Gotse Delchev, and so by foot to the Papazchair Hut (1462 m.). Mt. Orelyak (2099 m.) to the north-west of the hut yielded *Astragalus angustifolius* and a large expanse of the showy yellow-flowered *Linum capitatum*. In the alpine zone were *Saxifraga* *ferdinandi-coburgi, S. sempervivum, Sempervivum zeleborii, Genista depressa, Campanula alpina orbelica* and *Saxifraga marginata* on western slopes near the summit. From near this point there is a tantalising distant glimpse of the famous Gocev Vrah, formerly Ali Botusch, the home of several notable endemics such as *Dianthus* "simulans"*, *Pulsatilla halleri slavica, Fritillaria drenovskii* and *Saxifraga stribrnyi zollikoferi.* Unfortunately, because of its location on the frontier with Greece it is not possible to visit it without a special permit.

The Pirin Mountains seem to accumulate a good deal of snow, and early July is quite soon enough to visit them. For mountain walking, September can be an ideal time. The weather then is often very good indeed, and not quite so hot, and a surprising number of flowers are still to be found.

Bulgaria in the *Bulletin*:

4, 191 Ingwersen, W. E. Th.   **40,** 231 Barrett, G. E.
     Bulgaria   Moussalla
10, 112 Ingwersen, W. E. Th.   **42,** 193 Barrett, G. E. Vitosha,
     Pirin   Rila
16, 178 Schacht, W. Pirin

Other reading:

Schacht, W., Plant Hunting in Bulgaria and Macedonia, 1951 *Conference Report*

* Found only on this mountain, *Dianthus* "simulans" seems to be accepted by gardeners but not by botanists as a distinct plant

13

ROMANIA*

Romania is an interesting country, and sufficiently little-known to make it especially attractive to the more adventurous plant-seeker.

The Romanian people are very friendly and lively. Local costumes are often worn in country districts. There is much of architectural interest, such as the many fine castles and the famous painted monasteries.

As to language, English is frequently and often avidly spoken by the many who have been taught it at school or university, and French is also widely understood.

A network of railways traverses the country. Trains are liable to be crowded, but if 'meeting the people' is not your aim, first-class travel will avoid this. Roads generally are very good, and traffic is light although it builds up considerably at week-ends. You can travel by car everywhere in Romania on any itinerary with no previous arrangements, and cars may be hired there. A leaflet 'Motor-car Map' issued by the Ministry of Tourism gives full details in English regarding travel by car in Romania, and other leaflets dealing with motoring holidays are also available from the Romanian National Tourist Office.

The great range of the Carpathian Mountains sweeps through the centre of the country, effectively dividing it in two. The Romanian Carpathians have many fine peaks, the highest reaching 2543 m. Many of the flowers here are similar to those in other parts of the

* Contributed by Mr. G. E. Barrett

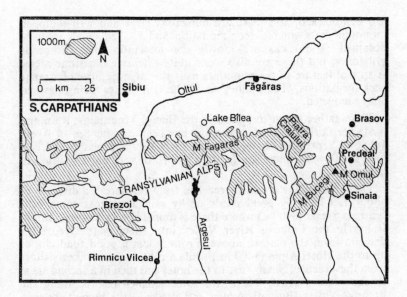

Carpathian chain (often species not found in the Alps) and in addition there are also a number of species endemic to Romania itself.

The weather in the mountains about to be described tends to be wet and sometimes misty in late June and early July, the time when most of the flowers are at their best. In the higher mountains it is likely that there will still be some snow. September frequently provides a warm sunny spell, and is not too late for finding interesting flowers.

Many interesting areas of the Romanian Carpathian Mountains remain undescribed in the following pages. The Rodnei Mountains in the extreme north of the country and the Cibin Mountains in the west in particular would appear to offer many exciting possibilities, while several of the Romanian gorges too, such as the Turda, Bicaz and Cazane Gorges, have their own local or even endemic flowers such as the yellow-flowered *Tulipa hungarica*. It is to be hoped that further exploration of such areas may be possible before they are overtaken by development programmes which seem now to be proceeding rapidly in so many parts of Romania.

THE BUCEGI MOUNTAINS

Part of the long Carpathian Range, the Bucegi Mountains mark the beginning of that abrupt change to an east-west direction which the Carpathians make as they become the Transylvanian Alps. They form a high-level plateau at about 2000 m., with occasional higher peaks culminating in Mt. Omul (2507 m.). Paths on the mountains are well-marked, and there are numerous large and well-equipped mountain huts where accommodation and cooked meals may be obtained. The rocks are mostly conglomerates and micaceous gritstones, but there are also some quite extensive limestone areas. A special feature of these mountains is the large number of strange rock-formations, 'The Sphinx' and 'The Old Ladies' being particularly renowned.

The weather is not too good in the Bucegi Mountains. Rain and mists are fairly frequent, and snow has been experienced in April, July and September. Late June and early July is probably the best time for flowers, and there is often a spell of very good weather in September.

These mountains are easily reached from Bucharest, a distance of about 130 km., by good roads or by rail. The most convenient centre is **Sinaia** (800 m.) where there is ample hotel accommodation. It lies in the Prahova River Valley into which very steep cliffs descend from the plateau above. From Sinaia a good road climbs up to the Hotel Alpin (1400 m.) while a cablecar now takes visitors from the streets of Sinaia first to the hotel and then in a second stage to the plateau itself. There are some smaller resorts along the Prahova Valley (Busteni, Azuga and Predeal—the highest town in Romania) but from these access to the mountains is more difficult. Near the old town of Brasov the resort of Poiana Brasov is popular with English visitors and has a cable railway up to Mt. Postăvaru (1802 m.), but here the mountains are lower and somewhat apart from the main Bucegi Range.

There are many fine walks in these mountains, and once on the plateau itself the going is fairly easy and distances are not too great. With the help of the cable-car it is now possible to reach the summit of Mt. Omul and to return to Sinaia the same day. Most of the plateau is heavily grazed, but *Campanula alpina* is widespread, often appearing here in an unusual pink form. *Gentiana brachyphylla favratii*, *Primula halleri*, *P. minima*, *Iris ruthenica* and *Bruckenthalia spiculifolia* are to be found here, while the interesting *Rhododendron myrtifolium* (*kotschyi*), a close relative of the 'alpenrose', covers considerable areas. On rocky outcrops the curious flowers and flat rosettes of *Saxifraga luteoviridis* are often to be seen. In the thick woods that cover the lower slopes of the mountains, *Digitalis grandiflora*, *Dianthus barbatus*, the scarce *Symphytum cordatum*, the very curious *Centaurea atropurpurea* and attractive *Pulmonaria rubra* may be found. In April the forests are filled with *Corydalis solida* (unfortunately not the 'George Baker' form which occurs rather further to the west, but still beautiful), *Corydalis bulbosa* (*cava*) in both its pink and its exquisite white form, *Anemone ranunculoides*, and the little-known dwarf purple-flowered *Cardamine glanduligera*. There is a very steep path descending from the Piatra Arsă Hut to the town of Busteni, and in April the woods at the lower end of this path are full of the huge blue flowers of *Hepatica transsylvanica*, the largest and finest of all the hepaticas.

The alpine meadow of Poiana Stinii is particularly noted for its flowers. Although spectacular in summer, they are mostly of the commoner 'hay-meadow' varieties. In early spring, however, the meadow is covered with myriads of mauve *Crocus vernus heuffelianus*, the typical form in the Carpathians of *Crocus vernus*, while *Scilla bifolia* and *Galanthus nivalis*, and the lovely dusky *Helleborus purpurascens*, appear in quantity around its edges. In the autumn, growing here with the local form of *Colchicum autumnale*, is that most beautiful crocus, *C. banaticus*. It is not however confined to this meadow, and by September it is already appearing in enormous numbers in Sinaia itself in the fields beside the river and indeed in river meadows along the whole length of the Prahova Valley.

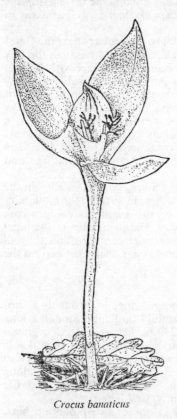

Crocus banaticus

One plant of outstanding interest, *Daphne blagayana*, rare in these mountains, grows in a particularly sheltered spot near the rock of St. Ann at an altitude of only about 1100 m. It is an especially good form, and can be found in full flower in April in company with a magnificent large local form of *Primula veris*.

In the steep gully behind the small Costila Shelter (1670 m.) on the crags above Busteni, snow lingers late in spite of its low altitude, and even in autumn there are still many flowers. Even *Primula veris columnae* is likely to be still in flower, together with dainty *Aquilegia transsilvanica*, *Dianthus spiculifolius* (a deliciously scented fringed pink with white or pale pink flowers), *Iris graminea*, *Anemone narcissiflora*, *Cortusa matthioli* in very good form, an interesting dwarf form of *Symphytum tuberosum* with yellow flowers, *Leontopodium alpinum* and the magnificent *Trollius europaeus transsylvanicus*.

Higher in the mountains the path leading from the 'Heroes' Cross', just beneath the summit of Mt. Caraiman (2325 m.), to the Caraiman

Hut is particularly rich in flowers and has been declared a Nature Reserve. Here are the lovely *Dianthus glacialis gelidus*, very dwarf but with huge deep pink flowers, *Primula halleri*, *Saxifraga luteoviridis*, the endemic dwarf yellow 'wallflower', *Erysimum witmannii transsilvanicum*, *Pulsatilla alba* (like a small *P. alpina*), *Scabiosa lucida* with very large pink flowers, *Centaurea uniflora nervosa*, *Alyssum repens*, *Soldanella pusilla*, the showy purplish-red *Pedicularis verticillata*, *Gypsophila petraea*, *Potentilla aurea chrysocraspeda*, and a diminutive form of *Leontopodium alpinum* as well as many of the 'basic alpine' plants.

On the rocky summits of the mountains, particularly near the Omul Wall and the final peak of Omul itself, are many treasures; the tiny *Viola jooi* (a Romanian endemic), *Pedicularis oederi* with brown-tipped yellow flowers, *Doronicum carpaticum* with small very hairy leaves, the delightful yellow alpine poppy, *Papaver corona-sancti-stephani* (also endemic), blue *Oxytropis carpatica*, and on the very summit of Omul, growing in limestone as it sometimes does in Jugoslavia, *Eritrichium nanum*—probably the subspecies *jankae*. Less likely to be found but well worth searching for are *Saxifraga marginata coriophylla*, *Draba haynaldii*, *Anthemis carpatica*, and *Linum perenne extraaxillare*.

Another area worth exploring is the lovely Ialomita Valley in the western half of the Bucegi Mountains. Here in autumn the mountainsides are covered with multitudes of the small annual 'gentian', *Gentianella bulgarica*, with pink flowers, and in crevices in the limestone rocks grows the beautiful *Campanula carpatica* and the tall endemic *Delphinium simonkaianum* may occasionally be seen on the wooded banks of mountain streams.

PIATRA CRAIULUI

About 23 km. distant from the Bucegi Range in a roughly north-westerly direction lies the Piatra Craiului (the King's Stone), a long white ridge of limestone reaching 2239 m. between the Bucegi and the Fagaras Mountains. This curious mountain has a remarkable flora, including its own unique and very beautiful flower, and is also very popular with mountaineers. It is approached by rail or along good roads from Brasov, or from Sinaia via Predeal and the interesting old fortified town of Risnov, to Zărnesti.

Accommodation is available only in one of two mountain huts. The Plaiul Foii Hut (849 m.) on the west side can be reached by road from Zărnesti, and meals are served here. Sleeping accommodation is somewhat rough however and rooms must usually be shared. It is at comparatively low altitude and about 5 km. from the mountain, whose west face is very steep. Even the normal route to the summit (La Om) requires the use of fixed wire ropes and iron pegs. The Curmatura Hut (1470 m.) on the east side of the mountain is fairly comfortable but much smaller with fewer amenities. It is reached by road from Zărnesti to the Fintina lui Botorog and thence by footpath, a walk of five or six hours in all. This hut is on the easier side of the mountain. It is higher, and the summit ridge is much more easily accessible.

The greatest treasure of this mountain is the beautiful endemic *Dianthus callizonus*. It is somewhat straggling but its rose-pink flowers have speckled inner zones which gives them a unique beauty. The flowers are variable, and hybrids occur with *Dianthus tenuifolius* and *D. spiculifolius* which also grow on the mountain. The true plant as it is found here in its best forms is seldom seen in cultivation. It flowers from July until September.

There is a great wealth of flowers on this mountain, some of the

Viola alpina

more outstanding being *Daphne blagayana*, *D. cneorum*, *Viola declinata*, *V. jooi*, *V. alpina*, *Campanula patula abietina*, *Dianthus glacialis gelidus*, dwarf dark blue *Geranium sylvaticum caeruleatum*, *Eritrichium nanum*, *Androsace arachnoidea*, *Saxifraga luteoviridis*, *Campanula carpatica*, *Papaver corona-sancti-stephani* and *Gypsophila petraea*. *Gladiolus imbricatus* is plentiful in the meadows, and *Hepatica transsylvanica* and *Cardamine glanduligera* in the woods.

THE FAGARAS MOUNTAINS

These mountains, still further to the west, extend from Piatra Craiului to the Olt Valley, a distance of some 80 km. They are the highest and probably the finest in Romania, the two dominant peaks being Moldoveanu (2543 m.) and Negoiu (2535 m.). The region is very picturesque and there are many mountain lakes. The initial approach is by the excellent Brasov-Sibiu road or by the railway that runs alongside it. To reach the main ridge of the Fǎgǎras Mountains is, however, more difficult. A new road runs to the Bilea Lake area, and indeed continues by a tunnel through the mountains to Lake Vidraru on the south side. The Bilea Lake is also accessible by cable-car from Bilea-Cascadǎ (1239 m.) on the north side of the range.

There is limited hotel accommodation at **Bilea-Cascada**, and further accommodation at **Bilea Lake** (2034 m.) in the Bilea Lake Hut, picturesquely but strangely situated in the middle of the lake, or preferably in the newer luxurious Palatinul Hut.

Besides being scenically very beautiful the Bilea Lake area is an excellent one for flowers, and is designated a Nature Reserve. Plants to be found here include *Doronicum carpaticum* near the lake, *Cortusa matthioli* in fine form on the slopes, and high up on the rocky peaks *Ranunculus crenatus*, *Saxifraga pedemontana cymosa*, *Viola*

253

alpina, Gentiana brachyphylla favratii, Pulsatilla alba, Silene dinarica (dwarf with small dark red flowers), the attractive, blue-flowered *Centaurea pinnatifida,* and many plants typical of the Eastern Alps.

Moldoveanu (2543 m.), the highest mountain in Romania, may be ascended from the Podragul Hut (2163 m.), some way to the east of Bilea Lake. It is a long walk but interesting and there is no real difficulty. *Trollius europaeus transsylvanicus* is especially good here. This hut is usually reached from Arpasul de Jos, spending a night at the Arpas Hut (accessible by rough roads) on the way. Some especially fine forms of *Saxifraga rotundifolia heucherifolia* may be seen on this route.

THE RETEZAT MOUNTAINS

These are wild and impressive mountains near the western end of the Transylvanian Alps as they approach the Danube. They cover a large area, with many rocky peaks exceeding 2300 m. The heart of the Retezat Massif is a vast National Park covering some 50 square miles. It is unique in having within it a strict Scientific Reservation of about 18 square km. where grazing, fishing, shooting and tree-felling are forbidden and even walkers must obtain special permits to enter. Here scientific study of the flora and fauna of the Retezat Mountains and of a completely natural environment undisturbed by man is carried out. These mountains are also particularly noted for the grandeur of their many glacial lakes. Unfortunately it is also one of the wettest areas in Romania.

Approach by road from the south is via Petrosani and Cimpul lui Neag to the Buta Hut (1580 m.); from the north from Pui through Hobita to the Baleia Hut (1450 m.); from Ohaba de sub Piatră to the Pietrele Hut (1480 m.) and from Hateg to the Gura Zlata Hut. Pui and Ohaba de sub Piatra may also be reached by rail. There may be a considerable walking distance between the nearest approach by road and the huts themselves. In the case of the Pietrele Hut for example a walk of about one and a half hours is necessary. The only accommodation is in these mountain huts, of which the largest and best-known is the Pietrele Hut, where conditions generally are somewhat primitive, a state of affairs not aided by the frequent wet weather.

One fine expedition from the Pietrele Hut is to cross the Curmatura Bucurei (a pass of about 2360 m.) to the Bucura Lake, Romania's largest alpine lake. A much shorter and easier walk is to the attractive Lacul Galesul (1990 m.) and into the cirque of mountains beyond. Access to the Scientific Reserve is over the Retezat Saddle just below the Retezat Peak (2484 m.), which may easily be climbed from the saddle. Near to this point are to be found the endemic *Draba dorneri* and really magnificent forms of *Rhododendron myrtifolium (kotschyi).* Most of the flowers already mentioned as occurring in the Bucegi and Făgăras Mountains are also to be found in the Retezat Range, with in addition the large pale yellow *Pedicularis exaltata,* beautiful pale blue *Campanula transsylvanica*, and in the limestone areas of the Retezatul Mic, *Pulsatilla vulgaris grandis*, *Lilium carniolicum jankae*, *Erysimum comatum* (*saxosum*) and the very rare *Pedicularis baumgartenii* with creamy white flowers and pinnate leaves.

One unusual hazard in these mountains is the presence of small black spiders (European Black Widow), said to be very venomous, which scuttle about on the rocks.

Romania in the *Bulletin:*

38, 253 Barrett, G. E.   **39,** 12 Schacht, W.
Carpathians   Carpathians

Other reading:

Bichiceanu, M. & R. R. *Flowers of Romania*. Meridiane Publishing House, Bucharest

Pop, E. & Salageanu, N. *Nature Reserves in Romania*. Meridiane Publishing House, Bucharest

14

THE HIGH TATRA

The main Carpathian Range north of Romania crosses the south-west corner of the Ukraine at no great altitude, and then forms the frontier between Czechoslovakia and Poland, gaining heights exceeding 2000 m. in one relatively small area, the High Tatra. From the following accounts it would seem that this area has more to offer to the plant-seeker on the Polish (northern) side than the Czechoslovakian. It should perhaps be said that Mr. and Mrs. Hilton's visits to the Czechoslovakian side were made more than ten years ago, and it is possible that the facilities have improved since then. Nevertheless the fact remains that the High Tatra is a small area to accommodate a large summer-holidaying and mountaineering population, as well as winter sports, and that July and August are likely to be times when both the accommodation and the transport facilities are over-burdened. Other writers in the *Bulletin* have however suggested that visits in June or September would avoid these difficulties, and in the former month at least the flowers should be in good form. The language problem may be expected to have eased now in that there is probably less reluctance to speak German.

Readers of Roger-Smith's book will see that he has remarkably little to say about the flowers of the High Tatra, but he does empha-sise the beauty and interest of the range and its various tourist attractions, as well as some of the outstanding architectural and other interests of Czechoslovakia as a whole.

THE CZECHOSLOVAKIAN SIDE*

The main ridge of the High Tatra Mountains has a length of only 25 km., and its greatest breadth is no more than 16, but the peaks rise steeply from the plains, and four of them exceed a height of 2500 m., and Gerlach (2655 m.) is the highest peak in the Carpathian chain. They are not very readily reached by car, being 500 km. from

* Contributed by Mr. E. Hilton

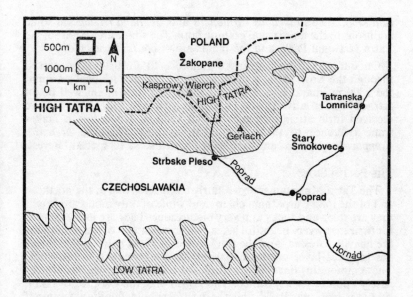

Prague, but one can fly to Poprad. There are few plants which cannot be found in the much more readily accessible European mountains.

The main tourist centres are **Strbske Pleso** (1355 m.), **Stary Smokovec** (1010 m.) and **Tatranska Lomnica** (850 m.). The Tatra is the principal holiday area available to the Czechs themselves and they flock to the mountains in great numbers. The hotels are relatively few, and foreign visitors seem to be rather crowded out. I would suggest that anyone contemplating a holiday here would do well to communicate with one of the members of the thriving Alpine Garden Club of Czechoslovakia, many of whom are also Members of our Society. We stayed at Tatranska Lomnica, attracted by the presence of a cable-railway running into the mountains. Our visit was however a disappointment. The hotel was very crowded and the service bad. No one spoke English, nor would anyone admit to speaking German, so we could get very little information of practical value concerning access to the mountains. Our car was of little use, for the only road merely linked the three main tourist centres. The cable-car was so heavily booked in advance that we were not able to obtain places on it, nor could we obtain a map of large enough scale to indicate the footpaths.

Both granite and limestone formations are represented in the High Tatra, and as usual it is the latter which provide the greater wealth of plants. *Viola lutea sudetica, Soldanella hungarica, S. carpatica, Draba dubia, Oxytropis halleri, O. carpatica* and *Hedysarum hedysaroides* are some of the less common calcareous plants, while *Pulsa-*

257

tilla alba, Senecio incanus carniolicus and *Gentiana frigida* are some additions to the more usual granitic flora. The whole area is part of the Tatra National Park, and the plants are of course protected.

On our way from Tatranska Lomnica to Bratislava we passed through the Low Tatra, a more extensive region with peaks around the 2000 m. mark, and it seemed to us that they might well be an attractive alternative to the High Tatra, though they seem to have received little attention from foreign visitors. Roger-Smith makes some reference to them, but mentions only *Jovibarba arenaria*, *Campanula carpatica* and *Gladiolus imbricatus* as of special interest.

THE POLISH SIDE*

The Tatra Mountains form a fairly compact group at the northern end of the long Carpathian chain, and while of only moderate height they are steep and rocky and very picturesque. They are justly famous for their many very beautiful lakes. The lower slopes of the mountains are heavily forested, and the thick cover of *Pinus mugo* which forms the topmost layer creates a barrier for walkers that is notorious. These mountains have a reputation for bad weather which unfortunately appears to be justified. The Polish, like the Czechoslovakian, side is a National Park, and the visitor should familiarise himself with the regulations governing this great nature reserve.

Zakopane is a very convenient centre from which to explore the Polish side of these mountains. It can be reached in about two hours by road from the small airport at Cracow. Roads in the area are very good. Car hire services are available, and there are no restrictions regarding routes. There are also good bus and train services throughout the country.

There is ample good hotel accommodation in Zakopane, and the 'Orbis' (Polish Tourist Organisation) Pensions are surprisingly good and often more conveniently placed for exploring the mountains. Zakopane is quite a large town, and it becomes very crowded in the holiday season. There is a very good cable-car service from Kunice (about 5 km. from Zakopane) to the summit of Kasprowy Wierch (1985 m.). Local buses provide frequent services to all the main valleys at very low fares. Footpaths in the mountains are good and very well-marked. There are a number of mountain huts, some rather small, some large and ornate.

A recommended time to visit is the latter half of June.

There are many walkers in these mountains, and the visitor will receive a friendly welcome. Only in the Chochlowska Valley where some sheep are kept largely to enable tourists better to visualise conditions here in earlier times is any grazing allowed, so there is usually an abundance of mountain flowers. Typical of the Carpathian Mountains is the beautiful *Campanula alpina*, which here in the Tatra

* Contributed by Mr. G. E. Barrett

is very large and fine. Very attractive too are the little-known *Doronicum clusii* with showy orange-yellow flowers, and dainty free-flowering *Soldanella carpatica*. Other flowers to be seen here include *Ranunculus platanifolius*, *Cardamine glanduligera*, *Swertia perennis*, *Senecio abrotanifolius*, *Trollius europaeus transsylvanicus*, *Pedicularis exaltata*, and many flowers characteristic of the Eastern Alps. Other rather scarcer flowers that may possibly be found are *Gentiana frigida*, *G. pannonica*, *Campanula carpatica* and *Dianthus glacialis*.

Pedicularis oederi

On an excursion to the mountain Giewont (1909 m.), a splendid rocky peak, the interesting *Pedicularis oederi* was seen in a very large and fine form, together with the smaller but more showy *P. verticillata*. The high frontier ridge, most easily accessible from the Kondratowa Valley, is a delightful walk and rich in flowers. Other attractive excursions are to the Roztok, Chocholowska and Koscieliska Valleys. The limestone peak of Kominiarska Wierch (1829 m.), situated between the two latter valleys, is noted for its rich flora. Roads are very good, but access to some of the valleys is prohibited for motor vehicles and the traveller must proceed on foot or in one of the special horse-drawn carriages provided.

The High Tatra in the *Bulletin:*

34, 93 Philipson, W. R. The High Tatra

36, 57 Cheyne, G. The Tatras

39, 181 Tyller, Ing. Z. Czechoslovakia

44, 20 Barrett, G. E. The Polish Tatra

15

SCANDINAVIA

A Viking Church

This great area of Northern Europe presents a problem to the compiler of a book such as this. It is largely mountainous and scenically attractive, and contains some beautiful flowers, many of them more or less confined to the area, so that it unquestionably qualifies for a place in the book. Yet, truth to tell, the number of species of gardening interest is not very great, and of these many are representatives of the 'Arctic-Alpine' flora, well-known and often more abundant in the Alps. Consequently it is unlikely that many Members of our Society would wish to visit Scandinavia for the flowers alone, but the mountains are beautiful and interesting, and the people friendly, so that there are excellent reasons for going there. An intriguing element in the flora is a group of North American species, and another interesting feature is that many of the more special plants are found, even if only rarely, in Northern Britain, so that they may be found illustrated in Keble Martin's and other British Floras.

NORWAY

The main mountain mass of Norway is near its southern end and the mountains reach their greatest heights in the Jotunheim. South of the Jotunheim is 'Fjordland', the scenically beautiful area of mountains surrounding the fjords that penetrate deeply in from the west coast, the main area visited by tourists. At the extreme north, within the Arctic Circle, where Norway curls round to the north of Sweden, there is another area of special interest. Great parts of the Scandinavian mountains are composed of primary rock, but in this northern area there are limestones and calcareous schists.

SOUTHERN NORWAY*

Access to Southern Norway is by sea (there are car-ferries) from Newcastle or Harwich to Bergen, Stavanger or Oslo, or by air to Bergen or Oslo, where cars can be hired. Anyone setting out for Norway expecting to find the profusion of flowers and colour seen in the Alps will be profoundly disappointed. The higher parts are still fairly bleak and snow-covered even in July and August. In consequence the flora is sparse and in some instances to be found only by

* Contributed by Mr. E. M. Upward

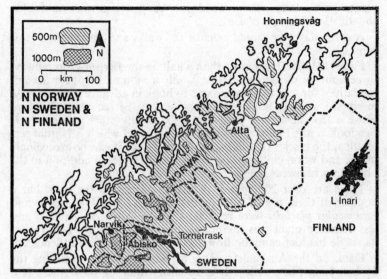

walking in very wet boggy conditions. Also the weather is extremely
unreliable and a standard item of equipment seems to be the
umbrella.

The first two centres to be described, Geilo and Finse, both lie
on the Bergen-Oslo road and railway, so that they can readily be
approached from either end.

Geilo is a small ski resort, well provided with comfortable hotels.
It is some four hours by rail from Bergen. Only one chair-lift operates
during the summer, to Geilo-hogda (1200 m.), where there are
magnificent views south to Usteldalfjord and north to the mountain
range of Hallingskarvet. The terrain towards Prestholtsaeter looks
flat, but is intersected with wet ditches which make it uncomfortable
for walking but interesting for plants. There are many clubmosses,
rushes, sedges, grasses, cotton-grasses, and parsley fern; *Betula nana*
and several species of dwarf willow, and many old friends from the
Alps—moss campion (*Silene acaulis*), *Lychnis alpina*, *Ranunculus
platanifolius*, *Rhodiola rosea*, *Saxifraga stellaris*, *S. aizoides* (both
yellow and orange), *Parnassia palustris*, black bearberry (*Arctostaphylos alpinus*), *Dryas octopetala*, *Potentilla crantzii*, *Loiseleuria
procumbens*, *Gentiana nivalis*, *Bartsia alpina* and *Pinguicula vulgaris*
—among other representatives of the Arctic-Alpine flora. Of yet
greater interest, in that they are plants with a mainly Scandinavian
distribution, are *Aconitum septentrionale*, *Rubus chamaemorus* (the
cloudberry), *Phyllodoce caerulea*, *Cassiope hypnoides*, *Cornus suecica*
and *Pedicularis lapponica*.

In and around Geilo itself can be found *Cirsium helenioides*
(*heterophyllum*), the 'melancholy' thistle—not in any way a cheerful

261

plant, particularly when found in the pouring rain—and blue sow-thistle (*Cicerbita alpina*).

A seven-day stay should exhaust the walks and excursions of this centre.

Finse (1214 m.) is no more than a halt on the Bergen-Oslo railway, three hours from Bergen. There is only a mountain hut for accommodation, for which it is advisable to book in advance. For the fit, a mountain walking holiday in Norway is to be recommended, and Finse is the starting-off point for walks to the north and south. It overlooks Lake Finsevatn to the south, beyond which is Hardangerjokulen, the glacier that feeds Hardangerfjord. It can be exceedingly bleak, and warm clothing is necessary at all times in addition to the obligatory rainwear.

There are over 200 species of plant endemic to the area, but a number of them are of little gardening interest. *Silene acaulis* and *Ranunculus glacialis* were reminders of the Alps. An unusual and less common plant was the nodding campion, *Silene wahlbergella*: its single bladder-campion flower is at first nodding and then erect.

Flam, on the Aurlandsfjord, is a good centre for exploring the 15 km. long Flam valley. It is reached either by boat (there is a car-ferry) from the fjord, or by rail from Myrdal which is at the head of the Flam valley and is also on the Bergen-Oslo railway line.

From Myrdal the whole 15 km. can be walked, but there are numerous intermediate stations from which the walk down the valley can be started. The descent is gentle and the valley is wooded,

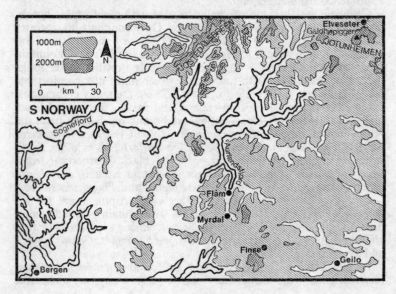

with lower alpine-belt flora such as monkshood, *Geranium sylvaticum, Polemonium caeruleum,* and the inevitable willow-herb. The outstanding plant in this valley was *Saxifraga cotyledon,* whose hundreds of flowering rosettes were well out of reach and best observed through binoculars.

The public transport system in Norway is unequalled. The timing of trains, buses and boats is pure perfection, with never a moment wasted. Thus it is with comparative ease that the Jotunheim Mountains can be reached.

Elveseter is a good centre in the Jontunheim. The hotel is comfortable and attractively decorated. The energetic can climb Galdhopiggen (2468 m.), Norway's highest peak, but a guide is necessary. Short comfortable walks will provide floral interest, mostly of plants already noted at Geilo, together with *Dianthus deltoides, Botrychium lunaria* (moonwort), *Chamorchis alpina, Pyrola norvegica, Gentianella campestris* and *G. amarella.* It is worth spending two or three days at Leirvassbu, above Elveseter, to see the higher flowers such as *Cassiope hypnoides, Pulsatilla vernalis, Draba fladnizensis, Saxifraga oppositifolia* and *Epilobium anagallidifolium,* the prostrate nodding alpine willow-herb.

Further to the north (but still in Southern Norway) is Dovre-fjell, an area renowned for its rich flora. It is a protected area.

NORTHERN NORWAY—THE NORTH CAPE AND ALTA FJORD*

This area in the extreme north of Norway can be reached either by the E6 road through Sweden, which is fast with a good surface, and then through Finland, or by the E5 through Norway, which is pot-holed, slow, and expensive because of all the ferries across the fjords. After motoring 1500 km. through Swedish forests and then the bleak tundra region of Finland one reaches the very spectacular scenery of mountains and sea islands of Norwegian Finnmark. On the coast the sea breezes blow away the midges and mosquitoes which are such a plague in Northern Sweden and Finland. It has to be experienced to be appreciated—the misery of perpetual daylight seen through a perpetual cloud of biting insects! Though it was cold at the time of our visit in early July, there was plenty of sunshine in the North Cape and Alta Fjord region, a delightful contrast to the mist and rain of Western Norway.

Plants of the boggy inland permafrost region include *Ledum palustre* growing in the birch forest with *Linnaea borealis,* a very slow-growing form of *Andromeda polifolia* with deep purple leaves, *Vaccinium oxycoccos* (cranberry), *Rubus arcticus, Cornus suecica* with very large flowers, and *Phyllodoce caerulea.* On the better-drained coastal cliffs adjacent to the Alta Fjord are a form of *Viola biflora* with deep brown veining on the yellow petals, *Astragalus alpinus arcticus* with showy purple-blue flowers, *Mertensia maritima*

* Contributed by Mr. H. Taylor

on pebbly beaches and, perhaps the most striking plant of the Alta fjord, *Primula nutans** (*finmarchica*), growing in quantity in a salt-marsh by the seaside. It looks rather like *P. farinosa*, but is completely devoid of farina.

Mageraya Island, site of the North Cape, is reached by ferry to the town of Honningsvag. Perpetual daylight here extends from 14th May to 30th July. In early July there were extensive snow-fields just above sea-level. The ground is carpeted with lichens and very short grass, but some areas are natural rock-gardens with low-growing flowers. *Cassiope hypnoides* with its pink-flushed flowers is sometimes so thick on the ground that you have to step on 'Farrer Medal plants' to study the *Diapensia lapponica*, which here forms small hummocks rather than large mats. *Saxifraga oppositifolia* too is remarkably small and compact here, though with good-sized flowers, and there is a small-leaved form of *Dryas octopetala*.

SWEDEN

Sweden, like Norway, is a vast, elongated country. Its frontier with Norway is formed by a chain of mountains which reach their maximum height of around 2000 m. near their northern end, in the area of **Abisko** by Lake Tornetrask and south from there in the Stora Sjofallets and Sareks National Parks.

This area is reached by rail, either from Narvik in Norway or from Stockholm, which itself is reached either by air, or by road or rail from Goteborg. There is no road into the Abisko area: the nearest road appears to end at Kiruna, some sixty miles away. Distances in Scandinavia are great; Northern Sweden is about as far, as the crow flies, from London as is Northern Greece.

There is an interesting account of the Abisko area in the *Bulletin* (Vol. 5, p. 130), and I am indebted to Mrs. D. Graiff for a list of plants in the area. These are, as would be expected, very much the same as those that we have encountered in Norway, but the list is an impressive one and includes a number of additional plants. Among those of special interest in that their distribution in Europe is more or less confined to Scandinavia are *Draba alpina*, *Saxifraga nivalis*, *S. rivularis*, *Rhododendron lapponicum*, *Cassiope tetragona*, *Primula stricta*, *Pedicularis sceptrum-carolinum*, *P. lapponica* and *P. hirsuta*. The rhododendron and cassiope are of special interest in being calcicolous species in predominantly lime-hating genera. A number of other interesting plants are mentioned in the *Bulletin* article referred to above, including *Campanula uniflora*, *Ranunculus sulphureus* and *Papaver radicatum*.

FINLAND†

Finland is a land of lakes, forests and mires, northern and cold in winter—summer is quite different. I can remember landing at an

---

* This is *P. nutans* Georgi, not to be confused with *P. nutans* Delavay, the Asiatic primula of our gardens, which is now correctly *P. flaccida*.

† Contributed by Dr. F. M. Tayler

airfield north of the Arctic Circle where the temperature was 94°F. It is a remote and sparsely populated country and so still has a profusion of wild flowers: most of these occur in the British Isles, but many of our rarities are not rare there.

Finland is mainly a low-lying country, but in the north (part of Lappland) there are mountains rising to 1000 m. near the Norwegian and Swedish borders. These hills are bare-topped and rise from forests of *Betula pubescens tortuosa* and *B. nana*. Summer here is short and eventful, and autumn a riot of colour. Permafrost is everywhere; the ground is frozen solid a foot or two down at all times. It is the zone where the birch forest gives way to the open fells that holds some of the finest alpine flowers, such as saxifrages, veronicas, *Cicerbita alpina*, *Erigeron uniflorus*, and *Chamorchis alpina*, all growing fast in the first few frost-free weeks.

Long-distance travel is by train, car and bus. Remember that the distances are great and that north of the Arctic Circle there are few tarmac roads. Why not travel by Post Office canoe with the Lapp postman down the fast-flowing Tana River along the Norwegian border to see the charming endemic *Thymus serpyllum tanaensis*?

ICELAND*

Iceland is a large and remote country, costly to get to and to travel in. Parts of it are accessible only with special vehicles and equipment. Large areas, though not so large as the name perhaps suggests, are covered with ice or snow, and other vast areas consist of accumulations of volcanic debris: here are few plants, or none at all. Most roads are dreadful, most prices seem outrageous, and the traditional dishes include rotted shark, and a revolting parody of black pudding, supposed to be eaten with porridge. Yet it is one of the most exciting countries on earth, colourful beyond expectation: not a country for the alpine plant fanatic, but an enduring delight and excitement for anyone who tempers that fanaticism with an interest in birds, and with the ability to respond to one of the most evocative of landscapes.

You can fly expensively to Reykjavik via Glasgow, or, if time is unimportant, take a boat from Scrabster via the Faroes to Seydhis-fjordhur on the east coast of Iceland. There are also occasional boats from Felixstowe. If you go by sea you can take your car, laden with tinned food and a Gaz cooker. If you fly you will have to buy most of your food and must, at high cost, hire a car, but you may think it better to subject a hired car rather than your own to the vicissitudes of Icelandic 'roads'.

Within the island there are good air services, and in clear weather the views from a plane are breath-taking. If you want to visit the north or east you can fly from Reykjavik to Akureyri or Egilsstadhir and hire a car there. (You could go by bus—but I wouldn't!). Organised tours and day-trips are available from the larger towns,

* Contributed by Mr. F. R. Smith

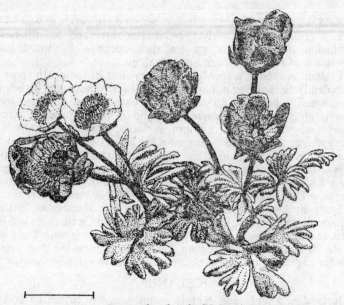

Ranunculus glacialis (Norway)

but it is a reasonable generalisation to say that the areas to which most of the tours go would be less good for plants than the areas accessible to fairly venturesome tourists who carry walking-boots in their cars. My suggestion would be to go it alone with a car to one of the following areas:

Akureyri (chief town of the north) with Myvatn and its surroundings; the area accessible from **Reykjavik**, including Gullfoss, the Geysir area, Keridh and Thingvellir (on the way, call at the greenhouses in the hot spring area at Hveragerdhi); the **Skaftafell National Park**, remotely situated in the south-east.

The Icelandic Tourist Board in Reykjavik is most helpful, and will book accommodation for you for a nominal fee. There are hotels in most towns and villages.

Summer in Iceland is generally cool, but it can be cold, because of the penetrating winds, or very hot. Before June, snow could impede movement, and then, and after mid-September, it could be uncomfortably cold. There is little darkness during the summer months.

Geologically, the island is wholly volcanic, and much of it is of very recent origin. It is one of the evocative wonders of the country to see the start of colonisation—widely spaced clumps of *Silene acaulis* or *Thymus serpyllum* smothered in flowers among a sea of pumice, or wisps of *Betula nana* sprouting from clefts in a great sea of red lava. But it is in the older rocks that the main plant interest

266

is to be found. There are clefts rich in ferns and colourful with *Geranium sylvaticum* and *Potentilla crantzii*, and the valleys have a varied and interesting flora including *Phyllodoce caerulea, Cassiope hypnoides, Ranunculus glacialis* and *Koenigia islandica*. But be warned that there are only some 450 species of vascular plant in Iceland, and that 85% of them occur also in Britain. There is how-

Epilobium latifolium

ever a small number of western species, not found elsewhere in Europe, of which the arctic fire-weed, or river beauty (*Epilobium latifolium*), is the most spectacular. It is not uncommon in river gravels, and flowers rather late in the summer. Another is the northern green orchid, *Platanthera* (*Limnorchis*) *hyperborea*, which is locally common, especially in the north, where on lake-sides there are colonies of *Lomatogonium* (*Pleurogyne*) *rotatum* and sometimes patches of an unusual and luminous reddish-purple form of *Viola tricolor*. The true Iceland poppy, *Papaver radicatum*, is no-where common but is a delight to be sought. There is unusual vegetation around the hot springs, but it is of more interest to the botanist than to the gardener.

SPITSBERGEN

We have travelled far since entering the Bernese Oberland 236 pages ago, and now we finish (for we could hardly travel further in Europe) with a brief visit to Spitsbergen, a group of Norwegian islands 650 km. north of the North Cape. The following notes are abstracted from information contributed by Mr. D. P. Spicer.

The Spitsbergen archipelago is a spectacular land of mountains, ice-caps and glaciers dissected by fjords. It is the only European habitat for some of the extreme northern circumpolar plants.

The Norwegian coastal steamers from Bergen link one with an excellent 11-day cruise from Tromso, with a choice of staying at Longyearbyen or continuing around the north-west coast with a number of trips ashore. It is possible to fly London-Oslo-Tromso-

267

Longyearbyen. The only hotel is run by the coal company and is difficult to get into, so longer stays have to be arranged on an expedition basis, taking tents, food, fuel and preferably a boat. Permission must be obtained from the authorities.

The larger islands are mountainous, reaching about 1680 m. The Gulf Stream helps to keep the west and north-west coasts snow-free for a few summer months, allowing plant-growth. There are attractive grasses, sedges and rushes, and a few familiar plants like *Saxifraga oppositifolia*, *Silene acaulis* and *Dryas octopetala* make large sheets of colour. Other 'Arctic Alpines' are *Ranunculus glacialis*, *Potentilla crantzii* and the tiny annual *Gentianella tenella* whose single sky-blue trumpets, barely 2 cm. high, are found in only one valley in Spitsbergen, but how remarkable that it should be both here and on the Sierra Nevada in southern Spain! Other plants more restricted to Scandinavia include *Papaver dahlianum*, the rare dwarf blue *Polemonium boreale*, *Arenaria ciliata pseudofrigida*, *Ranunculus sulphureus*, *Draba bellii* and *D. subcapitata*, respectively yellow and white, *Potentilla nivea* and *Campanula uniflora*.

Mr. Spicer ends with a note of warning—avoid lone bull musk-oxen and polar bears!

Scandinavia in the *Bulletin*:

5, 130 Fries, R. E. Sweden
7, 344 Fiedler, S. G. Norway, Sweden
35, 48 Lewis, Dr. M. Spitsbergen
35, 88 Stocken, C. M. Iceland

36, 258 Jones, E. L. Iceland
38, 110 Crum, M. Iceland
39, 6 Webb, R. Iceland
39, 7 Faegri, K. Norway, Sweden

Other reading:

Faegri, K., *Plant World at Finse, Norway*. Bergen Line, 1953
'Icelandair', *The Flora and Vegetation of Iceland*
Lid, D. T. (Illustrator), *Mountain Flowers of Scandinavia* (available in English in Bergen bookshops)
Ostenfeld & Grontved, *The Flora of Iceland and the Faroes* (1917, reprinted 1934)

16

SOME THOUGHTS ON PHOTOGRAPHING FLOWERS*

Equipment. Keep it simple. One Member goes abroad loaded with two camera bodies, five lenses (wide angle to telephoto) and a bag of knick-knacks. Another takes a compact 35 mm. reflex with macro lens. The plant photos taken by the latter are every bit as good as the former's, though of course his mountain views are less so. A lightweight tripod is vital, as is a light meter if your camera does not incorporate one. A small electronic, battery-operated flash is desirable, and an ultra-violet filter should be kept permanently on the camera in the mountains.

Lenses. Never buy a camera complete with standard lens without considering your personal type of photography. A standard, or long-focus, lens is at its best at infinity and definition falls off as the subject gets closer. A macro lens is exactly the opposite, so if flowers take priority to scenery, choose a macro lens in preference to a standard one. Zoom lenses are costly, bulky and unwieldy. Standard lenses will need close-up attachments or extension tubes.

Films. One must choose between colour prints (negative material) or transparencies (positive) or, of course, black and white, which calls for infinitely more skill where flowers are concerned. But times are fast changing, and the new Cibachrome A process (at present very costly) gives a degree of sharpness unattainable with colour negative film, also non-fading prints directly from colour transparencies. Such prints are easily produced in the amateur's darkroom without expensive equipment. For black and white photos a fine grain film around ASA 64 is preferable to a very fast film.

The Four Rules of Flower Photography

1. Learn to recognise a potential photograph . . . particularly difficult where black and white is concerned. Taking shots in the mountains is quite different from the garden. You cannot come back for another go, and it may be raining, windy or misty. Mist diffuses light and often provides ideal conditions, especially for contra-jour shots. The ideal plant photograph shows the whole plant, flowers and foliage; close-ups are often very beautiful, but give no idea of scale.

2. Compose and frame the picture. With colour, this is a vital exercise; with black and white, the final composition can be in the darkroom. Choose a subdued background, and decide whether it is to be blurred or sharp (see rule 3). Do a bit of 'gardening' if necessary to clean up odd twigs, but refrain from adding extra flowers . . . it generally shows! Carry a background cloth of neutral grey . . . it can also serve as a windshield. Colour photography needs bright sunlight (but shade off the direct sunlight when taking blue flowers); black and white needs a subdued light. Do not hesitate to use flash

* Contributed by Roy Elliott, A.R.P.S.

to 'fill in' shadows, but never let the flash predominate; a reflector (say the foil from the hotel sandwiches) will also serve the purpose. Remember that many of the finest shots are taken into the light, and that your treatment of the background will make or mar the picture.

3. Focus. The lens should be focussed on a point roughly one third of the distance from front to back of subject. The smaller the f stop, the greater the depth of field. The closer the camera is to the subject, the smaller the depth of field and the more critical the focussing. The shorter the focal length of the lens, the greater the depth of field; a wide angle lens with a small f stop will give almost unlimited depth of field (and a degree of distortion), whereas a long focus lens with a larger f stop will need highly critical focussing. With a hand-held camera, an absolute minimum of 1/60th of a second is called for with an equivalent f stop.

The dilemma between choosing a fast shutter speed for a flower that is moving in the wind and a small f stop to give depth of field can be solved up to a point by using a fast film. Such films used to lack the definition required in plant photography, but colour films are improving almost annually in this respect.

4. Exposure. Correct exposure in a negative or transparency is obtained by finding the right balance between f stop and shutter speed for a particular ASA rating of film. A fast shutter speed will arrest movement, and the closer the camera-subject distance, the faster the shutter speed needed for a similar degree of movement. Flash will also arrest movement, but unless the background is close behind the subject, a stark 'night time' effect is produced. With advanced modern 35 mm. cameras (and 35 mm. is the only convenient format when toiling around mountains), the f stop can be chosen in advance and electronic circuits coupled to the T.T.L. (through the lens) metering will automatically adjust the speed. This shows great advantage over earlier cameras with separate exposure meters (where users of extension tubes so often forget to increase the exposure time). For close-up work, do not be afraid of using the camera at full aperture, for if the focus is critical the background will be so blurred as to be immaterial.

Don't forget to adjust the camera for the ASA value of the film you are using: if you use two camera bodies, for colour and mono-chrome, choose films with similar ASA values.

Don't try to get 22 shots off a 20 exposure film; watch the perfora-tions engage on both sides . . . and in any case the processors will probably lop off the extras when they splice the films together for processing.

Don't take colour film in bad light, or white flowers in monochrome in direct sunshine if it can be avoided.

Do use a tripod; if it is a bit unstable and you have no cable release, use the self-timing device on the camera if it has one.

Do remember to tension the film with the re-wind lever before embarking on the first exposure.

Do take spare batteries for your camera and flash unit.

Finally, when your holiday is over, don't send all your film to the processors at once . . . mistakes can happen in the very best circles.

Plant Photography in the *Bulletin*:

29, 42 Downward, J. E.   **34,** 324 Tomlinson, A. J. H.
32, 101 Elliott, R. C.   **39,** 50 Fabb, G. N.
33, 143 Read, P.

Other reading:
Angel, H., *Photographing Nature—Flowers.* Fountain Press

LONDON TOURIST OFFICES

All these offices have proved helpful, and liberal with their 'handouts'—though these vary a good deal in their value. In general detailed local information, e.g. as to bus routes, seasons when chairlifts operate, etc., are not available at these head offices, but they will obtain the information on request. In addition to the informative leaflets, booklets and brochures mentioned below the offices hold large numbers of brochures relating to specific areas, generally designed to attract rather than to inform. Nearly all the leaflets, etc., mentioned below are available in English.

Austria. 30, St. George St., W1. Hotel list. Motoring. Address of Austrian Alpine Club (OAV): Longcroft Ho., Fretherne Rd., Welwyn Garden City, AL8 6PQ.

Bulgaria. 126, Regent St., W1. Motoring leaflet with map. More information from 'Balkantourist', Sofia, 1 Lenin Square, Bulgaria.

Czechoslovakia. Czechoslovak Travel Bureau (Cedok), 17 Old Bond St., W1X 3DA. Limited hotel list: fuller booklet on Cedok Interhotels. General information leaflet. Camping and motoring.

France. 178, Piccadilly, W1. Area hotel guides. Book '*Guides des Hotels*' (Logis de France & Auberges Rurales) published annually and purchasable in book-shops. Address of Club Alpin Français: 7 Rue de la Boetie, 75008 Paris.

Greece. 195, Regent St., W1R 8DL. Full hotel list. Car-hire. Routes to and from Greece. Mountaineering. Flowers. Map-book.

Iceland. Icelandair, 73, Grosvenor St., W1.

Italy. 201, Regent St., W1R 8AY. Traveller's Handbook. Mountain Holidays. (Hotel lists must be obtained from provincial tourist offices). Address of Club Alpino Italiano: Corso Italia 10, Milano.

Jugoslavia. 143, Regent St., W1. Hotel list. Car-ferries (Italy-Jugoslavia-Greece).

Norway. 20, Pall Mall, SW1. Ferry-services (international and internal). Motoring (with map). Car hire. Hotel list.

Poland. Polish Travel Office (Orbis), 313, Regent St., W1.

Portugal. New Bond St. House, W1. Hotels, food and eating-places. Pousadas.

Romania. 98, Jermyn St., SW1. General information booklet. Hotel lists.

Spain. 57, St. James St., SW1. Paradores and albergues. Shipping services. Bus services. General information booklet.

Sweden. 3, Cork St., W1. Hotel list. National Parks. Hiking.

Switzerland. 1, New Coventry St., W1V 3HG. Hotel Guides. Rail travel and concessions. Passes. Mountain flowers.

Appendix II

MAPS*

The basic reference guide is *"International Maps and Atlases in Print"* Ed. K. L. Winch, published by Bowker, which is in its 2nd edition 1976. Reference may also be made to the following regularly published material:

Bibliographie Cartographique Internationale (Armand Colin) (Annual)

New Geographical Literature and Maps (Royal Geographical Society) (twice yearly)

Current Geographical Publications (American Geographical Society) (10 times yearly)

The principal U.K. retail agents are Stanfords International Map Centre, 12–14 Long Acre, London WC2E 9LP. Large stocks are maintained and most other maps are obtainable by order. Maps may be more readily available and up-to-date from Stanfords than in the country of origin!

"Winch" includes map indices to the major series, and most national cartographic institutions issue their own catalogues or indices. Given your area of interest, Stanfords will suggest relevant maps if you are unable to visit the shop or consult "Winch". They will also supply appropriate indices on request.

Where large scale maps are not generally available (e.g. most East European countries), national tourist office free brochures and locally available guides may prove the only alternatives. The larger detailed country guides often have adequate maps, and the pre-war Baedekers have detailed information on walking routes.

It should be noted that geological maps may be available at scales larger than topographic ones. They are, however, usually expensive.

The listing which follows is a selection of the more important maps available in 1978 of value (a) for route planning and touring (scales 1/1 million to 1/200,000), and (b) for walking (scales 1/100,000 to 1/15,000).

ANDORRA
1/80,000	La Principauté d'Andorre (IGN—French Official Survey)
1/50,000	Carte de la France XXI-49 (IGN)
1/40,000	Andorra I Sectors Fronterers (Editorial Alpina)

AUSTRIA
1/1 m.	Philip International 1/1 m. Road Map to Alpine Countries (covers area from Paris—Brno and Marseilles—Foggia)
1/1 m.	Michelin 987—Austria, Benelux, Germany, Italy
1/850,000	Shell Reisekarte Österreich
1/600,000	Hallwag Alpina—Eastern and Central Alps (Hallwag)
1/500,000	Austria (Geographia)
1/400,000	Michelin 426
1/250,000	Kompass Autocarte—2 sheets
1/200,000	Generalkarte Österreich (OAMTC—Mair) (7 sheets)
1/200,000	Oberbayern, Tirol, Dolomiten RV51 (RV Reise-und-Verkehrsverlag)
1/100,000	Freytag und Berndt Wanderkarten (52 sheets)
1/50,000	Freytag und Berndt Wanderkarten
1/50,000	Kompass Wanderkarten (118 sheets)
1/50,000 & 1/25,000	O. Müller Verlag Wanderkarten (33 sheets—selected areas of Alps)
1/25,000	Alpenvereinskarten (Österreichischer Alpenverein (45 sheets)—selected areas)
1/15,000 to 1/30,000	Kompass Umgebungskarten (10 sheets)

* Contributed by Mr. R. E. Metcalfe

Official surveys at 1/200,000 (23 sheets); 1/50,000 (213 sheets); and 1/25,000 (800 sheets) are available, but the additional information on the Wanderkarten type maps (based on the official surveys) makes the latter more useful.

Vegetation maps are available at 1/400,000 and selected areas are at a larger scale.

BULGARIA

1/1 m.	Rumänien, Bulgarien (Freytag und Berndt)
1/1 m.	Rumänien—Bulgarien (Kümmerly & Frey)
1/800,000	Road map of Bulgaria

CZECHOSLOVAKIA

1/1 m.	Tschechoslowakei-Ungarn (Hallwag)
1/600,000	Czechoslovakia (Ravenstein)
1/600,000	Czechoslovakia (Geographia)
1/100,000	Soubor Turistickych Map CSSR (Tourist area including Tatras)
1/50,000	Covering High Tatras (Slovenska, Karl—Bratislava)

FINLAND

1/500,000	Shell Reisekarte Finnland
1/200,000	Suomen tiekartta vägkarta över Finland (Maanmittaushallitus) (19 sheets)
1/50,000	Ulkoilukartat (Mann) (9 sheets—in progress)
Official Surveys	
1/200,000	Suomen yleiskarten Suurennos (76 sheets)
1/100,000	Topografinen Kartta (In progress)
1/50,000	Topografinen Kartta (In progress)

FRANCE

1/1 m.	Michelin 916
	Michelin 989 Grandes Routes
—	Michelin 400 Motorways (small atlas)
1/500,000	Shell Reisekarte Frankreich
1/200,000	Michelin Carte de France (38 sheets)—also three special sheets including Jura/Savoie
1/100,000	Michelin 195 Cote d'Azur
	96 Environs de Paris
1/50,000	Carte Touristique Mont Blanc (Tobacco)
1/50,000 & 1/25,000	Cartes de Savoie et Dauphiné (Didier-Richard) (15 sheets)
	Generally to be preferred to the official surveys since they have an overlay of recommended paths
Official Surveys (I.G.N.)	
1/250,000	Cartes touristiques (Série Rouge) (16 sheets)
1/100,000	Cartes touristiques (Série Verte) (74 sheets)
1/25,000	Cartes touristiques (Série Violette—Massifs montagneux) (17 sheets) Includes Vercors (4), Mont Blanc (2), Vanoise (3), Ecrins (3), Haute Vésubie, Sancy, Massif du Cantal, Mont Lozère
1/50,000	Carte de France (In progress)
1/25,000	Carte de France (In progress)
1/100,000	Cartes des parcs nationaux—Cévennes (No. 3⁵⁴)
1/25,000	Cartes des parcs nationaux—Pyrénées (4 sheets) (Nos. 3⁵⁰ to 3⁵³)
1/100,000 to 1/25,000	Cartes des parcs naturels regionaux (12 sheets)—includes 3¹⁰ Haut Languedoc and 3⁰⁵ Vercors
1/1 m.	Sentiers de grande randonnée—903 (same base as 901—Routes/ autoroutes)
1/200,000	Carte de la végétation de la France (In progress)
1/100,000 & 1/50,000	Cartes de la végétation des alpes (In progress—24 published)

| 1/100,000 | Carte Écologique des Alpes Occidentales (Grenoble University) (In progress) |
| 1/20,000 | Col du Lautaret et versant Sud du Grand Galibier (Ecological map) (Editions du Centre National de la Recherche Scientifique) |

GREECE
1/650,000	Greece Road Map (Freytag und Berndt)
1/500,000	Shell Reisekarte
1/300,000	Road map of Crete
1/200,000	Corfou (Al-Ma)
1/100,000	Road and tourist map of Corfu
1/100,000	Fairey Leisure map of Corfu
No scale	Fairey Leisure maps of Crete and Rhodes

Official surveys
| 1/200,000 | Maps of the Nomi of Greece (52 sheets) |
| 1/50,000 | Geological maps (105 sheets). This is the only large scale map and is based on a United States Army mapping series which do not appear to be available to the public. |

Maps of smaller islands often locally available, but usually crude. Best source guide books and brochures.

ICELAND
| 1/750,000 | Tourist road map of Iceland (Touring Club of Iceland) |
| 1/600,000 | Shell Vegakort Island |

Official surveys
1/250,000	Adelkort Yfir Island Turiskaort (4 sheets)
1/100,000	Atlas Blodin (87 sheets)
1/50,000	Fjordungsblodn Ny Utgafa (In progress)
1/50,000	Myvatan
1/25,000	National Parks (2 sheets)
1/40,000	Grodurkort Af Island (430 sheets). Classification into 60 vegetation types

ITALY (Including Sardinia and Sicily)
1/1 m.	Philip International
1/1 m.	Hallwag (Kümmerly & Frey)
1/1 m.	Michelin 988—Italie-Suisse. Grandes Routes
1/750,000	Shell Autokarte
1/650,000	Carta panoramica e stradale Dolomite (Tobacco)
1/250,000	Dolomiti (Kompass)
1/200,000	Carta automobilistica (Touring Club Italiano) (30 sheets)
1/150,000 to 1/350,000	Carta Regionale (Litografia e Artistica) (18 sheets)
1/100,000	For northern Dolomites see Austria (Freytag und Berndt Wanderkarten)
1/50,000	Kompass Wanderkarten (35 sheets south to Garda)
1/50,000	Carte sentieri e rifugi—Dolomites/Alps (Tobacco) (7 sheets)
1/50,000	Carte delle zone turistiche d'Italia (Touring Club Italiano)

Official Surveys
1/200,000	Carta stradale d'Italia (67 sheets)
1/100,000	Carta cartografica d'Italia (278 sheets)
1/50,000	Carta cartografica d'Italia (In progress)
1/25,000	Carta cartografica d'Italia (3556 sheets)
1/25,000	Monte Bianco
	Monte Cervino
	Cortina d'Ampezzo

JUGOSLAVIA
1/1 m.	Michelin 991
1/800,000	Large Road Map (Reise und Verkersverlag)
1/800,000	Motoring Map (Geographia)

1/500,000	Shell Yugoslavia, Bulgaria, Romania, Hungary
1/500,000	Autokarte Jugoslavije (4 sheets)
1/500,000	Auto Atlas (Jugoslavenski Leksikografski Zavod)
1/200,000	Generalkarte Dalmatinische Küste (Dalmatian Coast) (Shell) (3 sheets)
1/100,000	Wanderkarten Julian, Ostkarawanken und Steiner Alpen
1/50,000	Julijske Alpe

NORWAY

1/800,000	Norway and Sweden (Geographia)
1/325,000 &	
1/400,000	Norge Bil-og Turistkarte (Cappelen) (5 sheets)
1/325,000	Regional Maps—mountain areas (Cappelen) (4 sheets)
1/25,000 to	
1/50,000	Turistkart (Norges geografiske oppmaling—NGO—)(40 sheets)
Official Surveys	
1/250,000	Norge Serie 1501 (46 sheets)
1/100,000	Topografisk Kart over Norge
1/50,000	Topografisk Kart over Norge Serie M711

POLAND

1/1 m.	Mapa Samochochdowy Polski
1/1 m.	Poland (Ravenstein)
1/750,000	Road Map Poland (Freytag & Berndt)
1/75,000	Mapy Turystyczne Tatras (2 sheets) (PPWK)
1/30,000	Mapy Turystyczne National Park (PPWK)
1/1 m.	Nature Parks and Reserves (PPWK)

PORTUGAL (See also Spain)

1/1 m.	Carta de Portugal (IGC)
1/500,000	Michelin 37
1/500,000	Mapas de Carreteras (Sheets 7 and 10) (Firestone Hispania)
1/200,000	Carta de Portugal (IGC) (9 sheets)
1/100,000	Carta de Portugal (IGC) (53 sheets)
1/50,000	Carta Corografica de Portugal (IGC) (171 sheets)

ROMANIA

1/1 m.	Romania and Bulgaria (Freytag und Berndt)
1/1 m.	Romania and Bulgaria (Kümmerly & Frey)
	Geological maps at 1/500,000; 1/200,000 (50 sheets) and 1/100,000

SPAIN

1/1 m.	Spanien-Portugal (Kümmerly & Frey)
1/1 m.	Michelin 990 Spain and Portugal
1/600,000	Spain and Portugal (Foldex) (6 sheets)
1/500,000	Shell Reisekarte Spanien-Portugal
1/500,000	Mapas de Carreteras (Firestone-Hispania) (10 sheets including Portugal
1/400,000	Michelin 42 and 43 (Southern Pyrenees)
1/200,000	Mapas Turisticos (Firestone-Hispania) (11 sheets including E. and W. Pyrenees, Picos and Andalucia)
1/50,000	Mapa de los Tres Macizos de los Picos de Europa (Federation Española de Montanismo)
1/25,000	Guias cartograficas—Cordillera Cantabrica (Editorial alpina)
	Picos de Europa I Macizo Occidental
	II Macizo Central-Oriental
1/25,000 &	
1/40,000	Guias cartográficas —Pyrenees (Editorial alpina) (17 sheets)
	—Sierra de Guadarrama

Official Surveys
1/400,000	Mapa militar de España
1/200,000	Mapa militar de España
1/100,000	Mapa militar de España
1/50,000	Mapa militar de España

Additional maps for Balearics
1/175,000	Islas Baleares (Firestone-Hispania)
1/75,000	Mapa Turistico—Majorca (Firestone-Hispania)
No scale	Fairey Leisure Map—Majorca

SWEDEN
1/500,000	Shell Map of Sweden
1/300,000	Svenska Turist Karten (Tourist map of Sweden) (10 sheets)
1/250,000	Bil-Og Turistkarten
1/25,000 to	
1/200,000	Svenska Fjallkarten (mountain areas) (23 sheets)
1/100,000	Neya Fjallkarte (mountain areas) (8 sheets)
1/100,000	Stora Fritidskarten (Leisure map) (10 sheets)
1/50,000 to	
1/300,000	Fjallkarte (mountain areas) (8 sheets)

Official Surveys
1/100,000	Topografiska Karten (In progress)
1/50,000	Topografiska Karten Over Sverige (In progress)

SWITZERLAND
1/1 m.	Michelin 988 Italie et Suisse
1/500,000	Shell Reisekarte Schweiz
1/400,000	Michelin 427
1/350,000	Geographia
1/250,000	Schweiz (Automobil Club der Schweiz)
1/200,000	Michelin 21, 23, 24, 26
1/25,000 to	
1/50,000	Schweiz Teilgebiete (Tourist areas) (Kümmerly & Frey) (53 sheets)

Official Surveys
1/500,000	Carte géographique (13 colours)
1/300,000	Carte murale (enlargement of above)
1/200,000	Carte nationale de la Suisse (4 sheets)
	Landeskarten der Schweiz
1/100,000	—do— (23 sheets + 3 special areas)
1/50,000	—do— (76 sheets + 16 special areas)
1/25,000	—do— (250 sheets + 12 special areas)
1/200,000	Vegetation karte der Schweiz (4 sheets)

INDEX OF PLANT NAMES

In this Index the currently accepted correct botanical names (as given in *Flora Europaea*) are in Roman type and synonyms are in *italics*. The page numbers of illustrations are in **bold** type. ssp. = subspecies var. = variety f. = form. Some only of the text references are included in this Index.

283

291